GEOFFREY CHAUCER

The Canterbury Tales

A Selection
Modernized by J. U. Nicolson

BORDERS.
CLASSICS

Please direct sales or editorial inquiries to:
BordersTradeBookInventoryQuestions@bordersgroupinc.com

This edition is published by
Borders Classics, an imprint of Borders Group, Inc.,
by special arrangement with
Ann Arbor Media Group, LLC
2500 South State Street, Ann Arbor, MI 48104

Printed and bound in the United States of America
by Edwards Brothers, Inc.

Quality Paperback ISBN 13: 978-1-58726-485-6
ISBN 10: 1-58726-485-4

11   10   09   08   07   10 9 8 7 6 5 4 3 2 1

CONTENTS

THE CANTERBURY TALES

The Prologue

When April with his showers sweet with fruit
The drought of March has pierced unto the root
And bathed each vein with liquor that has power
To generate therein and sire the flower;
When Zephyr also has, with his sweet breath,
Quickened again, in every holt and heath,
The tender shoots and buds, and the young sun
Into the Ram one half his course has run,
And many little birds make melody
That sleep through all the night with open eye
(So Nature pricks them on to ramp and rage)—
Then do folk long to go on pilgrimage,
And palmers to go seeking out strange strands,
To distant shrines well known in sundry lands.
And specially from every shire's end
Of England they to Canterbury wend,
The holy blessed martyr there to seek
Who helped them when they lay so ill and weak.
   Befell that, in that season, on a day
In Southwark, at the Tabard, as I lay
Ready to start upon my pilgrimage
To Canterbury, full of devout homage,
There came at nightfall to that hostelry
Some nine and twenty in a company
Of sundry persons who had chanced to fall
In fellowship, and pilgrims were they all
That toward Canterbury town would ride.
The rooms and stables spacious were and wide,
And well we there were eased, and of the best.
And briefly, when the sun had gone to rest,
So had I spoken with them, every one,
That I was of their fellowship anon,

And made agreement that we'd early rise
To take the road, as you I will apprise.
　　But none the less, whilst I have time and space,
Before yet farther in this tale I pace,
It seems to me accordant with reason
To inform you of the state of every one
Of all of these, as it appeared to me,
And who they were, and what was their degree,
And even how arrayed there at the inn;
And with a knight thus will I first begin.

The Knight

A knight there was, and he a worthy man,
Who, from the moment that he first began
To ride about the world, loved chivalry,
Truth, honour, freedom and all courtesy.
Full worthy was he in his liege-lord's war,
And therein had he ridden (none more far)
As well in Christendom as heathenesse,
And honoured everywhere for worthiness.
　　At Alexandria, he, when it was won;
Full oft the table's roster he'd begun
Above all nations' knights in Prussia.
In Latvia raided he, and Russia,
No christened man so oft of his degree.
In far Granada at the siege was he
Of Algeciras, and in Belmarie.
At Ayas was he and at Satalye
When they were won; and on the Middle Sea
At many a noble meeting chanced to be.
Of mortal battles he had fought fifteen,
And he'd fought for our faith at Tramissene
Three times in lists, and each time slain his foe.
This self-same worthy knight had been also
At one time with the lord of Palatye
Against another heathen in Turkey:
And always won he sovereign fame for prize.
Though so illustrious, he was very wise

And bore himself as meekly as a maid.
He never yet had any vileness said,
In all his life, to whatsoever wight.
He was a truly perfect, gentle knight.
But now, to tell you all of his array,
His steeds were good, but yet he was not gay.
Of simple fustian wore he a jupon
Sadly discoloured by his habergeon;
For he had lately come from his voyage
And now was going on this pilgrimage.

The Squire

With him there was his son, a youthful squire,
A lover and a lusty bachelor,
With locks well curled, as if they'd laid in press.
Some twenty years of age he was, I guess.
In stature he was of an average length,
Wondrously active, aye, and great of strength.
He'd ridden sometime with the cavalry
In Flanders, in Artois, and Picardy,
And borne him well within that little space
In hope to win thereby his lady's grace.
Prinked out he was, as if he were a mead,
All full of fresh-cut flowers white and red.
Singing he was, or fluting, all the day;
He was as fresh as is the month of May.
Short was his gown, with sleeves both long and wide.
Well could he sit on horse, and fairly ride.
He could make songs and words thereto indite,
Joust, and dance too, as well as sketch and write.
So hot he loved that, while night told her tale,
He slept no more than does a nightingale.
Courteous he, and humble, willing and able,
And carved before his father at the table.

The Yeoman

A yeoman had he, nor more servants, no,
At that time, for he chose to travel so;

And he was clad in coat and hood of green.
A sheaf of peacock arrows bright and keen
Under his belt he bore right carefully
(Well could he keep his tackle yeomanly:
His arrows had no draggled feathers low),
And in his hand he bore a mighty bow.
A cropped head had he and a sun-browned face.
Of woodcraft knew he all the useful ways.
Upon his arm he bore a bracer gay,
And at one side a sword and buckler, yea,
And at the other side a dagger bright,
Well sheathed and sharp as spear point in the light;
On breast a Christopher of silver sheen.
He bore a horn in baldric all of green;
A forester he truly was, I guess.

The Prioress

There was also a nun, a prioress,
Who, in her smiling, modest was and coy;
Her greatest oath was but "By Saint Eloy!"
And she was known as Madam Eglantine.
Full well she sang the services divine,
Intoning through her nose, becomingly;
And fair she spoke her French, and fluently,
After the school of Stratford-at-the-Bow,
For French of Paris was not hers to know.
At table she had been well taught withal,
And never from her lips let morsels fall,
Nor dipped her fingers deep in sauce, but ate
With so much care the food upon her plate
That never driblet fell upon her breast.
In courtesy she had delight and zest.
Her upper lip was always wiped so clean
That in her cup was no iota seen
Of grease, when she had drunk her draught of wine.
Becomingly she reached for meat to dine.
And certainly delighting in good sport,
She was right pleasant, amiable—in short.

She was at pains to counterfeit the look
Of courtliness, and stately manners took,
And would be held worthy of reverence.
   But, to say something of her moral sense,
She was so charitable and piteous
That she would weep if she but saw a mouse
Caught in a trap, though it were dead or bled.
She had some little dogs, too, that she fed
On roasted flesh, or milk and fine white bread.
But sore she'd weep if one of them were dead,
Or if men smote it with a rod to smart:
For pity ruled her, and her tender heart.
Right decorous her pleated wimple was;
Her nose was fine; her eyes were blue as glass;
Her mouth was small and therewith soft and red;
But certainly she had a fair forehead;
It was almost a full span broad, I own,
For, truth to tell, she was not undergrown.
Neat was her cloak, as I was well aware.
Of coral small about her arm she'd bear
A string of beads and gauded all with green;
And therefrom hung a brooch of golden sheen
Whereon there was first written a crowned "A,"
And under, *Amor vincit omnia.*

The Nun

Another little nun with her had she,

The Three Priests

Who was her chaplain; and of priests she'd three.

The Monk

A monk there was, one made for mastery,
An outrider, who loved his venery;
A manly man, to be an abbot able.
Full many a blooded horse had he in stable:

And when he rode men might his bridle hear
A-jingling in the whistling wind as clear,
Aye, and as loud as does the chapel bell
Where this brave monk was master of the cell.
The rule of Maurus or Saint Benedict,
By reason it was old and somewhat strict,
This said monk let such old things slowly pace
And followed new-world manners in their place.
He cared not for that text a clean-plucked hen
Which holds that hunters are not holy men;
Nor that a monk, when he is cloisterless,
Is like unto a fish that's waterless;
That is to say, a monk out of his cloister.
But this same text he held not worth an oyster;
And I said his opinion was right good.
What? Should he study as a madman would
Upon a book in cloister cell? Or yet
Go labour with his hands and swink and sweat,
As Austin bids? How shall the world be served?
Let Austin have his toil to him reserved.
Therefore he was a rider day and night;
Greyhounds he had, as swift as bird in flight.
Since riding and the hunting of the hare
Were all his love, for no cost would he spare.
I saw his sleeves were purfled at the hand
With fur of grey, the finest in the land;
Also, to fasten hood beneath his chin,
He had of good wrought gold a curious pin:
A love-knot in the larger end there was.
His head was bald and shone like any glass,
And smooth as one anointed was his face.
Fat was this lord, he stood in goodly case.
His bulging eyes he rolled about, and hot
They gleamed and red, like fire beneath a pot;
His boots were soft; his horse of great estate.
Now certainly he was a fine prelate:
He was not pale as some poor wasted ghost.
A fat swan loved he best of any roast.
His palfrey was as brown as is a berry.

The Friar

A friar there was, a wanton and a merry,
A limiter, a very festive man.
In all the Orders Four is none that can
Equal his gossip and his fair language.
He had arranged full many a marriage
Of women young, and this at his own cost.
Unto his order he was a noble post.
Well liked by all and intimate was he
With franklins everywhere in his country,
And with the worthy women of the town:
For at confessing he'd more power in gown
(As he himself said) than a good curate,
For of his order he was licentiate.
He heard confession gently, it was said,
Gently absolved too, leaving naught of dread.
He was an easy man to give penance
When knowing he should gain a good pittance;
For to a begging friar, money given
Is sign that any man has been well shriven.
For if one gave (he dared to boast of this),
He took the man's repentance not amiss.
For many a man there is so hard of heart
He cannot weep however pains may smart.
Therefore, instead of weeping and of prayer,
Men should give silver to poor friars all bare.
His tippet was stuck always full of knives
And pins, to give to young and pleasing wives.
And certainly he kept a merry note:
Well could he sing and play upon the rote.
At balladry he bore the prize away.
His throat was white as lily of the May;
Yet strong he was as ever champion.
In towns he knew the taverns, every one,
And every good host and each barmaid too—
Better than begging lepers, these he knew.
For unto no such solid man as he

Accorded it, as far as he could see,
To have sick lepers for acquaintances.
There is no honest advantageousness
In dealing with such poverty-stricken curs;
It's with the rich and with big victuallers.
And so, wherever profit might arise,
Courteous he was and humble in men's eyes.
There was no other man so virtuous.
He was the finest beggar of his house;
A certain district being farmed to him,
None of his brethren dared approach its rim;
For though a widow had no shoes to show,
So pleasant was his *In principio*,
He always got a farthing ere he went.
He lived by pickings, it is evident.
And he could romp as well as any whelp.
On love days could he be of mickle help.
For there he was not like a cloisterer,
With threadbare cope as is the poor scholar,
But he was like a lord or like a pope.
Of double worsted was his semi-cope,
That rounded like a bell, as you may guess.
He lisped a little, out of wantonness,
To make his English soft upon his tongue;
And in his harping, after he had sung,
His two eyes twinkled in his head as bright
As do the stars within the frosty night.
This worthy limiter was named Hubert.

The Merchant

There was a merchant with forked beard, and girt
In motley gown, and high on horse he sat,
Upon his head a Flemish beaver hat;
His boots were fastened rather elegantly.
His spoke his notions out right pompously,
Stressing the times when he had won, not lost.
He would the sea were held at any cost
Across from Middleburgh to Orwell town.

At money-changing he could make a crown.
This worthy man kept all his wits well set;
There was no one could say he was in debt,
So well he governed all his trade affairs
With bargains and with borrowings and with shares.
Indeed, he was a worthy man withal,
But, sooth to say, his name I can't recall.

The Clerk

A clerk from Oxford was with us also,
Who'd turned to getting knowledge, long ago.
As meagre was his horse as is a rake,
Nor he himself too fat, I'll undertake,
But he looked hollow and went soberly.
Right threadbare was his overcoat; for he
Had got him yet no churchly benefice,
Nor was so worldly as to gain office.
For he would rather have at his bed's head
Some twenty books, all bound in black and red,
Of Aristotle and his philosophy
Than rich robes, fiddle, or gay psaltery.
Yet, and for all he was philosopher,
He had but little gold within his coffer;
But all that he might borrow from a friend
On books and learning he would swiftly spend,
And then he'd pray right busily for the souls
Of those who gave him wherewithal for schools.
Of study took he utmost care and heed.
Not one word spoke he more than was his need;
And that was said in fullest reverence
And short and quick and full of high good sense.
Pregnant of moral virtue was his speech;
And gladly would he learn and gladly teach.

The Lawyer

A sergeant of the law, wary and wise,
Who'd often gone to Paul's walk to advise,

There was also, compact of excellence.
Discreet he was, and of great reverence;
At least he seemed so, his words were so wise.
Often he sat as justice in assize,
By patent or commission from the crown;
Because of learning and his high renown,
He took large fees and many robes could own.
So great a purchaser was never known.
All was fee simple to him, in effect,
Wherefore his claims could never be suspect.
Nowhere a man so busy of his class,
And yet he seemed much busier than he was.
All cases and all judgments could he cite
That from King William's time were apposite.
And he could draw a contract so explicit
Not any man could fault therefrom elicit;
And every statute he'd verbatim quote.
He rode but badly in a medley coat,
Belted in a silken sash, with little bars,
But of his dress no more particulars.

The Franklin

There was a franklin in his company;
White was his beard as is the white daisy.
Of sanguine temperament by every sign,
He loved right well his morning sop in wine.
Delightful living was the goal he'd won,
For he was Epicurus' very son,
That held opinion that a full delight
Was true felicity, perfect and right.
A householder, and that a great, was he;
Saint Julian he was in his own country.
His bread and ale were always right well done;
A man with better cellars there was none.
Baked meat was never wanting in his house,
Of fish and flesh, and that so plenteous
It seemed to snow therein both food and drink

Of every dainty that a man could think.
According to the season of the year
He changed his diet and his means of cheer.
Full many a fattened partridge did he mew,
And many a bream and pike in fish-pond too.
Woe to his cook, except the sauces were
Poignant and sharp, and ready all his gear.
His table, waiting in his hall alway,
Stood ready covered through the livelong day.
At county sessions was he lord and sire,
And often acted as a knight of shire.
A dagger and a trinket bag of silk
Hung from his girdle, white as morning milk.
He had been sheriff and been auditor;
And nowhere was a worthier vavasor.

The Haberdasher and the Carpenter

A haberdasher and a carpenter,

The Weaver, The Dyer, and The Arras-Maker

An arras-maker, dyer, and weaver
Were with us, clothed in similar livery,
All of one sober, great fraternity.
Their gear was new and well adorned it was;
Their weapons were not cheaply trimmed with brass,
But all with silver; chastely made and well
Their girdles and their pouches too, I tell.
Each man of them appeared a proper burgess
To sit in guildhall on a high dais.
And each of them, for wisdom he could span,
Was fitted to have been an alderman;
For chattels they'd enough, and, too, of rent;
To which their goodwives gave a free assent,
Or else for certain they had been to blame.
It's good to hear "Madam" before one's name,
And go to church when all the world may see,
Having one's mantle borne right royally.

The Cook

A cook they had with them, just for the nonce,
To boil the chickens with the marrow-bones,
And flavour tartly and with galingale.
Well could he tell a draught of London ale.
And he could roast and seethe and broil and fry,
And make a good thick soup, and bake a pie.
But very ill it was, it seemed to me,
That on his shin a deadly sore had he;
For sweet blanc-mange, he made it with the best.

The Sailor

There was a sailor, living far out west;
For aught I know, he was of Dartmouth town.
He sadly rode a hackney, in a gown,
Of thick rough cloth falling to the knee.
A dagger hanging on a cord had he
About his neck, and under arm, and down.
The summer's heat had burned his visage brown;
And certainly he was a good fellow.
Full many a draught of wine he'd drawn, I trow,
Of Bordeaux vintage, while the trader slept.
Nice conscience was a thing he never kept.
If that he fought and got the upper hand,
By water he sent them home to every land.
But as for craft, to reckon well his tides,
His currents and the dangerous watersides,
His harbours, and his moon, his pilotage,
There was none such from Hull to far Carthage.
Hardy, and wise in all things undertaken,
By many a tempest had his beard been shaken.
He knew well all the havens, as they were,
From Gottland to the Cape of Finisterre,
And every creek in Brittany and Spain;
His vessel had been christened *Madeleine*.

The Physician

With us there was a doctor of physic;
In all this world was none like him to pick
For talk of medicine and surgery;
For he was grounded in astronomy.
He often kept a patient from the pall
By horoscopes and magic natural.
Well could he tell the fortune ascendent
Within the houses for his sick patient.
He knew the cause of every malady,
Were it of hot or cold, of moist or dry,
And where engendered, and of what humour;
He was a very good practitioner.
The cause being known, down to the deepest root,
Anon he gave to the sick man his boot.
Ready he was, with his apothecaries,
To send him drugs and all electuaries;
By mutual aid much gold they'd always won—
Their friendship was a thing not new begun.
Well read was he in Esculapius,
And Deiscorides, and in Rufus,
Hippocrates, and Hali, and Galen,
Serapion, Rhazes, and Avicen,
Averrhoës, Gilbert, and Constantine,
Bernard, and Gatisden, and John Damascene.
In diet he was measured as could be,
Including naught of superfluity,
But nourishing and easy. It's no libel
To say he read but little in the Bible.
In blue and scarlet he went clad, withal,
Lined with a taffeta and with sendal;
And yet he was right chary of expense;
He kept the gold he gained from pestilence.
For gold in physic is a fine cordial,
And therefore loved he gold exceeding all.

The Wife of Bath

There was a housewife come from Bath, or near,
Who—sad to say—was deaf in either ear.
At making cloth she had so great a bent
She bettered those of Ypres and even of Ghent.
In all the parish there was no goodwife
Should offering make before her, on my life;
And if one did, indeed, so wroth was she
It put her out of all her charity.
Her kerchiefs were of finest weave and ground;
I dare swear that they weighed a full ten pound
Which, of a Sunday, she wore on her head.
Her hose were of the choicest scarlet red,
Close gartered, and her shoes were soft and new.
Bold was her face, and fair, and red of hue.
She'd been respectable throughout her life,
With five churched husbands bringing joy and strife,
Not counting other company in youth;
But thereof there's no need to speak, in truth.
Three times she'd journeyed to Jerusalem;
And many a foreign stream she'd had to stem;
At Rome she'd been, and she'd been in Boulogne,
In Spain at Santiago, and at Cologne.
She could tell much of wandering by the way:
Gap-toothed was she, it is no lie to say.
Upon an ambler easily she sat,
Well wimpled, aye, and over all a hat
As broad as is a buckler or a targe;
A rug was tucked around her buttocks large,
And on her feet a pair of sharpened spurs.
In company well could she laugh her slurs.
The remedies of love she knew, perchance,
For of that art she'd learned the old, old dance.

The Parson

There was a good man of religion, too,
A country parson, poor, I warrant you;
But rich he was in holy thought and work.

He was a learned man also, a clerk,
Who Christ's own gospel truly sought to preach;
Devoutly his parishioners would he teach.
Benign he was and wondrous diligent,
Patient in adverse times and well content,
As he was ofttimes proven; always blithe,
He was right loath to curse to get a tithe,
But rather would he give, in case of doubt,
Unto those poor parishioners about,
Part of his income, even of his goods.
Enough with little, coloured all his moods.
Wide was his parish, houses far asunder,
But never did he fail, for rain or thunder,
In sickness, or in sin, or any state,
To visit to the farthest, small and great,
Going afoot, and in his hand a stave.
This fine example to his flock he gave,
That first he wrought and afterward he taught;
Out of the gospel then that text he caught,
And this figure he added thereunto—
That, if gold rust, what shall poor iron do?
For if the priest be foul, in whom we trust,
What wonder if a layman yield to lust?
And shame it is, if priest take thought for keep,
A shitty shepherd, shepherding clean sheep.
Well ought a priest example good to give,
By his own cleanness, how his flock should live.
He never let his benefice for hire,
Leaving his flock to flounder in the mire,
And ran to London, up to old Saint Paul's
To get himself a chantry there for souls,
Nor in some brotherhood did he withhold;
But dwelt at home and kept so well the fold
That never wolf could make his plans miscarry;
He was a shepherd and not mercenary.
And holy though he was, and virtuous,
To sinners he was not impiteous,
Nor haughty in his speech, nor too divine,
But in all teaching prudent and benign.
To lead folk into Heaven but by stress

Of good example was his busyness.
But if some sinful one proved obstinate,
Be who it might, of high or low estate,
Him he reproved, and sharply, as I know.
There is nowhere a better priest, I trow.
He had no thirst for pomp or reverence,
Nor made himself a special, spiced conscience,
But Christ's own lore, and His apostles' twelve
He taught, but first he followed it himselve.

The Plowman

With him there was a plowman, was his brother,
That many a load of dung, and many another
Had scattered, for a good true toiler, he,
Living in peace and perfect charity.
He loved God most, and that with his whole heart,
At all times, though he played or plied his art,
And next, his neighbour, even as himself.
He'd thresh and dig, with never thought of pelf,
For Christ's own sake, for every poor wight,
All without pay, if it lay in his might.
He paid his taxes, fully, fairly, well,
Both by his own toil and by stuff he'd sell.
In a tabard he rode upon a mare.
    There were also a reeve and miller there;
A summoner, manciple and pardoner,
And these, beside myself, made all there were.

The Miller

The miller was a stout churl, be it known,
Hardy and big of brawn and big of bone;
Which was well proved, for when he went on lam
At wrestling, never failed he of the ram.
He was a chunky fellow, broad of build;
He'd heave a door from hinges if he willed,
Or break it through, by running, with his head.

His beard, as any sow or fox, was red,
And broad it was as if it were a spade.
Upon the coping of his nose he had
A wart, and thereon stood a tuft of hairs,
Red as the bristles in an old sow's ears;
His nostrils they were black and very wide.
A sword and buckler bore he by his side.
His mouth was like a furnace door for size.
He was a jester and could poetize,
But mostly all of sin and ribaldries.
He could steal corn and full thrice charge his fees;
And yet he had a thumb of gold, begad.
A white coat and blue hood he wore, this lad.
A bagpipe he could blow well, be it known,
And with that same he brought us out of town.

The Manciple

There was a manciple from an inn of court,
To whom all buyers might quite well resort
To learn the art of buying food and drink;
For whether he paid cash or not, I think
That he so knew the markets, when to buy,
He never found himself left high and dry.
Now is it not of God a full fair grace
That such a vulgar man has wit to pace
The wisdom of a crowd of learned men?
Of masters had he more than three times ten,
Who were in law expert and curious;
Whereof there were a dozen in that house
Fit to be stewards of both rent and land
Of any lord in England who would stand
Upon his own and live in manner good,
In honour, debtless (save his head were wood),
Or live as frugally as he might desire;
These men were able to have helped a shire
In any case that ever might befall;
And yet this manciple outguessed them all.

The Reeve

The reeve he was a slender, choleric man,
Who shaved his beard as close as razor can.
His hair was cut round even with his ears;
His top was tonsured like a pulpiteer's.
Long were his legs, and they were very lean,
And like a staff, with no calf to be seen.
Well could he manage granary and bin;
No auditor could ever on him win.
He could foretell, by drought and by the rain,
The yielding of his seed and of his grain.
His lord's sheep and his oxen and his dairy,
His swine and horses, all his stores, his poultry,
Were wholly in this steward's managing;
And, by agreement, he'd made reckoning
Since his young lord of age was twenty years;
Yet no man ever found him in arrears.
There was no agent, hind, or herd who'd cheat
But he knew well his cunning and deceit;
They were afraid of him as of the death.
His cottage was a good one, on a heath;
By green trees shaded with this dwelling-place.
Much better than his lord could he purchase.
Right rich he was in his own private right,
Seeing he'd pleased his lord, by day or night,
By giving him, or lending, of his goods,
And so got thanked—but yet got coats and hoods.
In youth he'd learned a good trade, and had been
A carpenter, as fine as could be seen.
This steward sat a horse that well could trot,
And was all dapple-grey, and was named Scot.
A long surcoat of blue did he parade,
And at his side he bore a rusty blade.
Of Norfolk was this reeve of whom I tell,
From near a town that men call Badeswell.
Bundled he was like friar from chin to croup,
And ever he rode hindmost of our troop.

The Summoner

A summoner was with us in that place,
Who had a fiery red, cherubic face,
For eczema he had; his eyes were narrow,
As hot he was, and lecherous, as a sparrow;
With black and scabby brows and scanty beard;
He had a face that little children feared.
There was no mercury, sulphur, or litharge,
No borax, ceruse, tartar, could discharge,
Nor ointment that could cleanse enough, or bite,
To free him of his boils and pimples white,
Nor of the bosses resting on his cheeks.
Well loved he garlic, onions, aye and leeks,
And drinking of strong wine as red as blood.
Then would he talk and shout as madman would.
And when a deal of wine he'd poured within,
Then would he utter no word save Latin.
Some phrases had he learned, say two or three,
Which he had garnered out of some decree;
No wonder, for he'd heard it all the day;
And all you know right well that even a jay
Can call out "Wat" as well as can the pope.
But when, for aught else, into him you'd grope,
'Twas found he'd spent his whole philosophy;
Just "*Questio quid juris*" would he cry.
He was a noble rascal, and a kind;
A better comrade 'twould be hard to find.
Why, he would suffer, for a quart of wine,
Some good fellow to have his concubine
A twelvemonth, and excuse him to the full
(Between ourselves, though, he could pluck a gull).
And if he chanced upon a good fellow,
He would instruct him never to have awe,
In such a case, of the archdeacon's curse,
Except a man's soul lie within his purse;
For in his purse the man should punished be.
"The purse is the archdeacon's Hell," said he.

But well I know he lied in what he said;
A curse ought every guilty man to dread
(For curse can kill, as absolution save),
And 'ware *significavit* to the grave.
In his own power had he, and at ease,
The boys and girls of all the diocese,
And knew their secrets, and by counsel led.
A garland had he set upon his head,
Large as a tavern's winebush on a stake;
A buckler had he made of bread they bake.

The Pardoner

With him there rode a gentle pardoner
Of Rouncival, his friend and his compeer;
Straight from the court of Rome had journeyed he.
Loudly he sang "Come hither, love, to me,"
The summoner joining with a burden round;
Was never horn of half so great a sound.
This pardoner had hair as yellow as wax,
But lank it hung as does a strike of flax;
In wisps hung down such locks as he'd on head,
And with them he his shoulders overspread;
But thin they dropped, and stringy, one by one.
But as to hood, for sport of it, he'd none,
Though it was packed in wallet all the while.
It seemed to him he went in latest style,
Dishevelled, save for cap, his head all bare.
As shiny eyes he had as has a hare.
He had a fine veronica sewed to cap.
His wallet lay before him in his lap,
Stuffed full of pardons brought from Rome all hot.
A voice he had that bleated like a goat.
No beard had he, nor ever should he have,
For smooth his face as he'd just had a shave;
I think he was a gelding or a mare.
But in his craft, from Berwick unto Ware,
Was no such pardoner in any place.
For in his bag he had a pillowcase

The which, he said, was Our True Lady's veil:
He said he had a piece of the very sail
That good Saint Peter had, what time he went
Upon the sea, till Jesus changed his bent.
He had a latten cross set full of stones,
And in a bottle had he some pig's bones.
But with these relics, when he came upon
Some simple parson, then this paragon
In that one day more money stood to gain
Than the poor dupe in two months could attain.
And thus, with flattery and suchlike japes,
He made the parson and the rest his apes.
But yet, to tell the whole truth at the last,
He was, in church, a fine ecclesiast.
Well could he read a lesson or a story,
But best of all he sang an offertory;
For well he knew that when that song was sung,
Then might he preach, and all with polished tongue,
To win some silver, as he right well could;
Therefore he sang so merrily and so loud.

   Now have I told you briefly, in a clause,
The state, the array, the number, and the cause
Of the assembling of this company
In Southwark, at this noble hostelry
Known as the Tabard Inn, hard by the Bell.
But now the time is come wherein to tell
How all we bore ourselves that very night
When at the hostelry we did alight.
And afterward the story I engage
To tell you of our common pilgrimage.
But first, I pray you, of your courtesy,
You'll not ascribe it to vulgarity
Though I speak plainly of this matter here,
Retailing you their words and means of cheer;
Nor though I use their very terms, nor lie.
For this thing do you know as well as I:
When one repeats a tale told by a man,
He must report, as nearly as he can,

Every least word, if he remember it,
However rude it be, or how unfit;
Or else he may be telling what's untrue,
Embellishing and fictionizing too.
He may not spare, although it were his brother;
He must as well say one word as another.
Christ spoke right broadly out, in holy writ,
And, you know well, there's nothing low in it.
And Plato says, to those able to read:
"The word should be the cousin to the deed."
Also, I pray that you'll forgive it me
If I have not set folk, in their degree
Here in this tale, by rank as they should stand.
My wits are not the best, you'll understand.

    Great cheer our host gave to us, every one,
And to the supper set us all anon;
And served us then with victuals of the best.
Strong was the wine and pleasant to each guest.
A seemly man our good host was, withal,
Fit to have been a marshal in some hall;
He was a large man, with protruding eyes,
As fine a burgher as in Cheapside lies;
Bold in his speech, and wise, and right well taught,
And as to manhood, lacking there in naught.
Also, he was a very merry man,
And after meat, at playing he began,
Speaking of mirth among some other things,
When all of us had paid our reckonings;
And saying thus: "Now masters, verily
You are all welcome here, and heartily:
For by my truth, and telling you no lie,
I have not seen, this year, a company
Here in this inn, fitter for sport than now.
Fain would I make you happy, knew I how.
And of a game have I this moment thought
To give you joy, and it shall cost you naught.
    "You go to Canterbury; may God speed
And the blest martyr soon requite your meed.

And well I know, as you go on your way,
You'll tell good tales and shape yourselves to play;
For truly there's no mirth nor comfort, none,
Riding the roads as dumb as is a stone;
And therefore will I furnish you a sport,
As I just said, to give you some comfort.
And if you like it, all, by one assent,
And will be ruled by me, of my judgment,
And will so do as I'll proceed to say,
Tomorrow, when you ride upon your way,
Then, by my father's spirit, who is dead,
If you're not gay, I'll give you up my head.
Hold up your hands, nor more about it speak."
  Our full assenting was not far to seek;
We thought there was no reason to think twice,
And granted him his way without advice,
And bade him tell his verdict just and wise,
  "Masters," quoth he, "here now is my advice;
But take it not, I pray you, in disdain;
This is the point, to put it short and plain,
That each of you, beguiling the long day,
Shall tell two stories as you wend your way
To Canterbury town; and each of you
On coming home, shall tell another two,
All of adventures he has known befall.
And he who plays his part the best of all,
That is to say, who tells upon the road
Tales of best sense, in most amusing mode,
Shall have a supper at the others' cost
Here in this room and sitting by this post,
When we come back again from Canterbury.
And now, the more to warrant you'll be merry,
I will myself, and gladly, with you ride
At my own cost, and I will be your guide.
But whosoever shall my rule gainsay
Shall pay for all that's bought along the way.
And if you are agreed that it be so,
Tell me at once, or if not, tell me no,
And I will act accordingly. No more."

This thing was granted, and our oaths we swore,
With right glad hearts, and prayed of him, also,
That he would take the office, nor forgo
The place of governor of all of us,
Judging our tales; and by his wisdom thus
Arrange that supper at a certain price,
We to be ruled, each one, by his advice
In things both great and small; by one assent,
We stood committed to his government.
And thereupon, the wine was fetched anon;
We drank, and then to rest went every one,
And that without a longer tarrying.
　　Next morning, when the day began to spring,
Up rose our host, and acting as our cock,
He gathered us together in a flock,
And forth we rode, a jog trot being the pace,
Until we reached Saint Thomas' watering place.
And there our host pulled horse up to a walk,
And said: "Now, masters, listen while I talk.
You know what you agreed at set of sun.
If evensong and morningsong are one,
Let's here decide who first shall tell a tale.
And as I hope to drink more wine and ale,
Whoso proves rebel to my government
Shall pay for all that by the way is spent.
Come now, draw cuts, before we farther win,
And he that draws the shortest shall begin.
Sir knight," said he, "my master and my lord,
You shall draw first as you have pledged your word.
Come near," quoth he, "my lady prioress:
And you, sir clerk, put by your bashfulness,
Nor ponder more; out hands, now, every man!"
　　At once to draw a cut each one began,
And, to make short the matter, as it was,
Whether by chance or whatsoever cause,
The truth is, that the cut fell to the knight,
At which right happy then was every wight.
Thus that his story first of all he'd tell,
According to the compact, it befell,

As you have heard. Why argue to and fro?
And when this good man saw that it was so,
Being a wise man and obedient
To plighted word, given by free assent,
He said: "Since I must then begin the game,
Why, welcome be the cut, and in God's name!
Now let us ride, and hearken what I say."

 And at that word we rode forth on our way;
And he began to speak, with right good cheer,
His tale anon, as it is written here.

The Knight's Tale

Iamque domos patrias, Scithice post aspera gentis
Prelia, laurigero, etc.
                        –STATIUS, *Thebaid*, XII, 519.

Once on a time, as old tales tell to us,
There was a duke whose name was Thesëus;
Of Athens he was lord and governor,
And in his time was such a conqueror
That greater was there not beneath the sun.
Full many a rich country had he won;
What with his wisdom and his chivalry
He gained the realm of Femininity,
That was of old time known as Scythia.
There wedded he the queen, Hippolyta,
And brought her home with him to his country.
In glory great and with great pageantry,
And, too, her younger sister, Emily.
And thus, in victory and with melody,
Let I this noble duke to Athens ride
With all his armed host marching at his side.
    And truly, were it not too long to hear,
I would have told you fully how, that year,
Was gained the realm of Femininity
By Thesëus and by his chivalry;
And all of the great battle that was wrought
Where Amazons and the Athenians fought;
And how was wooed and won Hippolyta,
That fair and hardy queen of Scythia;
And of the feast was made at their wedding,
And of the tempest at their homecoming;
But all of that I must for now forbear.
I have, God knows, a large field for my share,
And weak the oxen, and the soil is tough.
The remnant of the tale is long enough.

I will not hinder any, in my turn;
Let each man tell his tale, until we learn
Which of us all the most deserves to win;
So where I stopped, again I'll now begin.
   This duke of whom I speak, of great renown,
When he had drawn almost unto the town,
In all well-being and in utmost pride,
He grew aware, casting his eyes aside,
That right upon the road, as suppliants do,
A company of ladies, two by two,
Knelt, all in black, before his cavalcade;
But such a clamorous cry of woe they made
That in the whole world living man had heard
No such a lamentation, on my word;
Nor would they cease lamenting till at last
They'd clutched his bridle reins and held them fast.
   "What folk are you that at my homecoming
Disturb my triumph with this dolorous thing?"
Cried Thesëus. "Do you so much envy
My honour that you thus complain and cry?
Or who has wronged you now, or who offended?
Come, tell me whether it may be amended;
And tell me, why are you clothed thus, in black?"
   The eldest lady of them answered back,
After she'd swooned, with cheek so deathly drear
That it was pitiful to see and hear,
And said: "Lord, to whom Fortune has but given
Victory, and to conquer where you've striven,
Your glory and your honour grieve not us;
But we beseech your aid and pity thus.
Have mercy on our woe and our distress.
Some drop of pity, of your gentleness,
Upon us wretched women, oh, let fall!
For see, lord, there is no one of us all
That has not been a duchess or a queen;
Now we are captives, as may well be seen:
Thanks be to Fortune and her treacherous wheel,
There's none can rest assured of constant weal.
And truly, lord, expecting your return,
In Pity's temple, where the fires yet burn,

We have been waiting through a long fortnight;
Now help us, lord, since it is in your might.
   "I, wretched woman, who am weeping thus,
Was once the wife of King Capanëus,
Who died at Thebes, oh, cursed be the day!
And all we that you see in this array,
And make this lamentation to be known,
All we have lost our husbands at that town
During the siege that round about it lay.
And now the old Creon, ah welaway!
The lord and governor of Thebes city,
Full of his wrath and all iniquity,
He, in despite and out of tyranny,
To do the dead a shame and villainy,
Of all our husbands, lying among the slain,
Has piled the bodies in a heap, amain,
And will not suffer them, nor give consent,
To buried be, or burned, nor will relent,
But sets his dogs to eat them, out of spite."
   And on that word, at once, without respite,
They all fell prone and cried out piteously:
"Have on us wretched women some mercy,
And let our sorrows sink into your heart!"
   This gentle duke down from his horse did start
With heart of pity, when he'd heard them speak.
It seemed to him his heart must surely break,
Seeing them there so miserable of state,
Who had been proud and happy but so late.
And in his arms he took them tenderly,
Giving them comfort understandingly:
And swore his oath, that as he was true knight,
He would put forth so thoroughly his might
Against the tyrant Creon as to wreak
Vengeance so great that all of Greece should speak
And say how Creon was by Thesëus served,
As one that had his death full well deserved.
This sworn and done, he no more there abode;
His banner he displayed and forth he rode
Toward Thebes, and all his host marched on beside;
Nor nearer Athens would he walk or ride,

Nor take his ease for even half a day,
But onward, and in camp that night he lay;
And thence he sent Hippolyta the queen
And her bright sister Emily, I ween,
Unto the town of Athens, there to dwell
While he went forth. There is no more to tell.
　The image of red Mars, with spear and shield,
So shone upon his banner's snow-white field
It made a billowing glitter up and down;
And by the banner borne was his pennon,
On which in beaten gold was worked, complete,
The Minotaur, which he had slain in Crete.
Thus rode this duke, thus rode this conqueror,
And in his host of chivalry the flower,
Until he came to Thebes and did alight
Full in the field where he'd intent to fight.
But to be brief in telling of this thing,
With Creon, who was Thebes' dread lord and king,
He fought and slew him, manfully, like knight,
In open war, and put his host to flight;
And by assault he took the city then,
Levelling wall and rafter with his men;
And to the ladies he restored again
The bones of their poor husbands who were slain,
To do for them the last rites of that day.
But it were far too long a tale to say
The clamour of great grief and sorrowing
Those ladies raised above the bones burning
Upon the pyres, and of the great honour
That Theseus, the noble conqueror,
Paid to the ladies when from him they went;
To make the story short is my intent.
When, then, this worthy duke, this Theseus
Had slain Creon and won Thebes city thus,
Still on the field he took that night his rest,
And dealt with all the land as he thought best.
　In searching through the heap of enemy dead,
Stripping them of their gear from heel to head,
The busy pillagers could pick and choose,
After the battle, what they best could use;

And so befell that in a heap they found,
Pierced through with many a grievous, bloody wound,
Two young knights lying together, side by side,
Bearing one crest, wrought richly, of their pride,
And of those two Arcita was the one,
The other knight was known as Palamon.
Not fully quick, nor fully dead they were,
But by their coats of arms and by their gear
The heralds readily could tell, withal,
That they were of the Theban blood royal,
And that they had been of two sisters born.
Out of the heap the spoilers had them torn
And carried gently over to the tent
Of Theseüs; who shortly had them sent
To Athens, there in prison cell to lie
For ever, without ransom, till they die.
And when this worthy duke had all this done,
He gathered host and home he rode anon,
With laurel crowned again as conqueror;
There lived he in all joy and all honour
His term of life; what more need words express?
And in a tower, in anguish and distress,
Palamon and Arcita, day and night,
Dwelt whence no gold might help them to take flight.
    Thus passed by year by year and day by day,
Till it fell out, upon a morn in May,
That Emily, far fairer to be seen
Than is the lily on its stalk of green,
And fresher than is May with flowers new
    (For with the rose's colour strove her hue,
I know not which was fairer of the two),
Before the dawn, as was her wont to do,
She rose and dressed her body for delight;
For May will have no sluggards of the night.
That season rouses every gentle heart
And forces it from winter's sleep to start,
Saying: "Arise and show thy reverence."
So Emily remembered to go thence
In honour of the May, and so she rose.
Clothed, she was sweeter than any flower that blows;

Her yellow hair was braided in one tress
Behind her back, a full yard long, I guess.
And in the garden, as the sun uprose,
She sauntered back and forth and through each close,
Gathering many a flower, white and red,
To weave a delicate garland for her head;
And like a heavenly angel's was her song.
The tower tall, which was so thick and strong,
And of the castle was the great donjon,
(Wherein the two knights languished in prison,
Of whom I told and shall yet tell, withal),
Was joined, at base, unto the garden wall
Whereunder Emily went dallying.
Bright was the sun and clear that morn in spring,
And Palamon, the woeful prisoner,
As was his wont, by leave of his gaoler,
Was up and pacing round that chamber high,
From which the noble city filled his eye,
And, too, the garden full of branches green,
Wherein bright Emily, fair and serene,
Went walking and went roving up and down.
This sorrowing prisoner, this Palamon,
Being in the chamber, pacing to and fro,
And to himself complaining of his woe,
Cursing his birth, he often cried "Alas!"
And so it was, by chance or other pass,
That through a window, closed by many a bar
Of iron, strong and square as any spar,
He cast his eyes upon Emilia,
And thereupon he blenched and cried out "Ah!"
As if he had been smitten to the heart.
And at that cry Arcita did upstart,
Asking: "My cousin, why what ails you now
That you've so deathly pallor on your brow?
Why did you cry out? Who's offended you?
For God's love, show some patience, as I do,
With prison, for it may not different be;
Fortune has given this adversity.
Some evil disposition or aspect
Of Saturn did our horoscopes affect

To bring us here, though differently 'twere sworn;
But so the stars stood when we two were born;
We must endure it; that, in brief, is plain."
    This Palamon replied and said again:
"Cousin, indeed in this opinion now
Your fancy is but vanity, I trow.
It's not our prison that caused me to cry.
But I was wounded lately through the eye
Down to my heart, and that my bane will be.
The beauty of the lady that I see
There in that garden, pacing to and fro,
Is cause of all my crying and my woe.
I know not if she's woman or goddess;
But Venus she is verily, I guess."
And thereupon down on his knees he fell,
And said: "O Venus, if it be thy will
To be transfigured in this garden, thus
Before me, sorrowing wretch, oh now help us
Out of this prison to be soon escaped.
And if it be my destiny is shaped,
By fate, to die in durance, in bondage,
Have pity, then, upon our lineage
That has been brought so low by tyranny."
    And on that word Arcita looked to see
This lady who went roving to and fro.
And in that look her beauty struck him so
That, if poor Palamon is wounded sore,
Arcita is as deeply hurt, and more.
And with a sigh he said then, piteously:
"The virgin beauty slays me suddenly
Of her that wanders yonder in that place;
And save I have her pity and her grace,
That I at least may see her day by day,
I am but dead; there is no more to say."
    This Palamon, when these words he had heard,
Pitilessly he watched him, and answered:
"Do you say this in earnest or in play?"
    "Nay," quoth Arcita, "earnest, now, I say!
God help me, I am in no mood for play!"
    Palamon knit his brows and stood at bay.

"It will not prove," he said, "to your honour
After so long a time to turn traitor
To me, who am your cousin and your brother,
Sworn as we are, and each unto the other,
That never, though for death in any pain,
Never, indeed, till death shall part us twain,
Either of us in love shall hinder other,
No, nor in any thing, O my dear brother;
But that, instead, you shall so further me
As I shall you. All this we did agree.
Such was your oath and such was mine also.
You dare not now deny it, well I know.
Thus you are of my party, beyond doubt.
And now you would all falsely go about
To love my lady, whom I love and serve,
And shall while life my heart's blood may preserve.
Nay, false Arcita, it shall not be so.
I loved her first, and told you all my woe,
As to a brother and to one that swore
To further me, as I have said before.
For which you are in duty bound, as knight,
To help me, if the thing lie in your might,
Or else you're false, I say, and downfallen."
    Then this Arcita proudly spoke again:
"You shall," he said, "be rather false than I;
And that you're so, I tell you utterly;
For *par amour* I loved her first, you know.
What can you say? You know not, even now,
Whether she is a woman or goddess!
Yours is a worship as of holiness,
While mine is love, as of a mortal maid;
Wherefore I told you of it, unafraid,
As to my cousin and my brother sworn.
Let us assume you loved her first, this morn;
Know you not well the ancient writer's saw
Of 'Who shall give a lover any law?'
Love is a greater law, aye by my pan,
Than man has ever given to earthly man.
And therefore statute law and such decrees
Are broken daily and in all degrees.

A man must needs have love, maugre his head.
He cannot flee it though he should be dead,
And be she maid, or widow, or a wife.
And yet it is not likely that, in life,
You'll stand within her graces; nor shall I;
For you are well aware, aye verily,
That you and I are doomed to prison drear
Perpetually; we gain no ransom here.
We strive but as those dogs did for the bone;
They fought all day, and yet their gain was none.
Till came a kite while they were still so wroth
And bore the bone away between them both.
And therefore, at the king's court, O my brother,
It's each man for himself and not for other.
Love if you like; for I love and aye shall;
And certainly, dear brother, that is all.
Here in this prison cell must we remain
And each endure whatever fate ordain."
    Great was the strife, and long, betwixt the two,
If I had but the time to tell it you,
Save in effect. It happened on a day
(To tell the tale as briefly as I may),
A worthy duke men called Pirithous,
Who had been friend unto Duke Thesëus,
Since each had been a little child, a chit,
Was come to visit Athens and visit
His playfellow, as he was wont to do,
For in this whole world he loved no man so;
And Thesëus loved him as truly—nay,
So well each loved the other, old books say,
That when one died (it is but truth I tell),
The other went and sought him down in Hell;
But of that tale I have no wish to write.
Pirithous loved Arcita, too, that knight,
Having known him in Thebes full many a year;
And finally, at his request and prayer,
And that without a coin of ransom paid,
Duke Thesëus released him out of shade,
Freely to go where'er he wished, and to
His own devices, as I'll now tell you.

The compact was, to set it plainly down,
As made between those two of great renown:
That if Arcita, any time, were found,
Ever in life, by day or night, on ground
Of any country of this Thesëus,
And he were caught, it was concerted thus,
That by the sword he straight should lose his head.
He had no choice, so taking leave he sped
Homeward to Thebes, lest by the sword's sharp edge
He forfeit life. His neck was under pledge.
　How great a sorrow is Arcita's now!
How through his heart he feels death's heavy blow;
He weeps, he wails, he cries out piteously;
He thinks to slay himself all privily.
Said he: "Alas, the day that I was born!
I'm in worse prison, now, and more forlorn;
Now am I doomed eternally to dwell
No more in Purgatory, but in Hell.
Alas, that I have known Pirithous!
For else had I remained with Thesëus,
Fettered within that cell; but even so
Then had I been in bliss and not in woe.
Only the sight of her that I would serve,
Though I might never her dear grace deserve,
Would have sufficed, oh well enough for me!
O my dear cousin Palamon," said he,
"Yours is the victory, and that is sure,
For there, full happily, you may endure.
In prison? Never, but in Paradise!
Oh, well has Fortune turned for you the dice,
Who have the sight of her, I the absence.
For possible it is, in her presence,
You being a knight, a worthy and able,
That by some chance, since Fortune's changeable,
You may to your desire sometime attain.
But I, that am in exile and in pain,
Stripped of all hope and in so deep despair
That there's no earth nor water, fire nor air,
Nor any creature made of them there is
To help or give me comfort, now, in this—

Surely I'll die of sorrow and distress;
Farewell, my life, my love, my joyousness!
    "Alas! Why is it men so much complain
Of what great God, or Fortune, may ordain,
When better is the gift, in any guise,
Than men may often for themselves devise?
One man desires only that great wealth
Which may but cause his death or long ill-health.
One who from prison gladly would be free,
At home by his own servants slain might be.
Infinite evils lie therein, 'tis clear;
We know not what it is we pray for here.
We fare as he that's drunken as a mouse;
A drunk man knows right well he has a house,
But he knows not the right way leading thither;
And a drunk man is sure to slip and slither.
And certainly, in this world so fare we;
We furiously pursue felicity,
Yet we go often wrong before we die.
This may we all admit, and specially I,
Who deemed and held, as I were under spell,
That if I might escape from prison cell,
Then would I find again what joy might heal,
Who now am only exiled from my weal.
For since I may not see you, Emily,
I am but dead; there is no remedy."
    And on the other hand, this Palamon,
When that he found Arcita truly gone,
Such lamentation made he, that the tower
Resounded of his crying, hour by hour.
The very fetters on his legs were yet
Again with all his bitter salt tears wet.
"Alas!" said he, "Arcita, cousin mine,
With all our strife, God knows, you've won the wine.
You're walking, now, in Theban streets, at large,
And all my woe you may from mind discharge.
You may, too, since you've wisdom and manhood,
Assemble all the people of our blood
And wage a war so sharp on this city
That by some fortune, or by some treaty,

You shall yet have that lady to your wife
For whom I now must needs lay down my life.
For surely 'tis in possibility,
Since you are now at large, from prison free,
And are a lord, great is your advantage
Above my own, who die here in a cage.
For I must weep and wail, the while I live,
In all the grief that prison cell may give,
And now with pain that love gives me, also,
Which doubles all my torment and my woe."
    Therewith the fires of jealousy upstart
Within his breast and burn him to the heart
So wildly that he seems one, to behold,
Like seared box tree, or ashes, dead and cold.
Then said he: "O you cruel Gods, that sway
This world in bondage of your laws, for aye,
And write upon the tablets adamant
Your counsels and the changeless words you grant,
What better view of mankind do you hold
Than of the sheep that huddle in the fold?
For man must die like any other beast,
Or rot in prison, under foul arrest,
And suffer sickness and misfortune sad,
And still be ofttimes guiltless, too, by gad!
    "What management is in this prescience
That, guiltless, yet torments our innocence?
And this increases all my pain, as well,
That man is bound by law, nor may rebel,
For fear of God, but must repress his will,
Whereas a beast may all his lust fulfill.
And when a beast is dead, he feels no pain;
But, after death, man yet must weep amain,
Though in this world he had but care and woe:
There is no doubt that it is even so.
The answer leave I to divines to tell,
But well I know this present world is hell.
Alas! I see a serpent or a thief,
That has brought many a true man unto grief,
Going at large, and where he wills may turn,
But I must lie in gaol, because Saturn,

And Juno too, both envious and mad,
Have spilled out well-nigh all the blood we had
At Thebes, and desolated her wide walls.
And Venus slays me with the bitter galls
Of fear of Arcita, and jealousy."
   Now will I leave this Palamon, for he
Is in his prison, where he still must dwell,
And of Arcita will I forthwith tell.

   Summer being passed away and nights grown long,
Increased now doubly all the anguish strong
Both of the lover and the prisoner.
I know not which one was the woefuller.
For, to be brief about it, Palamon
Is doomed to lie for ever in prison,
In chains and fetters till he shall be dead;
And exiled (on the forfeit of his head)
Arcita must remain abroad, nor see,
For evermore, the face of his lady.
   You lovers, now I ask you this question:
Who has the worse, Arcita or Palamon?
The one may see his lady day by day,
But yet in prison must he dwell for aye.
The other, where he wishes, he may go,
But never see his lady more, ah no.
Now answer as you wish, all you that can.
For I will speak right on as I began.

           Explicit prima pars.
           Sequitur pars secunda.

Now when Arcita unto Thebes was come,
He lay and languished all day in his home,
Since he his lady nevermore should see,
But telling of his sorrow brief I'll be.
Had never any man so much torture,
No, nor shall have while this world may endure.
Bereft he was of sleep and meat and drink,
That lean he grew and dry as shaft, I think.
His eyes were hollow and ghastly to behold,
His face was sallow, all pale and ashen cold,

And solitary kept he and alone,
Wailing the whole night long, making his moan.
And if he heard a song or instrument,
Then he would weep ungoverned and lament;
So feeble were his spirits, and so low,
And so changed was he, that no man could know
Him by his words or voice, whoever heard.
And in this change, for all the world he fared
As if not troubled by malady of love,
But by that humor dark and grim, whereof
Springs melancholy madness in the brain,
And fantasy unbridled holds its reign.
And shortly, all was turned quite upside down,
Both habits and the temper all had known
Of him, this woeful lover, Dan Arcite.
    Why should I all day of his woe indite?
When he'd endured all this a year or two,
This cruel torment and this pain and woe,
At Thebes, in his own country, as I said,
Upon a night, while sleeping in his bed,
He dreamed of how the winged God Mercury
Before him stood and bade him happier be.
His sleep-bestowing wand he bore upright;
A hat he wore upon his ringlets bright.
Arrayed this god was (noted at a leap)
As he'd been when to Argus he gave sleep.
And thus he spoke: "To Athens shall you wend;
For all your woe is destined there to end."
And on that word Arcita woke and started.
"Now truly, howsoever sore I'm smarted,"
Said he, "to Athens right now will I fare;
Nor for the dread of death will I now spare
To see my lady, whom I love and serve;
I will not reck of death, with her, nor swerve."
    And with that word he caught a great mirror,
And saw how changed was all his old colour,
And saw his visage altered from its kind.
And right away it ran into his mind
That since his face was now disfigured so,
By suffering endured (as well we know),

He might, if he should bear him low in town,
Live there in Athens evermore, unknown,
Seeing his lady well-nigh every day.
And right anon he altered his array,
Like a poor labourer in mean attire,
And all alone, save only for a squire,
Who knew his secret heart and all his case,
And who was dressed as poorly as he was,
To Athens was he gone the nearest way.
And to the court he went upon a day,
And at the gate he proffered services
To drudge and drag, as any one devises.
And to be brief herein, and to be plain,
He found employment with a chamberlain
Was serving in the house of Emily;
For he was sharp and very soon could see
What every servant did who served her there.
Right well could he hew wood and water bear,
For he was young and mighty, let me own,
And big of muscle, aye and big of bone,
To do what any man asked, in a trice.
A year or two he was in this service,
Page of the chamber of Emily the bright;
He said "Philostrates" would name him right.
But half so well beloved a man as he
Was never in that court, of his degree;
His gentle nature was so clearly shown,
That throughout all the court spread his renown.
They said it were but kindly courtesy
If Theseus should heighten his degree
And put him in more honourable service
Wherein he might his virtue exercise.
And thus, anon, his name was so up-sprung,
Both for his deeds and sayings of his tongue,
That Theseus had brought him nigh and nigher
And of the chamber he had made him squire,
And given him gold to maintain dignity.
Besides, men brought him, from his own country,
From year to year, clandestinely, his rent;
But honestly and slyly it was spent,

And no man wondered how he came by it.
And three years thus he lived, with much profit,
And bore him so in peace and so in war
There was no man that Theseus loved more.
And in such bliss I leave Arcita now,
And upon Palamon some words bestow.
    In darksome, horrible, and strong prison
These seven years has now sat Palamon,
Wasted by woe and by his long distress.
Who has a twofold evil heaviness
But Palamon? whom love yet tortures so
That half out of his wits he is for woe;
And joined thereto he is a prisoner,
Perpetually, not only for a year.
And who could rhyme in English, properly,
His martyrdom? Forsooth, it is not I;
And therefore I pass lightly on my way.
    It fell out in the seventh year, in May,
On the third night (as say the books of old
Which have this story much more fully told),
Were it by chance or were it destiny
(Since, when a thing is destined, it must be),
That, shortly after midnight, Palamon,
By helping of a friend, broke from prison,
And fled the city, fast as he might go;
For he had given his guard a drink that so
Was mixed of spice and honey and certain wine
And Theban opiate and anodyne,
That all that night, although a man might shake
This gaoler, he slept on, nor could awake.
And thus he flees as fast as ever he may.
The night was short and it was nearly day,
Wherefore he needs must find a place to hide;
And to a grove that grew hard by, with stride
Of furtive foot, went fearful Palamon.
In brief, he'd formed his plan, as he went on,
That in the grove he would lie fast all day,
And when night came, then would he take his way
Toward Thebes, and there find friends, and of them pray
Their help on Theseus in war's array;

And briefly either he would lose his life,
Or else win Emily to be his wife;
This is the gist of his intention plain.
　Now I'll return to Arcita again,
Who little knew how near to him was care
Till Fortune caught him in her tangling snare.
　The busy lark, the herald of the day,
Salutes now in her song the morning grey;
And fiery Phoebus rises up so bright
That all the east is laughing with the light,
And with his streamers dries, among the greves,
The silver droplets hanging on the leaves.
And so Arcita, in the court royal
With Theseüs, and his squire principal,
Is risen, and looks on the merry day.
And now, to do his reverence to May,
Calling to mind the point of his desire,
He on a courser, leaping high like fire,
Is ridden to the fields to muse and play,
Out of the court, a mile or two away;
And to the grove, whereof I lately told,
By accident his way began to hold,
To make him there the garland that one weaves
Of woodbine leaves and of green hawthorn leaves.
And loud he sang within the sunlit sheen:
"O May, with all thy flowers and all thy green,
Welcome be thou, thou fair and freshening May:
I hope to pluck some garland green today."
And from his courser, with a lusty heart,
Into the grove right hastily did start,
And on a path he wandered up and down,
Near which, and as it chanced, this Palamon
Lay in the thicket, where no man might see,
For sore afraid of finding death was he.
He knew not that Arcita was so near:
God knows he would have doubted eye and ear,
But it has been a truth these many years
That "Fields have eyes and every wood has ears."
It's well for one to bear himself with poise;
For every day unlooked-for chance annoys.

And little knew Arcita of his friend,
Who was so near and heard him to the end,
Where in the bush he sat now, keeping still.
   Arcita, having roamed and roved his fill,
And having sung his rondel, lustily,
Into a study fell he, suddenly,
As do these lovers in their strange desires,
Now in the trees, now down among the briers,
Now up, now down, like bucket in a well.
Even as on a Friday, truth to tell,
The sun shines now, and now the rain comes fast,
Even so can fickle Venus overcast
The spirits of her people; as her day
Is changeful, so she changes her array.
Seldom is Friday quite like all the week.
   Arcita, having sung, began to speak,
And sat him down, sighing like one forlorn.
"Alas," said he, "the day that I was born!
How long, O Juno, of thy cruelty,
Wilt thou wage bitter war on Thebes city?
Alas! Confounded beyond all reason
The blood of Cadmus and of Amphion;
Of royal Cadmus, who was the first man
To build at Thebes, and first the town began,
And first of all the city to be king;
Of his lineage am I, and his offspring,
By true descent, and of the stock royal:
And now I'm such a wretched serving thrall,
That he who is my mortal enemy,
I serve him as his squire, and all humbly.
And even more does Juno give me shame,
For I dare not acknowledge my own name;
But whereas I was Arcita by right,
Now I'm Philostrates, not worth a mite.
Alas, thou cruel Mars! Alas, Juno!
Thus have your angers all our kin brought low,
Save only me, and wretched Palamon,
Whom Theseus martyrs yonder in prison.
And above all, to slay me utterly,
Love has his fiery dart so burningly

Struck through my faithful and care-laden heart,
My death was patterned ere my swaddling shirt.
You slay me with your two eyes, Emily;
You are the cause for which I now must die.
For on the whole of all my other care
I would not set the value of a tare,
So I could do one thing to your pleasance!"
And with that word he fell down in a trance
That lasted long; and then he did up-start.
   This Palamon, who thought that through his heart
He felt a cold and sudden sword blade glide,
For rage he shook, no longer would he hide.
But after he had heard Arcita's tale,
As he were mad, with face gone deathly pale,
He started up and sprang out of the thicket,
Crying: "Arcita, oh you traitor wicked,
Now are you caught, that crave my lady so,
For whom I suffer all this pain and woe,
And are my blood, and know my secrets' store,
As I have often told you heretofore,
And have befooled the great Duke Theseüs,
And falsely changed your name and station thus:
Either I shall be dead or you shall die.
You shall not love my lady Emily,
But I will love her, and none other, no;
For I am Palamon, your mortal foe.
And though I have no weapon in this place,
Being but out of prison by God's grace,
I say again, that either you shall die
Or else forgo your love for Emily.
Choose which you will, for you shall not depart."
   This Arcita, with scornful, angry heart,
When he knew him and all the tale had heard,
Fierce as a lion, out he pulled a sword,
And answered thus: "By God that sits above!
Were it not you are sick and mad for love,
And that you have no weapon in this place,
Out of this grove you'd never move a pace,
But meet your death right now, and at my hand.
For I renounce the bond and its demand

Which you assert that I have made with you.
What, arrant fool, love's free to choose and do,
And I will have her, spite of all your might!
But in as much as you're a worthy knight
And willing to defend your love, in mail,
Hear now this word: tomorrow I'll not fail
(Without the cognizance of any wight)
To come here armed and harnessed as a knight,
And to bring arms for you, too, as you'll see;
And choose the better and leave the worse for me.
And meat and drink this very night I'll bring,
Enough for you, and clothes for your bedding.
And if it be that you my lady win
And slay me in this wood that now I'm in,
Then may you have your lady, for all of me."
    This Palamon replied: "I do agree."
And thus they parted till the morrow morn,
When each had pledged his honour to return.
    O Cupido, that know'st not charity!
O despot, that no peer will have with thee!
Truly, 'tis said, that love, like all lordship,
Declines, with little thanks, a partnership.
Well learned they that, Arcite and Palamon.
    Arcita rode into the town anon,
And on the morrow, ere the dawn, he bore,
Secretly, arms and armour out of store,
Enough for each, and proper to maintain
A battle in the field between the twain.
So on his horse, alone as he was born,
He carried out that harness as he'd sworn;
And in the grove, at time and place they'd set,
Arcita and this Palamon were met.
Each of the two changed colour in the face.
For as the hunter in the realm of Thrace
Stands at the clearing with his ready spear,
When hunted is the lion, or the bear,
And through the forest hears him rushing fast,
Breaking the boughs and leaves, and thinks aghast,
"Here comes apace my mortal enemy!
Now, without fail, he must be slain, or I;

For either I must kill him ere he pass,
Or he will make of me a dead carcass"—
So fared these men, in altering their hue,
So far as each the strength of other knew.
There was no "good-day" given, no saluting,
But without word, rehearsal, or such thing,
Each of them helping, so they armed each other
As dutifully as he were his own brother;
And afterward, with their sharp spears and strong,
They thrust each at the other wondrous long.
You might have fancied that this Palamon,
In battle, was a furious, mad lion,
And that Arcita was a tiger quite:
Like very boars the two began to smite,
Like boars that froth for anger in the wood.
Up to the ankles fought they in their blood.
And leaving them thus fighting fast and fell,
Forthwith of Thesëus I now will tell.

　　Great destiny, minister-general,
That executes in this world, and for all,
The needs that God foresaw ere we were born,
So strong it is that, though the world had sworn
The contrary of a thing, by yea or nay,
Yet sometime it shall fall upon a day,
Though not again within a thousand years.
For certainly our wishes and our fears,
Whether of war or peace, or hate or love,
All, all are ruled by that Foresight above.
This show I now by mighty Thesëus,
Who to go hunting is so desirous,
And specially of the hart of ten, in May,
That, in his bed, there dawns for him no day
That he's not clothed and soon prepared to ride
With hound and horn and huntsman at his side.
For in his hunting has he such delight,
That it is all his joy and appetite
To be himself the great hart's deadly bane:
For after Mars, he serves Diana's reign.

　　Clear was the day, as I have told ere this,
When Thesëus, compact of joy and bliss,

With his Hippolyta, the lovely queen,
And fair Emilia, clothed all in green,
A-hunting they went riding royally.
And to the grove of trees that grew hard by,
In which there was a hart, as men had told,
Duke Thesëus the shortest way did hold.
And to the glade he rode on, straight and right,
For there the hart was wont to go in flight,
And over a brook, and so forth on his way.
This duke would have a course at him today,
With such hounds as it pleased him to command.
　And when this duke was come upon that land,
Under the slanting sun he looked, anon,
And there saw Arcita and Palamon,
Who furiously fought, as two boars do;
The bright swords went in circles to and fro
So terribly, that even their least stroke
Seemed powerful enough to fell an oak;
But who the two were, nothing did he note.
This duke his courser with the sharp spurs smote,
And in one bound he was between the two,
And lugged his great sword out, and cried out: "Ho!
No more, I say, on pain of losing head!
By mighty Mars, that one shall soon be dead
Who smites another stroke that I may see!
But tell me now what manner of men ye be
That are so hardy as to fight out here
Without a judge or other officer,
As if you rode in lists right royally?"
　This Palamon replied, then, hastily,
Saying: "O Sire, what need for more ado?
We have deserved our death at hands of you.
Two woeful wretches are we, two captives
That are encumbered by our own sad lives;
And as you are a righteous lord and judge,
Give us not either mercy or refuge,
But slay me first, for sacred charity;
But slay my fellow here, as well, with me.
Or slay him first; for though you learn it late,
This is your mortal foe, Arcita—wait!—

That from the land was banished, on his head.
And for the which he merits to be dead.
For this is he who came unto your gate,
Calling himself Philostrates—nay, wait!—
Thus has he fooled you well this many a year,
And you have made him your chief squire, I hear:
And this is he that loves fair Emily.
For since the day is come when I must die,
I make confession plainly and say on,
That I am that same woeful Palamon
Who has your prison broken, viciously.
I am your mortal foe, and it is I
Who love so hotly Emily the bright
That I'll die gladly here within her sight.
Therefore do I ask death as penalty;
But slay my fellow with the same mercy,
For both of us deserve but to be slain."
    This worthy duke presently spoke again,
Saying: "This judgment needs but a short session:
Your own mouth, aye, and by your own confession,
Has doomed and damned you, as I shall record.
There is no need for torture, on my word.
But you shall die, by mighty Mars the red!"
    But then the queen, whose heart for pity bled,
Began to weep, and so did Emily
And all the ladies in the company.
Great pity must it be, so thought they all,
That ever such misfortune should befall:
For these were gentlemen, of great estate,
And for no thing, save love, was their debate.
They saw their bloody wounds, so sore and wide,
And all cried out—greater and less, they cried:
"Have mercy, lord, upon us women all!"
And down upon their bare knees did they fall,
And would have kissed his feet there where he stood,
Till at the last assuaged was his high mood;
For soon will pity flow through gentle heart.
And though he first for ire did shake and start,
He soon considered, to state the case in brief,
What cause they had for fighting, what for grief;

And though his anger still their guilt accused,
Yet in his reason he held them both excused;
In such wise: he thought well that every man
Will help himself in love, if he but can,
And will himself deliver from prison;
And, too, at heart he had compassion on
Those women, for they cried and wept as one;
And in his gentle heart he thought anon,
And softly to himself he said then: "Fie
Upon a lord that will have no mercy,
But acts the lion, both in word and deed,
To those repentant and in fear and need,
As well as to the proud and pitiless man
That still would do the thing that he began!
That lord must surely in discretion lack
Who, in such case, can no distinction make,
But weighs both proud and humble in one scale."
And shortly, when his ire was thus grown pale,
He looked up to the sky, with eyes alight,
And spoke these words, as he would promise plight:
"The god of love, ah *benedicite!*
How mighty and how great a lord is he!
Against his might may stand no obstacles,
A true god is he by his miracles;
For he can manage, in his own sweet wise,
The heart of anyone as he devise.
Lo, here, Arcita and this Palamon,
That were delivered out of my prison,
And might have lived in Thebes right royally,
Knowing me for their mortal enemy,
And also that their lives lay in my hand;
And yet their love has wiled them to this land,
Against all sense, and brought them here to die!
Look you now, is not that a folly high?
Who can be called a fool, except he love?
And see, for sake of God who sits above,
See how they bleed! Are they not well arrayed?
Thus has their lord, the god of love, repaid
Their wages and their fees for their service!
And yet they are supposed to be full wise

Who serve love well, whatever may befall!
But this is yet the best jest of them all,
That she for whom they have this jollity
Can thank them for it quite as much as me;
She knows no more of all this fervent fare,
By God! than knows a cuckoo or a hare.
But all must be essayed, both hot and cold,
A man must play the fool, when young or old;
I know it of myself from years long gone:
For of love's servants I've been numbered one.
And therefore, since I know well all love's pain,
And know how sorely it can man constrain,
As one that has been taken in the net,
I will forgive your trespass, and forget,
At instance of my sweet queen, kneeling here,
Aye, and of Emily, my sister dear.
And you shall presently consent to swear
That nevermore will you my power dare,
Nor wage war on me, either night or day,
But will be friends to me in all you may;
I do forgive this trespass, full and fair."
    And then they swore what he demanded there,
And, of his might, they of his mercy prayed,
And he extended grace, and thus he said:
"To speak for royalty's inheritress,
Although she be a queen or a princess,
Each of you both is worthy, I confess,
When comes the time to wed: but nonetheless,
I speak now of my sister Emily,
The cause of all this strife and jealousy—
You know yourselves she may not marry two,
At once, although you fight or what you do:
One of you, then, and be he loath or lief,
Must pipe his sorrows in an ivy leaf.
That is to say, she cannot have you both,
However jealous one may be, or wroth.
Therefore I put you both in this decree,
That each of you shall learn his destiny
As it is cast; and hear, now, in what wise

The word of fate shall speak through my device.
  "My will is this, to draw conclusion flat,
Without reply, or plea, or caveat
(In any case, accept it for the best),
That each of you shall follow his own quest,
Free of all ransom or of fear from me;
And this day, fifty weeks hence, both shall be
Here once again, each with a hundred knights,
Armed for the lists, who stoutly for your rights
Will ready be to battle, to maintain
Your claim to love. I promise you, again,
Upon my word, and as I am a knight,
That whichsoever of you wins the fight,
That is to say, whichever of you two
May with his hundred, whom I spoke of, do
His foe to death, or out of boundary drive,
Then he shall have Emilia to wive
To whom Fortuna gives so fair a grace.
The lists shall be erected in this place.
And God so truly on my soul have ruth
As I shall prove an honest judge, in truth.
You shall no other judgment in me waken
Than that the one shall die or else be taken.
And if you think the sentence is well said,
Speak your opinion, that you're well repaid.
This is the end, and I conclude hereon."
  Who looks up lightly now but Palamon?
Who leaps for you but Arcita the knight?
And who could tell, or who could ever write
The jubilation made within that place
Where Thesëus has shown so fair a grace?
But down on knee went each one for delight
And thanked him there with all his heart and might,
And specially those Thebans did their part.
And thus, with high hopes, being blithe of heart,
They took their leave; and homeward did they ride
To Thebes that sits within her old walls wide.

Explicit secunda pars.
Sequitur pars tercia.

I think that men would deem it negligence
If I forgot to tell of the expense
Of Thesëus, who went so busily
To work upon the lists, right royally;
For such an amphitheatre he made,
Its equal never yet on earth was laid.
The circuit, rising, hemmed a mile about,
Walled all of stone and moated deep without.
Round was the shape as compass ever traces,
And built in tiers, the height of sixty paces,
That those who sat in one tier, or degree,
Should hinder not the folk behind to see.
   Eastward there stood a gate of marble white,
And westward such another, opposite.
In brief, no place on earth, and so sublime,
Was ever made in so small space of time;
For in the land there was no craftsman quick
At plane geometry or arithmetic,
No painter and no sculptor of hard stone,
But Thesëus pressed meat and wage upon
To build that amphitheatre and devise.
And to observe all rites and sacrifice,
Over the eastern gate, and high above,
For worship of Queen Venus, god of love,
He built an altar and an oratory;
And westward, being mindful of the glory
Of Mars, he straightway builded such another
As cost a deal of gold and many a bother.
And northward, in a turret on the wall,
Of alabaster white and red coral,
An oratory splendid as could be,
In honour of Diana's chastity,
Duke Thesëus wrought out in noble wise.
   But yet have I forgot to advertise
The noble carvings and the portraitures,
The shapes, the countenances, the figures
That all were in these oratories three.
   First, in the fane of Venus, one might see,
Wrought on the wall, and piteous to behold,
The broken slumbers and the sighing cold,

The sacred tears and the lamenting dire,
The fiery throbbing of the strong desire,
That all love's servants in this life endure;
The vows that all their promises assure;
Pleasure and hope, desire, foolhardiness,
Beauty, youth, bawdiness, and riches, yes,
Charms, and all force, and lies, and flattery,
Expense, and labour; aye, and Jealousy
That wore of marigolds a great garland
And had a cuckoo sitting on her hand;
Carols and instruments and feasts and dances,
Lust and array, and all the circumstances
Of love that I may reckon or ever shall,
In order they were painted on the wall,
Aye, and more, too, than I have ever known.
For truly, all the Mount of Citheron,
Where Venus has her chief and favoured dwelling,
Was painted on that wall, beyond my telling,
With all the gardens in their loveliness.
Nor was forgot the gate-guard Idleness,
Nor fair Narcissus of the years long gone,
Nor yet the folly of King Solomon,
No, nor the giant strength of Hercules,
Nor Circe's and Medea's sorceries,
Nor Turnus with his hardy, fierce courage,
Nor the rich Croesus, captive in his age.
Thus may be seen that wisdom, nor largess,
Beauty, nor skill, nor strength, nor hardiness,
May with Queen Venus share authority;
For as she wills, so must the whole world be.
Lo, all these folk were so caught in her snare
They cried aloud in sorrow and in care.
Here let suffice examples one or two,
Though I might give a thousand more to you.
    The form of Venus, glorious as could be,
Was naked, floating on the open sea,
And from the navel down all covered was
With green waves, bright as ever any glass.
A citole in her small right hand had she,
And on her head, and beautiful to see,

A garland of red roses, sweet smelling;
Above her swirled her white doves, fluttering.
Before her stood her one son, Cupido,
Whose two white wings upon his shoulders grow;
And blind he was, as it is often seen;
A bow he bore, and arrows bright and keen.

   Why should I not as well, now, tell you all
The portraiture that was upon the wall
Within the fane of mighty Mars the red?
In length and breadth the whole wall was painted
Like the interior of that grisly place,
The mighty temple of great Mars in Thrace,
In that same cold and frosty region where
Mars to his supreme mansion may repair.

   First, on the wall was limned a vast forest
Wherein there dwelt no man nor any beast,
With knotted, gnarled, and leafless trees, so old
The sharpened stumps were dreadful to behold;
Through which there ran a rumbling, even now,
As if a storm were breaking every bough;
And down a hill, beneath a sharp descent,
The temple stood of Mars armipotent,
Wrought all of burnished steel, whereof the gate
Was grim like death to see, and long, and strait.
And therefrom raged a wind that seemed to shake
The very ground, and made the great doors quake.
The northern light in at those same doors shone,
For window in that massive wall was none
Through which a man might any light discern.
The doors were all of adamant eterne,
Rivetted on both sides, and all along,
With toughest iron; and to make it strong,
Each pillar that sustained this temple grim
Was thick as tun, of iron bright and trim.

   There saw I first the dark imagining
Of felony, and all the compassing;
And cruel anger, red as burning coal;
Pickpurses, and the dread that eats the soul;
The smiling villain, hiding knife in cloak;
The farm barns burning, and the thick black smoke;

The treachery of murder done in bed;
The open battle, with the wounds that bled;
Contest, with bloody knife and sharp menace;
And loud with creaking was that dismal place.
The slayer of himself, too, saw I there,
His very heart's blood matted in his hair;
The nail that's driven in the skull by night;
The cold plague corpse, with gaping mouth upright.
In middle of the temple sat Mischance,
With gloomy, grimly woeful countenance.
And saw I Madness laughing in his rage;
Armed risings, and outcries, and fierce outrage;
The carrion in the bush, with throat wide carved;
A thousand slain, nor one by plague, nor starved.
The tyrant, with the spoils of violent theft;
The town destroyed, in ruins, nothing left.
And saw I burnt the ships that dance by phares;
The hunter strangled by the fierce wild bears;
The sow chewing the child right in the cradle;
The cook well scalded, spite of his long ladle.
Nothing was lacking of Mars' evil part:
The carter overdriven by his cart,
Under a wheel he lay low in the dust.
There were likewise in Mars' house, as needs must,
The surgeon, and the butcher, and the smith
Who forges sharp swords and great ills therewith.
And over all, depicted in a tower,
Sat Conquest, high in honour and in power,
Yet with a sharp sword hanging o'er his head
But by the tenuous twisting of a thread.
Depicted was the death of Julius,
Of Nero great, and of Antonius;
And though at that same time they were unborn,
There were their deaths depicted to adorn
The menacing of Mars, in likeness sure;
Things were so shown, in all that portraiture,
As are fore shown among the stars above,
Who shall be slain in war or dead for love.
Suffice one instance from old plenitude,
I could not tell them all, even if I would.

Mars' image stood upon a chariot,
Armed, and so grim that mad he seemed, God wot;
And o'er his head two constellations shone
Of stars that have been named in writings known,
One being Puella, and one Rubeus.
This god of armies was companioned thus:
A wolf there was before him, at his feet,
Red-eyed, and of a dead man he did eat.
A cunning pencil there had limned this story
In reverence of Mars and of his glory.
    Now to the temple of Diana chaste,
As briefly as I can, I'll pass in haste,
To lay before you its description well.
In pictures, up and down, the wall could tell
Of hunting and of modest chastity.
There saw I how Callisto fared when she
(Diana being much aggrieved with her)
Was changed from woman into a she-bear,
And after, made into the lone Pole Star;
There was it; I can't tell how such things are.
Her son, too, is a star, as men may see.
There saw I Daphne turned into a tree
(I do not mean Diana, no, but she,
Penëus' daughter, who was called Daphne).
I saw Actaeon made a hart all rude
For punishment of seeing Diana nude;
I saw, too, how his fifty hounds had caught
And him were eating, since they knew him not.
And painted farther on, I saw before
How Atalanta hunted the wild boar;
And Meleager, and many another there,
For which Diana wrought him woe and care.
There saw I many another wondrous tale
From which I will not now draw memory's veil.
This goddess on an antlered hart was set,
With little hounds about her feet, and yet
Beneath her perfect feet there was a moon,
Waxing it was, but it should wane full soon.
In robes of yellowish green her statue was,
She'd bow in hand and arrows in a case.

Her eyes were downcast, looking at the ground,
Where Pluto in his dark realm may be found.
Before her was a woman travailing,
Who was so long in giving birth, poor thing,
That pitifully Lucina did she call,
Praying, "Oh help, for thou may'st best of all!"
Well could he paint, who had this picture wrought,
With many a florin he'd his colours bought,
   But now the lists were done, and Thesëus,
Who at so great cost had appointed thus
The temples and the circus, as I tell,
When all was done, he liked it wondrous well.
But hold I will from Thesëus, and on
To speak of Arcita and Palamon.
   The day of their return is forthcoming,
When each of them a hundred knights must bring
The combat to support, as I have told;
And into Athens, covenant to uphold,
Has each one ridden with his hundred knights,
Well armed for war, at all points, in their mights.
And certainly, 'twas thought by many a man
That never, since the day this world began,
Speaking of good knights hardy of their hands,
Wherever God created seas and lands,
Was, of so few, so noble company.
For every man that loved all chivalry,
And eager was to win surpassing fame,
Had prayed to play a part in that great game;
And all was well with him who chosen was.
For if there came tomorrow such a case,
You know right well that every lusty knight
Who loves the ladies fair and keeps his might,
Be it in England, aye or otherwhere,
Would wish of all things to be present there
To fight for some fair lady. *Ben'cite!*
'Twould be a pleasant goodly sight to see!
   And so it was with those with Palamon.
With him there rode of good knights many a one;
Some would be armoured in a habergeon
And in a breastplate, under light jupon;

And some wore breast- and back-plates thick and large;
And some would have a Prussian shield, or targe;
Some on their very legs were armoured well,
And carried axe, and some a mace of steel.
There is no new thing, now, that is not old.
And so they all were armed, as I have told,
To his own liking and design, each one.
  There might you see, riding with Palamon,
Lycurgus' self, the mighty king of Thrace;
Black was his beard and manly was his face.
The eyeballs in the sockets of his head,
They glowed between a yellow and a red.
And like a griffon glared he round about
From under bushy eyebrows thick and stout.
His limbs were large, his muscles hard and strong,
His shoulders broad, his arms both big and long,
And, as the fashion was in his country,
High in a chariot of gold stood he,
With four white bulls in traces, to progress.
Instead of coat-of-arms above harness,
With yellow claws preserved and bright as gold,
He wore a bear-skin, black and very old.
His long combed hair was hanging down his back,
As any raven's feather it was black:
A wreath of gold, arm-thick, of heavy weight,
Was on his head, and set with jewels great,
Of rubies fine and perfect diamonds.
About his car there circled huge white hounds,
Twenty or more, as large as any steer,
To hunt the lion or the antlered deer;
And so they followed him, with muzzles bound,
Wearing gold collars with smooth rings and round.
A hundred lords came riding in his rout,
All armed at point, with hearts both stern and stout.
  With Arcita, in tales men call to mind,
The great Emetrëus, a king of Ind,
Upon a bay steed harnessed all in steel,
Covered with cloth of gold, all diapered well,
Came riding like the god of arms, great Mars.
His coat-of-arms was cloth of the Tartars,

Begemmed with pearls, all white and round and great.
Of beaten gold his saddle, burnished late;
A mantle from his shoulders hung, the thing
Close-set with rubies red, like fire blazing.
His crisp hair all in bright ringlets was run,
Yellow as gold and gleaming as the sun.
His nose was high, his eyes a bright citrine,
His lips were full, his colouring sanguine,
And a few freckles on his face were seen,
None either black or yellow, but the mean;
And like a lion he his glances cast.
Not more than five-and-twenty years he'd past.
His beard was well beginning, now, to spring;
His voice was as a trumpet thundering.
Upon his brows he wore, of laurel green,
A garland, fresh and pleasing to be seen.
Upon his wrist he bore, for his delight,
An eagle tame, as any lily white.
A hundred lords came riding with him there,
All armed, except their heads, in all their gear,
And wealthily appointed in all things.
For, trust me well, that dukes and earls and kings
Were gathered in this noble company
For love and for increase of chivalry.
About this king there ran, on every side,
Many tame lions and leopards in their pride.
And in such wise these mighty lords, in sum,
Were, of a Sunday, to the city come
About the prime, and in the town did light.
   This Thesëus, this duke, this noble knight,
When he'd conducted them to his city,
And quartered them, according to degree,
He feasted them, and was at so much pains
To give them ease and honour, of his gains,
That men yet hold that never human wit,
Of high or low estate, could better it.
The minstrelsy, the service at the feast,
The great gifts to the highest and the least,
The furnishings of Thesëus' rich palace,
Who highest sat or lowest on the dais,

What ladies fairest were or best dandling,
Or which of them could dance the best, or sing,
Or who could speak most feelingly of love,
Or what hawks sat upon the perch above,
Or what great hounds were lying on the floor—
Of all these I will make no mention more;
But tell my tale, for that, I think, is best;
Now comes the point, and listen if you've zest.
    That Sunday night, ere day began to spring,
When Palamon the earliest lark heard sing,
Although it lacked two hours of being day,
Yet the lark sang, and Palamon sang a lay.
With pious heart and with a high courage
He rose, to go upon a pilgrimage
Unto the blessed Cytherea's shrine
(I mean Queen Venus, worthy and benign).
And at her hour he then walked forth apace
Out to the lists wherein her temple was,
And down he knelt in manner to revere,
And from a full heart spoke as you shall hear.
    "Fairest of fair, O lady mine, Venus,
Daughter of Jove and spouse to Vulcanus,
Thou gladdener of the Mount of Citheron,
By that great love thou borest to Adon,
Have pity on my bitter tears that smart
And hear my humble prayer within thy heart.
Alas! I have no words in which to tell
The effect of all the torments of my hell;
My heavy heart its evils can't bewray;
I'm so confused I can find naught to say.
But mercy, lady bright, that knowest well
My heart, and seëst all the ills I feel,
Consider and have ruth upon my sore
As truly as I shall, for evermore,
Well as I may, thy one true servant be,
And wage a war henceforth on chastity.
If thou wilt help, thus do I make my vow,
To boast of knightly skill I care not now,
Nor do I ask tomorrow's victory,
Nor any such renown, nor vain glory

Of prize of arms, blown before lord and churl,
But I would have possession of one girl,
Of Emily, and die in thy service;
Find thou the manner how, and in what wise.
For I care not, unless it better be,
Whether I vanquish them or they do me,
So I may have my lady in my arms.
For though Mars is the god of war's alarms,
Thy power is so great in Heaven above,
That, if it be thy will, I'll have my love.
In thy fane will I worship always, so
That on thine altar, where'er I ride or go,
I will lay sacrifice and thy fires feed.
And if thou wilt not so, O lady, cede,
I pray thee, that tomorrow, with a spear,
Arcita bear me through the heart, just here.
For I'll care naught, when I have lost my life,
That Arcita may win her for his wife.
This the effect and end of all my prayer,
Give me my love, thou blissful lady fair."
　　Now when he'd finished all the orison,
His sacrifice he made, this Palamon,
Right piously, with all the circumstance,
Albeit I tell not now his observance.
But at the last the form of Venus shook
And gave a sign, and thereupon he took
This as acceptance of his prayer that day.
For though the augury showed some delay,
Yet he knew well that granted was his boon;
And with glad heart he got him home right soon.
　　Three hours unequal after Palamon
To Venus' temple at the lists had gone,
Up rose the sun and up rose Emily,
And to Diana's temple did she hie.
Her maidens led she thither, and with them
They carefully took fire and each emblem,
And incense, robes, and the remainder all
Of things for sacrifice ceremonial.
There was not one thing lacking; I'll but add
The horns of mead, as was a way they had.

In smoking temple, full of draperies fair,
This Emily with young heart debonnaire,
Her body washed in water from a well;
But how she did the rite I dare not tell,
Except it be at large, in general;
And yet it was a thing worth hearing all;
When one's well meaning, there is no transgression;
But it is best to speak at one's discretion.
Her bright hair was unbound, but combed withal;
She wore of green oak leaves a coronal
Upon her lovely head. Then she began
Two fires upon the altar stone to fan,
And did her ceremonies as we're told
In Statius' *Thebaid* and books as old.
When kindled was the fire, with sober face
Unto Diana spoke she in that place.
    "O thou chaste goddess of the wildwood green,
By whom all heaven and earth and sea are seen,
Queen of the realm of Pluto, dark and low,
Goddess of maidens, that my heart dost know
For all my years, and knowest what I desire,
Oh, save me from thy vengeance and thine ire
That on Actaeon fell so cruelly.
Chaste goddess, well indeed thou knowest that I
Desire to be a virgin all my life,
Nor ever wish to be man's love or wife.
I am, thou know'st, yet of thy company,
A maid, who loves the hunt and venery,
And to go rambling in the greenwood wild,
And not to be a wife and be with child.
I do not crave the company of man.
Now help me, lady, since thou may'st and can,
By the three beings who are one in thee.
For Palamon, who bears such love to me,
And for Arcita, loving me so sore,
This grace I pray thee, without one thing more,
To send down love and peace between those two,
And turn their hearts away from me: so do
That all their furious love and their desire,
And all their ceaseless torment and their fire

Be quenched or turned into another place;
And if it be thou wilt not show this grace,
Or if my destiny be moulded so
That I must needs have one of these same two,
Then send me him that most desires me.
Behold, O goddess of utter chastity,
The bitter tears that down my two cheeks fall.
Since thou art maid and keeper of us all,
My maidenhead keep thou, and still preserve,
And while I live a maid, thee will I serve."
     The fires blazed high upon the altar there,
While Emily was saying thus her prayer,
But suddenly she saw a sight most quaint,
For there, before her eyes, one fire went faint,
Then blazed again; and after that, anon,
The other fire was quenched, and so was gone.
And as it died it made a whistling sound.
As do wet branches burning on the ground,
And from the brands' ends there ran out, anon,
What looked like drops of blood, and many a one;
At which so much aghast was Emily
That she was near dazed, and began to cry,
For she knew naught of what it signified;
But only out of terror thus she cried
And wept, till it was pitiful to hear.
But thereupon Diana did appear,
With bow in hand, like any right huntress,
And said: "My daughter, leave this heaviness.
Among the high gods it has been affirmed,
And by eternal written word confirmed,
That you shall be the wife of one of those
Who bear for you so many cares and woes;
But unto which of them I may not tell.
I can no longer tarry, so farewell.
The fires that on my altar burn incense
Should tell you everything, ere you go hence,
Of what must come of love in this your case."
     And with that word the arrows of the chase
The goddess carried clattered and did ring,
And forth she went in mystic vanishing;

At which this Emily astonished was,
And said she then: "Ah, what means this, alas!
I put myself in thy protection here,
Diana, and at thy disposal dear."
   And home she wended, then, the nearest way.
This is the purport; there's no more to say.
   At the next hour of Mars, and following this,
Arcita to the temple walked, that is
Devoted to fierce Mars, to sacrifice
With all the ceremonies, pagan-wise.
With sobered heart and high devotion, on
This wise, right thus he said his orison.
   "O mighty god that in the regions cold
Of Thrace art honoured, where thy lordships hold,
And hast in every realm and every land
The reins of battle in thy guiding hand,
And givest fortune as thou dost devise,
Accept of me my pious sacrifice.
If so it be that my youth may deserve,
And that my strength be worthy found to serve
Thy godhead, and be numbered one of thine,
Then pray I thee for ruth on pain that's mine.
For that same pain and even that hot fire
Wherein thou once did'st burn with deep desire,
When thou did'st use the marvelous beauty
Of fair young wanton Venus, fresh and free,
And had'st her in thine arms and at thy will
(Howbeit with thee, once, all the chance fell ill,
And Vulcan caught thee in his net, whenas
He found thee lying with his wife, alas!)—
For that same sorrow that was in thy heart,
Have pity, now, upon my pains that smart.
I'm young, and little skilled, as knowest thou,
With love more hurt and much more broken now
Than ever living creature was, I'm sure;
For she who makes me all this woe endure,
Whether I float or sink cares not at all,
And ere she'll hear with mercy when I call,
I must by prowess win her in this place;
And well I know, too, without help and grace

Of thee, my human strength shall not avail.
Then help me, lord, tomorrow not to fail,
For sake of that same fire that once burned thee,
The which consuming fire so now burns me;
And grant, tomorrow, I have victory.
Mine be the toil, and thine the whole glory!
Thy sovereign temple will I honour most
Of any spot, and toil and count no cost
To pleasure thee and in thy craft have grace,
And in thy fane my banner will I place,
And all the weapons of my company;
And evermore, until the day I die,
Eternal fire shalt thou before thee find.
Moreover, to this vow myself I bind:
My beard, my hair that ripples down so long,
That never yet has felt the slightest wrong
Of razor or of shears, to thee I'll give,
And be thy loyal servant while I live.
Now, lord, have pity on my sorrows sore;
Give me the victory. I ask no more."
    With ended prayer of Arcita the young,
The rings that on the temple door were hung,
And even the doors themselves, rattled so fast
That this Arcita found himself aghast.
The fires blazed high upon the altar bright,
Until the entire temple shone with light;
And a sweet odour rose up from the ground;
And Arcita whirled then his arm around,
And yet more incense on the fire he cast,
And did still further rites; and at the last
The armour of God Mars began to ring,
And with that sound there came a murmuring,
Low and uncertain, saying: "Victory!"
For which he gave Mars honour and glory.
And thus in joy and hope, which all might dare,
Arcita to his lodging then did fare,
Fain of the fight as fowl is of the sun.
    But thereupon such quarrelling was begun,
From this same granting, in the heaven above,
'Twixt lovely Venus, goddess of all love,

And Mars, the iron god armipotent,
That Jove toiled hard to make a settlement;
Until the sallow Saturn, calm and cold,
Who had so many happenings known of old,
Found from his full experience the art
To satisfy each party and each part.
For true it is, age has great advantage;
Experience and wisdom come with age;
Men may the old outrun, but not outwit.
Thus Saturn, though it scarcely did befit
His nature so to do, devised a plan
To quiet all the strife, and thus began:
   "Now my dear daughter Venus," quoth Saturn,
"My course, which has so wide a way to turn,
Has power more than any man may know.
Mine is the drowning in the sea below;
Mine is the dungeon underneath the moat;
Mine is the hanging and strangling by the throat;
Rebellion, and the base crowd's murmuring,
The groaning and the private poisoning,
And vengeance and amercement—all are mine,
While yet I dwell within the Lion's sign.
Mine is the ruining of all high halls,
And tumbling down of towers and of walls
Upon the miner and the carpenter.
I struck down Samson, that pillar shaker;
And mine are all the maladies so cold,
The treasons dark, the machinations old;
My glance is father of all pestilence.
Now weep no more. I'll see, with diligence,
That Palamon, who is your own true knight,
Shall have his lady, as you hold is right.
Though Mars may help his man, yet none the less
Between you two there must come sometime peace,
And though you be not of one temperament,
Causing each day such violent dissent,
I am your grandsire and obey your will;
Weep then no more, your pleasure I'll fulfill."
   Now will I cease to speak of gods above,
Of Mars and Venus, goddess of all love,

And tell you now, as plainly as I can,
The great result, for which I first began.

Explicit tercia pars.
Sequitur pars quarta.

Great was the fête in Athens on that day,
And too, the merry season of the May
Gave everyone such joy and such pleasance
That all that Monday they'd but joust and dance,
Or spend the time in Venus' high service.
But for the reason that they must arise
Betimes, to see the heralded great fight,
All they retired to early rest that night.
And on the morrow, when that day did spring,
Of horse and harness, noise and clattering,
There was enough in hostelries about.
And to the palace rode full many a rout
Of lords, bestriding steeds and on palfreys.
There could you see adjusting of harness,
So curious and so rich, and wrought so well
Of goldsmiths' work, embroidery, and of steel;
The shields, the helmets bright, the gay trappings,
The gold-hewn casques, the coat-of-arms, the rings,
The lords in vestments rich, on their coursers,
Knights with their retinues and also squires;
The rivetting of spears, the helm-buckling,
The strapping of the shields, and thong-lacing—
In their great need, not one of them was idle;
The frothing steeds, champing the golden bridle,
And the quick smiths, and armourers also,
With file and hammer spurring to and fro;
Yeoman, and peasants with short staves were out,
Crowding as thick as they could move about;
Pipes, trumpets, kettledrums, and clarions,
That in the battle sound such grim summons;
The palace full of people, up and down,
Here three, there ten, debating the renown
And questioning about these Theban knights,
Some put it thus, some said, "It's so by rights."

Some held with him who had the great black beard,
Some with the baldheads, some with the thick haired;
Some said, "He looks grim, and he'll fight like hate;
He has an axe of twenty pound in weight."
And thus the hall was full of gossiping
Long after the bright sun began to spring.
  The mighty Thesëus, from sleep awakened
By songs and all the noise that never slackened,
Kept yet the chamber of this rich palace,
Till the two Theban knights, with equal grace
And honour, were ushered in with flourish fitting.
Duke Thesëus was at a window sitting,
Arrayed as he were god upon a throne.
Then pressed the people thitherward full soon,
To see him and to do him reverence,
Aye, and to hear commands of sapience.
  A herald on a scaffold cried out "Ho!"
Till all the people's noise was stilled; and so,
When he observed that all were fallen still,
He then proclaimed the mighty ruler's will.
  "The duke our lord, full wise and full discreet,
Holds that it were but wanton waste to meet
And fight, these gentle folk, all in the guise
Of mortal battle in this enterprise.
Wherefore, in order that no man may die,
He does his earlier purpose modify.
No man, therefore, on pain of loss of life,
Shall any arrow, poleaxe, or short knife
Send into lists in any wise, or bring;
Nor any shortened sword, for point thrusting,
Shall a man draw, or bear it by his side.
Nor shall a knight against opponent ride,
Save one full course, with any sharp ground spear;
Unhorsed, a man may thrust with any gear.
And he that's overcome, should this occur,
Shall not be slain, but brought to barrier,
Whereof there shall be one on either side;
Let him be forced to go there and abide.
And if by chance the leader there must go,
Of either side, or slay his equal foe,

No longer, then, shall tourneying endure.
God speed you; go forth now, and lay on sure.
With long sword and with maces fight your fill.
Go now your ways; this is the lord duke's will."
   The voices of the people rent the skies,
Such was the uproar of their merry cries:
"Now God save such a lord, who is so good
He will not have destruction of men's blood!"
Up start the trumpets and make melody.
And to the lists rode forth the company,
In marshalled ranks, throughout the city large,
All hung with cloth of gold, and not with serge.
Full like a lord this noble duke did ride,
With the two Theban knights on either side;
And, following, rode the queen and Emily,
And, after, came another company
Of one and other, each in his degree.
And thus they went throughout the whole city,
And to the lists they came, all in good time.
The day was not yet fully come to prime
When throned was Thesëus full rich and high,
And Queen Hippolyta and Emily,
While other ladies sat in tiers about.
Into the seats then pressed the lesser rout.
And westward, through the gate of Mars, right hearty,
Arcita and the hundred of his party
With banner red is entering anon;
And in that selfsame moment, Palamon
Is under Venus, eastward in that place,
With banner white, and resolute of face.
In all the world, searching it up and down,
So equal were they all, from heel to crown,
There were no two such bands in any way.
For there was no man wise enough to say
How either had of other advantage
In high repute, or in estate, or age,
So even were they chosen, as I guess.
And in two goodly ranks they did then dress.
And when the name was called of every one,
That cheating in their number might be none,

Then were the gates closed, and the cry rang loud:
"Now do your devoir, all you young knights proud!"
    The heralds cease their spurring up and down;
Now ring the trumpets as the charge is blown;
And there's no more to say, for east and west
Two hundred spears are firmly laid in rest;
And the sharp spurs are thrust, now, into side.
Now see men who can joust and who can ride!
Now shivered are the shafts on bucklers thick;
One feels through very breastbone the spear's prick;
Lances are flung full twenty feet in height;
Out flash the swords like silver burnished bright.
Helmets are hewed, the lacings ripped and shred;
Out bursts the blood, gushing in stern streams red.
With mighty maces bones are crushed in joust.
One through the thickest throng begins to thrust.
There strong steeds stumble now, and down goes all.
One rolls beneath their feet as rolls a ball.
One flails about with club, being overthrown,
Another, on a mailed horse, rides him down.
One through the body's hurt, and haled, for aid,
Spite of his struggles, to the barricade,
As compact was, and there he must abide;
Another's captured by the other side.
At times Duke Thesëus orders them to rest,
To eat a bite and drink what each likes best.
And many times that day those Thebans two
Met in the fight and wrought each other woe;
Unhorsed each has the other on that day.
No tigress in the vale of Galgophey,
Whose little whelp is stolen in the light,
Is cruel to the hunter as Arcite
For jealousy is cruel to Palamon;
Nor in Belmarie, when the hunt is on
Is there a lion, wild for want of food,
That of his prey desires so much the blood
As Palamon the death of Arcite there.
Their jealous blows fall on their helmets fair;
Out leaps the blood and makes their two sides red.
    But sometime comes the end of every deed;

And ere the sun had sunk to rest in gold,
The mighty King Emetrëus did hold
This Palamon, as he fought with Arcite,
And made his sword deep in the flesh to bite;
And by the force of twenty men he's made,
Unyielded, to withdraw to barricade.
And, trying hard to rescue Palamon,
The mighty King Lycurgus is borne down;
And King Emetrëus, for all his strength,
Is hurled out of the saddle a sword's length,
So hits out Palamon once more, or ere
(But all for naught) he's brought to barrier.
His hardy heart may now avail him naught;
He must abide there now, being fairly caught
By force of arms, as by provision known.
   Who sorrows now but woeful Palamon,
Who may no more advance into the fight?
And when Duke Thesëus had seen this sight,
Unto the warriors fighting, every one,
He cried out: "Hold! No more! For it is done!
Now will I prove true judge, of no party.
Theban Arcita shall have Emily,
Who, by his fortune, has her fairly won."
   And now a noise of people is begun
For joy of this, so loud and shrill withal,
It seems as if the very lists will fall.
   But now, what can fair Venus do above?
What says she now? What does this queen of love
But weep so fast, for thwarting of her will,
Her tears upon the lists begin to spill.
She said: "Now am I shamed and over flung."
But Saturn said: "My daughter, hold your tongue.
Mars has his will, his knight has all his boon,
And, by my head, you shall be eased, and soon."
   The trumpeters and other minstrelsy,
The heralds that did loudly yell and cry,
Were at their best for joy of Arcita.
But hear me further while I tell you—ah!—
The miracle that happened there anon.
   This fierce Arcita doffs his helmet soon,

And mounted on a horse, to show his face,
He spurs from end to end of that great place,
Looking aloft to gaze on Emily;
And she cast down on him a friendly eye
(For women, generally speaking, go
Wherever Fortune may her favor show);
And she was fair to see, and held his heart.
But from the ground infernal furies start,
From Pluto sent, at instance of Saturn,
Whereat his horse, for fear, began to turn
And leap aside, all suddenly falling there;
And Arcita before he could beware
Was pitched upon the ground, upon his head,
And lay there, moving not, as he were dead,
His chest crushed in upon the saddlebow.
And black he lay as ever coal, or crow,
So ran the surging blood into his face.
Anon they carried him from out that place,
With heavy hearts, to Theseüs' palace.
There was his harness cut away, each lace,
And swiftly was he laid upon a bed,
For he was yet alive and some words said,
Crying and calling after Emily.

    Duke Theseüs, with all his company,
Is come again to Athens, his city,
With joyous heart and great festivity.
And though sore grieved for this unhappy fall,
He would not cast a blight upon them all.
Men said, too, that Arcita should not die,
But should be healed of all his injury.
And of another thing they were right fain,
Which was, that of them all no one was slain,
Though each was sore, and hurt, and specially one
Who'd got a lance head thrust through his breast bone.
For other bruises, wounds and broken arms,
Some of them carried salves and some had charms;
And medicines of many herbs, and sage
They drank, to keep their limbs from hemorrhage.
In all of which this duke, as he well can,
Now comforts and now honours every man,

And makes a revelry the livelong night
For all these foreign lords, as was but right.
Nor was there held any discomfiting,
Save from the jousts and from the tourneying.
For truly, there had been no cause for shame,
Since being thrown is fortune of the game;
Nor is it, to be led to barrier,
Unyielded, and by twenty knights' power,
One man alone, surrounded by the foe,
Driven by arms, and dragged out, heel and toe,
And with his courser driven forth with staves
Of men on foot, yeomen and serving knaves—
All this imputes to one no kind of vice,
And no man may bring charge of cowardice.
    For which, anon, Duke Thesëus bade cry,
To still all rancour and all keen envy,
The worth, as well of one side as the other,
As equal both, and each the other's brother;
And gave them gifts according to degree,
And held a three days' feast, right royally;
And then convoyed these kings upon their road
For one full day, and to them honour showed.
And home went every man on his right way.
There was naught more but "Farewell" and "Good-day."
I'll say no more of war, but turn upon
My tale of Arcita and Palamon.
    Swells now Arcita's breast until the sore
Increases near his heart yet more and more.
The clotted blood, in spite of all leech craft,
Rots in his bulk, and there is must be left,
Since no device of skillful bloodletting,
Nor drink of herbs, can help him in this thing.
The power expulsive, or virtue animal
Called from its use the virtue natural,
Could not the poison void, nor yet expel.
The tubes of both his lungs began to swell,
And every tissue in his breast, and down,
Is foul with poison and all rotten grown.
He gains in neither, in his strife to live,
By vomiting or taking laxative;

All is so broken in that part of him,
Nature retains no vigour there, nor vim.
And certainly, where Nature will not work,
It's farewell physic, bear the man to kirk!
The sum of all is, Arcita must die,
And so he sends a word to Emily,
And Palamon, who was his cousin dear;
And then he said to them as you shall hear.

"Naught may the woeful spirit in my heart
Declare one point of how my sorrows smart
To you, my lady, whom I love the most;
But I bequeath the service of my ghost
To you above all others, this being sure
Now that my life may here no more endure.
Alas, the woe! Alas, the pain so strong
That I for you have suffered, and so long!
Alas for death! Alas, my Emily!
Alas, the parting of our company!
Alas, my heart's own queen! Alas, my wife!
My soul's dear lady, ender of my life!
What is this world? What asks a man to have?
Now with his love, now in the cold dark grave
Alone, with never any company.
Farewell, my sweet foe! O my Emily!
Oh, take me in your gentle arms, I pray,
For love of God, and hear what I will say.

"I have here, with my cousin Palamon,
Had strife and rancour many a day that's gone,
For love of you and for my jealousy.
May Jove so surely guide my soul for me.
To speak about a lover properly,
With all the circumstances, faithfully—
That is to say, truth, honour, and knighthood,
Wisdom, humility and kinship good,
And generous soul and all the lover's art—
So now may Jove have in my soul his part
As in this world, right now, I know of none
So worthy to be loved as Palamon,
Who serves you and will do so all his life.
And if you ever should become a wife,

Forget not Palamon, the noble man."
    And with that word his speech to fail began,
For from his feet up to his breast had come
The cold of death, making his body numb.
And furthermore, from his two arms the strength
Was gone out, now, and he was lost, at length.
Only the intellect, and nothing more,
Which dwelt within his heart so sick and sore,
Began to fail now, when the heart felt death,
And his eyes darkened, and he failed of breath.
But on his lady turned he still his eye,
And his last word was, "Mercy, Emily!"
His spirit changed its house and went away.
As I was never there, I cannot say
Where; so I stop, not being a soothsayer;
Of souls here naught shall I enregister;
Nor do I wish their notions, now, to tell
Who write of them, though they say where they dwell.
Arcita's cold; Mars guides his soul on high;
Now will I speak forthwith of Emily.
    Shrieked Emily and howled now Palamon,
Till Theseus his sister took, anon,
And bore her, swooning, from the corpse away.
How shall it help, to dwell the livelong day
In telling how she wept both night and morrow?
For in like cases women have such sorrow,
When their good husband from their side must go,
And, for the greater part, they take on so,
Or else they fall into such malady
That, at the last, and certainly, they die.
    Infinite were the sorrows and the tears
Of all old folk and folk of tender years
Throughout the town, at death of this Theban;
For him there wept the child and wept the man;
So great a weeping was not, 'tis certain,
When Hector was brought back, but newly slain,
To Troy. Alas, the sorrow that was there!
Tearing of cheeks and rending out of hair.
"Oh why will you be dead," these women cry,
"Who had of gold enough, and Emily?"

No man might comfort then Duke Thesëus,
Excepting his old father, Ægëus,
Who knew this world's mutations, and men's own,
Since he had seen them changing up and down,
Joy after woe, and woe from happiness:
He showed them, by example, the process.
  "Just as there never died a man," quoth he,
"But he had lived on earth in some degree,
Just so there never lived a man," he said,
"In all this world, but must be sometime dead.
This world is but a thoroughfare of woe,
And we are pilgrims passing to and fro;
Death is the end of every worldly sore."
And after this, he told them yet much more
To that effect, all wisely to exhort
The people that they should find some comfort.
  Duke Thesëus now considered and with care
What place of burial he should prepare
For good Arcita, as it best might be,
And one most worthy of his high degree.
And at the last concluded, hereupon,
That where at first Arcita and Palamon
Had fought for love, with no man else between,
There, in that very grove, so sweet and green,
Where he mused on his amorous desires
Complaining of love's hot and flaming fires,
He'd make a pyre and have the funeral
Accomplished there, and worthily in all.
And so he gave command to hack and hew
The ancient oaks, and lay them straight and true
In split lengths that would kindle well and burn.
His officers, with sure swift feet, they turn
And ride away to do his whole intent.
And after this Duke Thesëus straightway sent
For a great bier, and had it all o'erspread
With cloth of gold, the richest that he had.
Arcita clad he, too, in cloth of gold;
White gloves were on his hands where they did fold;
Upon his head a crown of laurel green,
And near his hand a sword both bright and keen.

Then, having bared the dead face on the bier,
The duke so wept, 'twas pitiful to hear.
And, so that folk might see him, one and all,
When it was day he brought them to the hall,
Which echoed of their wailing cries anon.
   Then came this woeful Theban, Palamon,
With fluttery beard and matted, ash-strewn hair,
All in black clothes wet with his tears; and there,
Surpassing all in weeping, Emily,
The most affected of the company.
And so that every several rite should be
Noble and rich, and suiting his degree,
Duke Thesëus commanded that they bring
Three horses, mailed in steel all glittering,
And covered with Arcita's armour bright.
Upon these stallions, which were large and white,
There rode three men, whereof one bore the shield,
And one the spear he'd known so well to wield;
The third man bore his Turkish bow, nor less
Of burnished gold the quiver than harness;
And forth they slowly rode, with mournful cheer,
Toward that grove, as you shall further hear.
   The noblest Greeks did gladly volunteer
To bear upon their shoulders that great bier,
With measured pace and eyes gone red and wet,
Through all the city, by the wide main street,
Which was all spread with black, and, wondrous high,
Covered with this same cloth were houses nigh.
Upon the right hand went old Ægëus,
And on the other side Duke Thesëus,
With vessels in their hands, of gold right fine,
All filled with honey, milk, and blood, and wine;
And Palamon with a great company;
And after that came woeful Emily,
With fire in hands, as use was, to ignite
The sacrifice and set the pyre alight.
   Great labour and full great apparelling
Went to the service and the fire making,
For to the skies that green pyre reached its top,
And twenty fathoms did the arms outcrop,

That is to say, the branches went so wide.
Full many a load of straw they did provide.
But how the fire was made to climb so high;
Or what names all the different trees went by,
As oak, fir, birch, asp, alder, poplar, holm,
Willow, plane, ash, box, chestnut, linden, elm,
Laurel, thorn, maple, beech, yew, dogwood tree,
Or how they were felled, sha'n't be told by me.
Nor how the wood gods scampered up and down,
Driven from homes that they had called their own,
Wherein they'd lived so long at ease, in peace,
The nymphs, the fauns, the hamadryades;
Nor how the beasts, for fear, and the birds, all
Fled, when that ancient wood began to fall;
Nor how aghast the ground was in the light,
Not being used to seeing the sun so bright;
Nor how the fire was started first with straw,
And then with dry wood, riven thrice by saw,
And then with green wood and with spicery,
And then with cloth of gold and jewellery,
And garlands hanging with full many a flower,
And myrrh, and incense, sweet as rose in bower;
Nor how Arcita lies among all this,
Nor what vast wealth about his body is;
Nor how this Emily, as was their way,
Lighted the sacred funeral fire, that day,
Nor how she swooned when men built up the fire,
Nor what she said, nor what was her desire;
No, nor what gems men on the fire then cast,
When the white flame went high and burned so fast;
Nor how one cast his shield, and one his spear,
And some their vestments, on that burning bier,
With cups of wine, and cups of milk, and blood,
Into that flame, which burned as wildfire would;
Nor how the Greeks, in one huge wailing rout,
Rode slowly three times all the fire about,
Upon the left hand, with a loud shouting,
And three times more, with weapons clattering,
While thrice the women there raised up a cry;
Nor how was homeward led sad Emily;

Nor how Arcita burned to ashes cold;
Nor aught of how the lichwake they did hold
All that same night, nor how the Greeks did play
Who, naked, wrestled best, with oil anointed,
Nor who best bore himself in deeds appointed.
I will not even tell how they were gone
Home, into Athens, when the play was done;
But briefly to the point, now, will I wend
And make of this, my lengthy tale, an end.

With passing in their length of certain years,
All put by was the mourning and the tears
Of Greeks, as by one general assent;
And then it seems there was a parliament
At Athens, upon certain points in case;
Among the which points spoken of there was
The ratifying of alliances
That should hold Thebes from all defiances.
Whereat this noble Thesëus, anon,
Invited there the gentle Palamon,
Not telling him what was the cause and why;
But in his mourning clothes, and sorrowfully,
He came upon that bidding, so say I.
And then Duke Thesëus sent for Emily.
When they were seated and was hushed the place,
And Thesëus had mused a little space,
Ere any word came from his full wise breast,
His two eyes fixed on whoso pleased him best,
Then with a sad face sighed he deep and still,
And after that began to speak his will.

"The Primal Mover and the Cause above,
When first He forged the goodly chain of love,
Great the effect, and high was His intent;
Well knew He why, and what thereof He meant;
For with that goodly chain of love He bound
The fire, the air, the water, and dry ground
In certain bounds, the which they might not flee;
That same First Cause and Mover," then quoth he,
"Has stablished in this base world, up and down,
A certain length of days to call their own
For all that are engendered in this place,

Beyond the which not one day may they pace,
Though yet all may that certain time abridge;
Authority there needs none, I allege,
For it is well proved by experience,
Save that I please to clarify my sense.
Then may men by this order well discern
This Mover to be stable and eterne.
Well may man know, unless he be a fool,
That every part derives but from the whole.
For Nature has not taken his being
From any part and portion of a thing,
But from a substance perfect, stable aye,
And so continuing till changed away.
And therefore, of His Wisdom's Providence,
Has He so well established ordinance
That species of all things and all progressions,
If they'd endure, it must be by successions,
Not being themselves eternal, 'tis no lie:
This may you understand and see by eye.
      "Lo now, the oak, that has long nourishing
Even from the time that it begins to spring,
And has so long a life, as we may see,
Yet at the last all wasted is the tree.
      "Consider, too, how even the hard stone
Under our feet we tread each day upon
Yet wastes it, as it lies beside the way.
And the broad river will be dry some day.
And great towns wane; we see them vanishing.
Thus may we see the end to everything.
      "Of man and woman just the same is true:
Needs must, in either season of the two,
That is to say, in youth or else in age,
All men perish, the king as well as page;
Some in their bed, and some in the deep sea,
And some in the wide field—as it may be;
There's naught will help; all go the same way. Aye,
Then may I say that everything must die.
Who causes this but Jupiter the King?
He is the Prince and Cause of everything,
Converting all back to that primal well

From which it was derived, 'tis sooth to tell.
And against this, for every thing alive,
Of any state, avails it not to strive.
    "Then is it wisdom, as it seems to me,
To make a virtue of necessity,
And calmly take what we may not eschew,
And specially that which to all is due.
Whoso would balk at aught, he does folly,
And thus rebels against His potency.
And certainly a man has most honour
In dying in his excellence and flower,
When he is certain of his high good name;
For then he gives to friend, and self, no shame.
And gladder ought a friend be of his death
When, in much honour, he yields up his breath,
Than when his name's grown feeble with old age;
For all forgotten, then, is his courage.
Hence it is best for all of noble name
To die when at the summit of their fame.
The contrary of this is wilfulness.
Why do we grumble? Why have heaviness
That good Arcita, chivalry's fair flower,
Is gone, with honour, in his best-lived hour.
Out of the filthy prison of this life?
Why grumble here his cousin and his wife
About his welfare, who loved them so well?
Can he thank them? Nay, God knows, not! Nor tell
How they his soul and their own selves offend,
Though yet they may not their desires amend.
    "What may I prove by this long argument
Save that we all turn to merriment,
After our grief, and give Jove thanks for grace.
And so, before we go from out this place,
I counsel that we make, of sorrows two,
One perfect joy, lasting for aye, for you;
And look you now, where most woe is herein,
There will we first amend it and begin.
    "Sister," quoth he, "you have my full consent,
With the advice of this my Parliament,
That gentle Palamon, your own true knight,

Who serves you well with will and heart and might,
And so has ever, since you knew him first—
That you shall, of your grace, allay his thirst
By taking him for husband and for lord:
Lend me your hand, for this is our accord.
Let now your woman's pity make him glad.
For he is a king's brother's son, by gad;
And though he were a poor knight bachelor,
Since he has served you for so many a year,
And borne for you so great adversity,
This ought to weigh with you, it seems to me,
For mercy ought to dominate mere right."
    Then said he thus to Palamon the knight:
"I think there needs but little sermoning
To make you give consent, now, to this thing.
Come near, and take your lady by the hand."
    Between them, then, was tied that nuptial band,
Which is called matrimony or marriage,
By all the council and the baronage.
And thus, in all bliss and with melody,
Has Palamon now wedded Emily.
And God, Who all this universe has wrought,
Send him His love, who has it dearly bought.
For now has Palamon, in all things, wealth,
Living in bliss, in riches, and in health;
And Emily loved him so tenderly,
And he served her so well and faithfully,
That never word once marred their happiness,
No jealousy, nor other such distress.
Thus ends now Palamon and Emily;
And may God save all this fair company! Amen.

The Miller's Tale

The Miller's Prologue

Now when the knight had thus his story told,
In all the rout there was nor young nor old
But said it was a noble story, well
Worthy to be kept in mind to tell;
And specially the gentle folk, each one.
Our host, he laughed and swore, "So may I run,
But this goes well; unbuckled is the mail;
Let's see now who can tell another tale:
For certainly the game is well begun.
Now shall you tell, sir monk, if't can be done,
Something with which to pay for the knight's tale."
    The miller, who with drinking was all pale,
So that unsteadily on his horse he sat,
He would not take off either hood or hat,
Nor wait for any man, in courtesy,
But all in Pilate's voice began to cry,
And by the Arms and Blood and Bones he swore,
"I have a noble story in my store,
With which I will requite the good knight's tale."
    Our host saw, then, that he was drunk with ale,
And said to him: "Wait, Robin, my dear brother,
Some better man shall tell us first another:
Submit and let us work on profitably."
    "Now by God's soul," cried he, "that will not I!
For I will speak, or else I'll go my way."
    Our host replied: "Tell on, then, till doomsday!
You are a fool, your wit is overcome."
    "Now hear me," said the miller, "all and some!
But first I make a protestation round
That I'm quite drunk, I know it by my sound:
And therefore, if I slander or mis-say,
Blame it on ale of Southwark, so I pray;

For I will tell a legend and a life
Both of a carpenter and of his wife,
And how a scholar set the good wright's cap."
    The reeve replied and said: "Oh, shut your trap,
Let be your ignorant drunken ribaldry!
It is a sin, and further, great folly
To asperse any man, or him defame,
And, too, to bring upon a man's wife shame.
There are enough of other things to say."
    This drunken miller spoke on in his way,
And said: "Oh, but my dear brother Oswald,
The man who has no wife is no cuckold.
But I say not, thereby, that you are one:
Many good wives there are, as women run,
And ever a thousand good to one that's bad,
As well you know yourself, unless you're mad.
Why are you angry with my story's cue?
I have a wife, begad, as well as you,
Yet I'd not, for the oxen of my plow,
Take on my shoulders more than is enow,
By judging of myself that I am one;
I will believe full well that I am none.
A husband must not be inquisitive
Of God, nor of his wife, while she's alive.
So long as he may find God's plenty there,
For all the rest he need not greatly care."
    What should I say, except this miller rare
He would forgo his talk for no man there,
But told his churlish tale in his own way:
I think I'll here re-tell it, if I may.
And therefore, every gentle soul, I pray
That for God's love you'll hold not what I say
Evilly meant, but that I must rehearse
All of their tales, the better and the worse,
Or else prove false to some of my design.
Therefore, who likes not this, let him, in fine,
Turn over page and choose another tale:
For he shall find enough, both great and small,
Of stories touching on gentility,
And holiness, and on morality;

And blame not me if you do choose amiss.
The miller was a churl, you well know this;
So was the reeve, and many another more,
And ribaldry they told from plenteous store.
Be then advised, and hold me free from blame;
Men should not be too serious at a game.

The Miller's Tale

Once on a time was dwelling in Oxford
A wealthy lout who took in guests to board,
And of his craft he was a carpenter.
A poor scholar was lodging with him there,
Who'd learned the arts, but all his phantasy
Was turned to study of astrology;
And knew a certain set of theorems
And could find out by various stratagems,
If men but asked of him in certain hours
When they should have a drought or else have showers,
Or if men asked of him what should befall
To anything—I cannot reckon them all.
    This clerk was called the clever Nicholas;
Of secret loves he knew and their solace;
And he kept counsel, too, for he was sly
And meek as any maiden passing by.
He had a chamber in that hostelry,
And lived alone there, without company,
All garnished with sweet herbs of good repute;
And he himself sweet smelling as the root
Of licorice, valerian, or setwall.
His *Almagest*, and books both great and small,
His astrolabe, belonging to his art,
His algorism stones—all laid apart
On shelves that ranged beside his lone bed's head;
His press was covered with a cloth of red.
And over all there lay a psaltery
Whereon he made an evening's melody,
Playing so sweetly that the chamber rang;
And *Angelus ad virginem* he sang;

And after that he warbled the *King's Note*:
Often in good voice was his merry throat.
And thus this gentle clerk his leisure spends
Supported by some income and his friends.

   This carpenter had lately wed a wife
Whom he loved better than he loved his life;
And she was come to eighteen years of age.
Jealous he was and held her close in cage.
For she was wild and young and he was old,
And deemed himself as like to be cuckold.
He knew not Cato, for his lore was rude:
That vulgar man should wed similitude.
A man should wed according to estate,
For youth and age are often in debate.
But now, since he had fallen in the snare,
He must endure, like other folk, his care.

   Fair was this youthful wife, and therewithal
As weasel's was her body slim and small.
A girdle wore she, barred and striped, of silk.
An apron, too, as white as morning milk
About her loins, and full of many a gore;
White was her smock, embroidered all before
And even behind, her collar round about,
Of coal-black silk, on both sides, in and out;
The strings of the white cap upon her head
Were, like her collar, black silk worked with thread;
Her fillet was of wide silk worn full high:
And certainly she had a lickerish eye.
She'd thinned out carefully her eyebrows two,
And they were arched and black as any sloe.
She was a far more pleasant thing to see
Than is the newly budded young pear tree;
And softer than the wool is on a wether.
Down from her girdle hung a purse of leather,
Tasselled with silk, with latten beading sown.
In all this world, searching it up and down,
So gay a little doll, I well believe,
Or such a wench, there's no man can conceive.
Far brighter was the brilliance of her hue
Than in the Tower the gold coins minted new.

And songs came shrilling from her pretty head
As from a swallow's sitting on a shed.
Therewith she'd dance too, and could play and sham
Like any kid or calf about its dam.
Her mouth was sweet as bragget or as mead
Or hoard of apples laid in hay or weed.
Skittish she was as is a pretty colt,
Tall as a staff and straight as crossbow bolt.
A brooch she wore upon her collar low,
As broad as boss of buckler did it show;
Her shoes laced up to where a girl's legs thicken.
She was a primrose, and a tender chicken
For any lord to lay upon his bed,
Or yet for any good yeoman to wed.
   Now, sir, and then, sir, so befell the case,
That on a day this clever Nicholas
Fell in with this young wife to toy and play,
The while her husband was down Osney way,
Clerks being as crafty as the best of us;
And unperceived he caught her by the puss,
Saying: "Indeed, unless I have my will,
For secret love of you, sweetheart, I'll spill."
And held her hard about the hips, and how!—
And said: "O darling, love me, love me now,
Or I shall die, and pray you God may save!"
   And she leaped as a colt does in the trave,
And with her head she twisted fast away,
And said: "I will not kiss you, by my fay!
Why, let go," cried she, "let go, Nicholas!
Or I will call for help and cry 'alas!'
Do take your hands away, for courtesy!"
   This Nicholas for mercy then did cry,
And spoke so well, importuned her so fast
That she her love did grant him at the last,
And swore her oath, by Saint Thomas of Kent,
That she would be at his command, content,
As soon as opportunity she could spy.
   "My husband is so full of jealousy,
Unless you will await me secretly,
I know I'm just as good as dead," said she.

"You must keep all quite hidden in this case."
   "Nay, thereof worry not," said Nicholas,
"A clerk has lazily employed his while
If he cannot a carpenter beguile."
   And thus they were agreed, and then they swore
To wait a while, as I have said before.
When Nicholas had done thus every whit
And patted her about the loins a bit,
He kissed her sweetly, took his psaltery,
And played it fast and made a melody.
   Then fell it thus, that to the parish kirk,
The Lord Christ Jesus' own works for to work,
This good wife went, upon a holy day;
Her forehead shone as bright as does the May,
So well she'd washed it when she left off work.
   Now there was of that church a parish clerk
Whose name was (as folk called him) Absalom.
Curled was his hair, shining like gold, and from
His head spread fanwise in a thick bright mop;
'Twas parted straight and even on the top;
His cheek was red, his eyes grey as a goose;
With Saint Paul's windows cut upon his shoes,
He stood in red hose fitting famously.
And he was clothed full well and properly
All in a coat of blue, in which were let
Holes for the lacings, which were fairly set.
And over all he wore a fine surplice
As white as ever hawthorn spray, and nice.
A merry lad he was, so God me save,
And well could he let blood, cut hair, and shave,
And draw a deed or quitclaim, as might chance.
In twenty manners could he trip and dance,
After the school that reigned in Oxford, though,
And with his two legs swinging to and fro;
And he could play upon a violin;
Thereto he sang in treble voice and thin;
And as well could he play on his guitar.
In all the town no inn was, and no bar,
That he'd not visited to make good cheer,
Especially were lively barmaids there.

But, truth to tell, he was a bit squeamish
Of farting and of language haughtyish.
　This Absalom, who was so light and gay,
Went with a censer on the holy day,
Censing the wives like an enthusiast;
And on them many a loving look he cast,
Especially on this carpenter's goodwife.
To look at her he thought a merry life,
She was so pretty, sweet, and lickerous.
I dare well say, if she had been a mouse
And he a cat, he would have mauled her some.
　This parish clerk, this lively Absalom
Had in his heart, now, such a love longing
That from no wife took he an offering,
For courtesy, he said, he would take none.
The moon, when it was night, full brightly shone,
And his guitar did Absalom then take,
For in love watching he'd intent to wake.
And forth he went, jolly and amorous,
Until he came unto the carpenter's house
A little after cocks began to crow;
And took his stand beneath a shot window
That was let into the good wood-wright's wall.
He sang then, in his pleasant voice and small,
"Oh now, dear lady, if your will it be,
I pray that you will have some ruth on me,"
The words in harmony with his string plucking.
This carpenter awoke and heard him sing,
And called unto his wife and said, in sum:
"What, Alison! Do you hear Absalom,
Who plays and sings beneath our bedroom wall?"
　And she said to her husband, therewithal:
"Yes, God knows, John, I hear it, truth to tell."
　So this went on; what is there better than well?
From day to day this pretty Absalom
So wooed her he was woebegone therefrom.
He lay awake all night and all the day;
He combed his spreading hair and dressed him gay;
By go-betweens and agents, too, wooed he,
And swore her loyal page he'd ever be.

He sang as tremulously as nightingale;
He sent her sweetened wine and well-spiced ale
And waffles piping hot out of the fire,
And, she being town-bred, mead for her desire.
For some are won by means of money spent,
And some by tricks, and some by long descent.
Once, to display his versatility,
He acted Herod on a scaffold high.
  But what availed it him in any case?
She was enamoured so of Nicholas
That Absalom might go and blow his horn;
He got naught for his labour but her scorn.
And thus she made of Absalom her ape,
And all his earnestness she made a jape.
For truth is in this proverb, and no lie,
Men say well thus: It's always he that's nigh
That makes the absent lover seem a sloth.
For now, though Absalom be wildly wroth,
Because he is so far out of her sight,
This handy Nicholas stands in his light.
  Now bear you well, you clever Nicholas!
For Absalom may wail and sing "Alas!"
And so it chanced that on a Saturday
This carpenter departed to Osney;
And clever Nicholas and Alison
Were well agreed to this effect: anon
This Nicholas should put in play a wile
The simple, jealous husband to beguile;
And if it chanced the game should go a-right,
She was to sleep within his arms all night,
For this was his desire, and hers also.
Presently then, and without more ado,
This Nicholas, no longer did he tarry,
But softly to his chamber did he carry
Both food and drink to last at least a day,
Saying that to her husband she should say—
If he should come to ask for Nicholas—
Why, she should say she knew not where he was,
For all day she'd not seen him, far or nigh;
She thought he must have got some malady,

Because in vain her maid would knock and call;
He'd answer not, whatever might befall.
  And so it was that all that Saturday
This Nicholas quietly in chamber lay,
And ate and slept, or did what pleased him best,
Till Sunday when the sun had gone to rest.
  This simple man with wonder heard the tale,
And marvelled what their Nicholas might ail,
And said: "I am afraid, by Saint Thomas,
That everything's not well with Nicholas.
God send he be not dead so suddenly!
This world is most unstable, certainly;
I saw, today, the corpse being borne to kirk
Of one who, but last Monday, was at work.
Go up," said he unto his boy anon,
"Call at his door, or knock there with a stone,
Learn how it is and boldly come tell me."
  The servant went up, then, right sturdily,
And at the chamber door, the while he stood,
He cried and knocked as any madman would—
"What! How! What do you, Master Nicholay?
How can you sleep through all the livelong day?"
  But all for naught, he never heard a word;
A hole he found, low down upon a board,
Through which the house cat had been wont to creep;
And to that hole he stooped, and through did peep,
And finally he ranged him in his sight.
This Nicholas sat gaping there, upright,
As if he'd looked too long at the new moon.
Downstairs he went and told his master soon
In what array he'd found this self-same man.
  This carpenter to cross himself began,
And said: "Now help us, holy Frideswide!
Little a man can know what shall betide.
This man is fallen, with his astromy,
Into some madness or some agony;
I always feared that somehow this would be!
Men should not meddle in God's privity.
Aye, blessed always be the ignorant man,
Whose creed is all he ever has to scan!

So fared another clerk with astromy;
He walked into the meadows for to pry
Into the stars, to learn what should befall,
Until into a clay pit he did fall;
He saw not that. But yet, by Saint Thomas,
I'm sorry for this clever Nicholas.
He shall be scolded for his studying,
If not too late, by Jesus, Heaven's King!
    "Get me a staff, that I may pry before,
The while you, Robin, heave against the door.
We'll take him from this studying, I guess."
    And on the chamber door, then, he did press.
His servant was a stout lad, if a dunce,
And by the hasp he heaved it up at once;
Upon the floor that portal fell anon.
This Nicholas sat there as still as stone,
Gazing, with gaping mouth, straight up in air.
This carpenter thought he was in despair,
And took him by the shoulders, mightily,
And shook him hard, and cried out, vehemently:
"What! Nicholay! Why how now! Come, look down!
Awake, and think on Jesus' death and crown!
I cross you from all elves and magic wights!"
    And then the night-spell said he out, by rights,
At the four corners of the house about,
And at the threshold of the door, without—
    "O Jesus Christ and good Saint Benedict,
Protect this house from all that may afflict,
For the night hag the white Paternoster!—
Where hast thou gone, Saint Peter's sister?"
And at the last this clever Nicholas
Began to sigh full sore, and said: "Alas!
Shall all the world be lost so soon again?"
    This carpenter replied: "What say you, then?
What! Think on God, as we do, men that swink."
    This Nicholas replied: "Go fetch me drink;
And afterward I'll tell you privately
A certain thing concerning you and me;
I'll tell it to no other man or men."
    This carpenter went down and came again,

And brought of potent ale a brimming quart;
And when each one of them had drunk his part,
Nicholas shut the door fast, and with that
He drew a seat and near the carpenter sat.

He said: "Now, John, my good host, lief and dear,
You must upon your true faith swear, right here,
That to no man will you this word betray;
For it is Christ's own word that I will say,
And if you tell a man, you're ruined quite;
This punishment shall come to you, of right,
That if you're traitor you'll go mad—and should!"

"Nay, Christ forbid it, for His holy blood!"
Said then this simple man: "I am no blab,
Nor, though I say it, am I fond of gab.
Say what you will, I never will it tell
To child or wife, by Him that harried Hell!"

"Now, John," said Nicholas, "I will not lie;
But I've found out, from my astrology,
As I have looked upon the moon so bright,
That now, come Monday next, at nine of night,
Shall fall a rain so wildly mad as would
Have been, by half, greater than Noah's flood.
This world," he said, "in less time than an hour,
Shall all be drowned, so terrible is this shower;
Thus shall all mankind drown and lose all life."

This carpenter replied: "Alas, my wife!
And shall she drown? Alas, my Alison!"
For grief of this he almost fell. Anon
He said: "Is there no remedy in this case?"

"Why yes, good luck," said clever Nicholas,
"If you will work by counsel of the wise;
You must not act on what your wits advise.
For so says Solomon, and it's all true,
'Work by advice and thou shalt never rue.'
And if you'll act as counselled and not fail,
I undertake, without a mast or sail,
To save us all, aye you and her and me.
Haven't you heard of Noah, how saved was he,
Because Our Lord had warned him how to keep
Out of the flood that covered earth so deep?"

"Yes," said this carpenter, "long years ago."

"Have you not heard," asked Nicholas, "also
The sorrows of Noah and his fellowship
In getting his wife to go aboard the ship?
He would have rather, I dare undertake,
At that time, and for all the weather black,
That she had one ship for herself alone.
Therefore, do you know what would best be done?
This thing needs haste, and of a hasty thing
Men must not preach nor do long tarrying.

"Presently go, and fetch here to this inn
A kneading tub, or brewing vat, and win
One each for us, but see that they are large,
Wherein we may swim out as in a barge,
And have therein sufficient food and drink
For one day only; that's enough, I think.
The water will dry up and flow away
About the prime of the succeeding day.
But Robin must not know of this, your knave,
And even Jill, your maid, I may not save;
Ask me not why, for though you do ask me,
I will not tell you of God's privity.
Suffice you, then, unless your wits are mad,
To have as great a grace as Noah had.
Your wife I shall not lose, there is no doubt,
Go, now, your way, and speedily get about,
But when you have, for you and her and me,
Procured these kneading tubs, or beer vats, three,
Then you shall hang them near the roof-tree high,
That no man our purveyance may espy.
And when you thus have done, as I have said,
And have put in our drink and meat and bread,
Also an axe to cut the ropes in two
When the flood comes, that we may float and go,
And cut a hole, high up, upon the gable,
Upon the garden side, over the stable,
That we may freely pass forth on our way
When the great rain and flood are gone that day—
Then shall you float as merrily, I'll stake,
As does the white duck after the white drake.

Then I will call, 'Ho, Alison! Ho, John!
Be cheery, for the flood will pass anon.'
And you will say, 'Hail, Master Nicholay!
Good morrow, I see you well, for it is day!'
And then shall we be barons all our life
Of all the world, like Noah and his wife.
    "But of one thing I warn you now, outright.
Be well advised, that on that very night
When we have reached our ships and got aboard,
Not one of us must speak or whisper word,
Nor call, nor cry, but sit in silent prayer;
For this is God's own bidding, hence—don't dare!
    "Your wife and you must hang apart, that in
The night shall come no chance for you to sin
Either in looking or in carnal deed.
These orders I have told you, go, God speed!
Tomorrow night, when all men are asleep,
Into our kneading tubs will we three creep
And sit there, still, awaiting God's high grace.
Go, now, your way, I have no longer space
Of time to make a longer sermoning.
Men say thus: 'Send the wise and say no thing.'
You are so wise it needs not that I teach;
Go, save our lives, and that I do beseech."
    This silly carpenter went on his way.
Often he cried "Alas!" and "Welaway!"
And to his wife he told all, privately;
But she was better taught thereof than he
How all this rigmarole was to apply.
Nevertheless she acted as she'd die,
And said: "Alas! Go on your way anon,
Help us escape, or we are lost, each one;
I am your true and lawfully wedded wife;
Go, my dear spouse, and help to save our life."
    Lo, what a great thing is affection found!
Men die of imagination, I'll be bound,
So deep an imprint may the spirit take.
This hapless carpenter began to quake;
He thought now, verily, that he could see
Old Noah's flood come wallowing like the sea

To drown his Alison, his honey dear.
He wept, he wailed, he made but sorry cheer,
He sighed and made full many a sob and sough.
He went and got himself a kneading trough
And, after that, two tubs he somewhere found
And to his dwelling privately sent round,
And hung them near the roof, all secretly.
With his own hand, then, made he ladders three,
To climb up by the rungs thereof, it seems,
And reach the tubs left hanging to the beams;
And those he victualled, tubs and kneading trough,
With bread and cheese and good jugged ale, enough
To satisfy the needs of one full day.
But ere he'd put all this in such array,
He sent his servants, boy and maid, right down
Upon some errand into London town.
And on the Monday, when it came on night,
He shut his door, without a candlelight,
And ordered everything as it should be.
And shortly after up they climbed, all three;
They sat while one might plow a furlong way.
    "Now, by Our Father, hush!" said Nicholay,
And "Hush!" said John, and "Hush!" said Alison.
    This carpenter, his loud devotions done,
Sat silent, saying mentally a prayer,
And waiting for the rain, to hear it there.
    The deathlike sleep of utter weariness
Fell on this wood-wright even (as I guess)
About the curfew time, or little more;
For travail of his spirit he groaned sore,
And soon he snored, for badly his head lay.
Down by the ladder crept this Nicholay,
And Alison, right softly down she sped.
Without more words they went and got in bed
Even where the carpenter was wont to lie.
There was the revel and the melody!
And thus lie Alison and Nicholas,
In joy that goes by many an alias,
Until the bells for lauds began to ring
And friars to the chancel went to sing.

This parish clerk, this amorous Absalom,
Whom love has made so woebegone and dumb,
Upon the Monday was down Osney way,
With company, to find some sport and play;
And there he chanced to ask a cloisterer,
Privately, after John the carpenter.
This monk drew him apart, out of the kirk,
And said: "I have not seen him here at work
Since Saturday; I think well that he went
For timber, that the abbot has him sent;
For he is wont for timber thus to go,
Remaining at the grange a day or so;
Or else he's surely at his house today;
But which it is I cannot truly say."
     This Absalom right happy was and light,
And thought: "Now is the time to wake all night;
For certainly I saw him not stirring
About his door since day began to spring.
So may I thrive, as I shall, at cock's crow,
Knock cautiously upon that window low
Which is so placed upon his bedroom wall.
To Alison then will I tell of all
My love longing, and thus I shall not miss
That at the least I'll have her lips to kiss.
Some sort of comfort shall I have, I say,
My mouth's been itching all this livelong day;
That is a sign of kissing at the least.
All night I dreamed, too, I was at a feast.
Therefore I'll go and sleep two hours away,
And all this night then will I wake and play."
     And so when time of first cockcrow was come,
Up rose this merry lover, Absalom,
And dressed him gay and all at point-device,
But first he chewed some licorice and spice
So he'd smell sweet, ere he had combed his hair.
Under his tongue some bits of true-love rare,
For thereby thought he to be more gracious.
He went, then, to the carpenter's dark house.
And silent stood beneath the shot window;
Unto his breast it reached, it was so low;

And he coughed softly, in a low half tone:
"What do you, honeycomb, sweet Alison?
My cinnamon, my fair bird, my sweetie,
Awake, O darling mine, and speak to me!
It's little thought you give me and my woe,
Who for your love do sweat where'er I go.
Yet it's no wonder that I faint and sweat;
I long as does the lamb for mother's teat.
Truly, sweetheart, I have such love longing
That like a turtledove's my true yearning;
And I can eat no more than can a maid."
   "Go from the window, jackanapes," she said,
"For, s'help me God, it is not 'come kiss me.'
I love another, or to blame I'd be,
Better than you, by Jesus, Absalom!
Go on your way, or I'll stone you therefrom,
And let me sleep, the fiends take you away!"
   "Alas," quoth Absalom, "and welaway!
That true love ever was so ill beset!
But kiss me, since you'll do no more, my pet,
For Jesus' love and for the love of me."
   "And will you go, then, on your way?" asked she.
   "Yes truly, darling," said this Absalom.
   "Then make you ready," said she, "and I'll come!"
   And unto Nicholas said she, low and still:
"Be silent now, and you shall laugh your fill."
   This Absalom plumped down upon his knees,
And said: "I am a lord in all degrees;
For after this there may be better still!
Darling, my sweetest bird, I wait your will."
   The window she unbarred, and that in haste.
"Have done," said she, "come on, and do it fast,
Before we're seen by any neighbour's eye."
   This Absalom did wipe his mouth all dry;
Dark was the night as pitch, aye dark as coal,
And through the window she put out her hole,
And Absalom no better felt nor worse,
But with his mouth he kissed her naked arse
Right greedily, before he knew of this.
   Aback he leapt—it seemed somehow amiss,

For well he knew a woman has no beard;
He'd felt a thing all rough and longish haired,
And said, "Oh fie, alas! What did I do?"
    "Teehee!" she laughed, and clapped the window to;
And Absalom went forth a sorry pace.
    "A beard! A beard!" cried clever Nicholas,
"Now by God's *corpus*, this goes fair and well!"
    This hapless Absalom, he heard that yell,
And on his lip, for anger, he did bite;
And to himself he said, "I will requite!"
    Who vigorously rubbed and scrubbed his lips
With dust, with sand, with straw, with cloth, with chips,
But Absalom, and often cried "Alas!
My soul I give now unto Sathanas,
For rather far than own this town," said he,
"For this despite, it's well revenged I'd be.
Alas," said he, "from her I never blenched!"
    His hot love was grown cold, aye and all quenched;
For, from the moment that he'd kissed her arse,
For paramours he didn't care a curse,
For he was healed of all his malady;
Indeed all paramours he did defy,
And wept as does a child that has been beat.
With silent step he went across the street
Unto a smith whom men called Dan Jarvis,
Who in his smithy forged plow parts, that is
He sharpened shares and coulters busily.
This Absalom he knocked all easily,
And said: "Unbar here, Jarvis, for I come."
    "What! Who are you?"
    "It's I, it's Absalom."
    "What! Absalom! For Jesus Christ's sweet tree,
Why are you up so early? *Ben'cite!*
What ails you now, man? Some gay girl, God knows,
Has brought you on the jump to my bellows;
By Saint Neot, you know well what I mean."
    This Absalom cared not a single bean
For all this play, nor one word back he gave;
He'd more tow on his distaff, had this knave,
Than Jarvis knew, and said he: "Friend so dear,

This red-hot coulter in the fireplace here,
Lend it to me, I have a need for it,
And I'll return it after just a bit."
   Jarvis replied: "Certainly, were it gold
Or a purse filled with yellow coins untold,
Yet should you have it, as I am true smith;
But eh, Christ's foe! What will you do therewith?"
   "Let that," said Absalom, "be as it may;
I'll tell you all tomorrow, when it's day"—
And caught the coulter then by the cold steel
And softly from the smithy door did steal
And went again up to the wood-wright's wall.
He coughed at first, and then he knocked withal
Upon the window, as before, with care.
   This Alison replied: "Now who is there?
And who knocks so? I'll warrant it's a thief."
   "Why no," quoth he, "God knows, my sweet rose leaf,
I am your Absalom, my own darling!
Of gold," quoth he, "I have brought you a ring;
My mother gave it me, as I'll be saved;
Fine gold it is, and it is well engraved;
This will I give you for another kiss."
   This Nicholas had risen for a piss,
And thought that it would carry on the jape
To have his arse kissed by this jackanape.
And so he opened window hastily,
And put his arse out thereat, quietly,
Over the buttocks, showing the whole bum;
And thereto said this clerk, this Absalom,
"O speak, sweet bird, I know not where thou art."
This Nicholas just then let fly a fart
As loud as it had been a thunderclap,
And well-nigh blinded Absalom, poor chap;
But he was ready with his iron hot
And Nicholas right in the arse he got.
   Off went the skin a handsbreadth broad, about,
The coulter burned his bottom so, throughout,
That for the pain he thought that he should die.
And like one mad he started in to cry,
"Help! Water! Water! Help! For God's dear heart!"

This carpenter out of his sleep did start,
Hearing that "Water!" cried as madman would,
And thought, "Alas, now comes down Noel's flood!"
He struggled up without another word
And with his axe he cut in two the cord,
And down went all; he did not stop to trade
In bread or ale till he'd the journey made,
And there upon the floor he swooning lay.
   Up started Alison and Nicholay
And shouted "Help!" and "Hello!" down the street.
The neighbours, great and small, with hastening feet
Swarmed in the house to stare upon this man,
Who lay yet swooning, and all pale and wan;
For in the falling he had smashed his arm.
He had to suffer, too, another harm,
For when he spoke he was at once borne down
By clever Nicholas and Alison.
For they told everyone that he was odd;
He was so much afraid of "Noel's" flood,
Through fantasy, that out of vanity
He'd gone and bought these kneading tubs, all three,
And that he'd hung them near the roof above;
And that he had prayed them, for God's dear love,
To sit with him and bear him company.
The people laughed at all this fantasy;
Up to the roof they looked, and there did gape,
And so turned all his injury to a jape.
For when this carpenter got in a word,
'Twas all in vain, no man his reasons heard;
With oaths impressive he was so sworn down
That he was held for mad by all the town;
For every clerk did side with every other.
They said: "The man is crazy, my dear brother."
And everyone did laugh at all this strife.
   Thus futtered was the carpenter's goodwife,
For all his watching and his jealousy;
And Absalom has kissed her nether eye;
And Nicholas is branded on the butt.
This tale is done, and God save all the rout!

The Reeve's Tale

The Reeve's Prologue

When folk had laughed their fill at this nice pass
Of Absalom and clever Nicholas,
Then divers folk diversely had their say;
And most of them were well amused and gay,
Nor at this tale did I see one man grieve,
Save it were only old Oswald the reeve,
Because he was a carpenter by craft.
A little anger in his heart was left,
And he began to grouse and blame a bit.
    "S' help me," said he, "full well could I be quit
With blearing of a haughty miller's eye,
If I but chose to speak of ribaldry.
But I am old; I will not play, for age;
Grass time is done, my fodder is rummage,
This white top advertises my old years,
My heart, too, is as mouldy as my hairs,
Unless I fare like medlar, all perverse.
For that fruit's never ripe until it's worse,
And falls among the refuse or in straw.
We ancient men, I fear, obey this law:
Until we're rotten, we cannot be ripe;
We dance, indeed, the while the world will pipe.
Desire sticks in our nature like a nail
To have, if hoary head, a verdant tail,
As has the leek; for though our strength be gone,
Our wish is yet for folly till life's done.
For when we may not act, then will we speak;
Yet in our ashes is there fire to reek
    "Four embers have we, which I shall confess:
Boasting and lying, anger, covetousness;
These four remaining sparks belong to eld.
Our ancient limbs may well be hard to wield,

But lust will never fail us, that is truth.
And yet I have had always a colt's tooth,
As many years as now are past and done
Since first my tap of life began to run.
For certainly, when I was born, I know
Death turned my tap of life and let it flow;
And ever since that day the tap has run
Till nearly empty now is all the tun.
The stream of life now drips upon the chime;
The silly tongue may well ring out the time
Of wretchedness that passed so long before;
For oldsters, save for dotage, there's no more."
    Now when our host had heard this sermoning,
Then did he speak as lordly as a king;
He said: "To what amounts, now, all this wit?
Why should we talk all day of holy writ?
The devil makes a steward for to preach,
And of a cobbler, a sailor or a leech.
Tell forth your tale, and do not waste the time.
Here's Deptford! And it is half way to prime.
There's Greenwich town that many a scoundrel's in;
It is high time your story should begin."
    "Now, sirs," then said this Oswald called the reeve,
"I pray you all, now, that you will not grieve
Though I reply and somewhat twitch his cap;
It's lawful to meet force with force, mayhap.
    "This drunken miller has related here
How was beguiled and fooled a carpenter—
Perchance in scorn of me, for I am one.
So, by your leave, I'll him requite anon;
All in his own boor's language will I speak.
I only pray to God his neck may break.
For in my eye he well can see the mote,
But sees not in his own the beam, you'll note."

The Reeve's Tale

At Trumpington, not far from Cambridge town,
There is a bridge wherethrough a brook runs down,

Upon the side of which brook stands a mill;
And this is very truth that now I tell.
A miller dwelt there, many and many a day;
As any peacock he was proud and gay.
He could mend nets, and he could fish, and flute,
Drink and turn cups, and wrestle well, and shoot;
And in his leathern belt he did parade
A cutlass with a long and trenchant blade.
A pretty dagger had he in his pouch;
There was no man who durst this man to touch.
A Sheffield whittler bore he in his hose;
Round was his face and turned up was his nose.
As bald as any ape's head was his skull;
He was a market swaggerer to the full.
There durst no man a hand on him to lay,
Because he swore he'd make the beggar pay.
A thief he was, forsooth, of corn and meal,
And sly at that, accustomed well to steal.
His name was known as arrogant Simpkin.
A wife he had who came of gentle kin;
The parson of the town her father was.
With her he gave full many a pan of brass,
To insure that Simpkin with his blood ally.
She had been bred up in a nunnery;
For Simpkin would not have a wife, he said,
Save she were educated and a maid
To keep up his estate of yeomanry.
And she was proud and bold as is a pie.
A handsome sight it was to see those two;
On holy days before her he would go
With a broad tippet bound about his head;
And she came after in a skirt of red,
While Simpkin's hose were dyed to match that same.
There durst no man to call her aught but dame;
Nor was there one so hardy, in the way,
As durst flirt with her or attempt to play,
Unless he would be slain by this Simpkin
With cutlass or with knife or with bodkin.
For jealous folk are dangerous, you know,
At least they'd have their wives to think them so.

Besides, because she was a dirty bitch,
She was as high as water in a ditch;
And full of scorn and full of backbiting.
She thought a lady should be quite willing
To greet her for her kin and culture, she
Having been brought up in that nunnery.
    A daughter had they got between the two,
Of twenty years, and no more children, no,
Save a boy baby that was six months old;
It lay in cradle and was strong and bold.
This girl right stout and well developed was,
With nose tip-tilted and eyes blue as glass,
With buttocks broad, and round breasts full and high,
But golden was her hair, I will not lie.
    The parson of the town, since she was fair,
Was purposeful to make of her his heir,
Both of his chattels and of his estate,
But all this hinged upon a proper mate.
He was resolved that he'd bestow her high
Into some blood of worthy ancestry;
For Holy Church's goods must be expended
On Holy Church's blood, as it's descended.
Therefore he'd honour thus his holy blood,
Though Holy Church itself became his food.
    Large tolls this miller took, beyond a doubt,
With wheat and malt from all the lands about;
Of which I'd specify among them all
A Cambridge college known as Soler Hall;
He ground their wheat and all their malt he ground.
    And on a day it happened, as they found,
The manciple got such a malady
That all men surely thought that he should die.
Whereon this miller stole both flour and wheat
A hundredfold more than he used to cheat;
For theretofore he stole but cautiously,
But now he was a thief outrageously,
At which the warden scolded and raised hell;
The miller snapped his fingers, truth to tell,
And cracked his brags and swore it wasn't so.
    There were two poor young clerks, whose names I know,

That dwelt within this Hall whereof I say.
Willful they were and lusty, full of play,
And (all for mirth and to make revelry)
After the warden eagerly did they cry
To give them leave, at least for this one round,
To go to mill and see their produce ground;
And stoutly they proclaimed they'd bet their neck
The miller should not steal one half a peck
Of grain, by trick, nor yet by force should thieve;
And at the last the warden gave them leave.
John was the one and Alain was that other;
In one town were they born, and that called Strother,
Far in the north, I cannot tell you where.
    This Alain, he made ready all his gear,
And on a horse loaded the sack anon.
Forth went Alain the clerk, and also John,
With good sword and with buckler at their side.
John knew the way and didn't need a guide,
And at the mill he dropped the sack of grain.
"Ah, Simon, hail, good morn," first spoke Alain.
"How fares it with your fair daughter and wife?"
    "Alain! Welcome," said Simpkin, "by my life,
And John also. How now? What do you here?"
    "Simon," said John, "by God, need makes no peer;
He must himself serve who's no servant, eh?
Or else he's but a fool, as all clerks say.
Our manciple—I hope he'll soon be dead,
So aching are the grinders in his head—
And therefore am I come here with Alain
To grind our corn and carry it home again;
I pray you speed us thither, as you may."
    "It shall be done," said Simpkin, "by my fay.
What will you do the while it is in hand?"
    "By God, right by the hopper will I stand,"
Said John, "and see just how the corn goes in;
I never have seen, by my father's kin,
Just how the hopper waggles to and fro."
    Alain replied: "Well, John, and will you so?
Then will I get beneath it, by my crown,

To see there how the meal comes sifting down
Into the trough; and that shall be my sport.
For, John, in faith, I must be of your sort;
I am as bad a miller as you be."
  The miller smiled at this, their delicacy,
And thought: "All this is done but for a wile;
They think there is no man may them beguile;
But, by my thrift, I will yet blear their eyes,
For all the tricks in their philosophies.
The more odd tricks and stratagems they make,
The more I'll steal when I begin to take.
In place of flour I'll give them only bran.
'The greatest clerk is not the wisest man,'
As once unto the grey wolf said the mare.
But all their arts—I rate them not a tare."
  Out of the door he went, then, secretly,
When he had seen his chance, and quietly;
He looked up and looked down, until he found
The clerks' horse where it stood, securely bound,
Behind the mill, under an arbour green;
And to the horse he went, then, all unseen;
He took the bridle off him and anon,
When the said horse was free, why he was gone
Toward the fen, for wild mares ran therein,
And with a neigh he went, through thick and thin.
  This miller straight went back and no word said,
But did his business and with these clerks played,
Until their corn was fairly, fully ground.
But when the flour was sacked and the ears bound,
This John went out, to find his horse away,
And so he cried: "Hello!" and "Weladay!
Our horse is lost! Alain, for Jesus' bones
Get to your feet, come out, man, now, at once!
Alas, our warden's palfrey's lost and lorn!"
  This Alain forgot all, both flour and corn,
Clean out of mind was all his husbandry,
"What? Which way did he go?" began to cry.
  The wife came bounding from the house, and then
She said: "Alas! Your horse went to the fen,

With the wild mares, as fast as he could go.
A curse light on the hand that tied him so,
And him that better should have knotted rein!"

   "Alas!" quoth John, "Alain, for Jesus' pain,
Lay off your sword, and I will mine also;
I am as fleet, God knows, as is a roe;
By God's heart, he shall not escape us both!
Why didn't you put him in the barn? My oath!
Bad luck, by God, Alain, you are a fool!"

   These foolish clerks began to run and roll
Toward the marshes, both Alain and John.

   And when the miller saw that they were gone,
He half a bushel of their flour did take
And bade his wife go knead it and bread make.
He said: "I think those clerks some trickery feared;
Yet can a miller match a clerkling's beard,
For all his learning; let them go their way.
Look where they go, yea, let the children play,
They'll catch him not so readily, by my crown!"

   Those simple clerks went running up and down
With "Look out! Halt! Halt! Down here! 'Ware the rear!
Go whistle, you, and I will watch him here!"
But briefly, till it came to utter night,
They could not, though they put forth all their might,
That stallion catch, he always ran so fast,
Till in a ditch they trapped him at the last.

   Weary and wet, as beast is in the rain,
Came foolish John and with him came Alain.
"Alas," said John, "the day that I was born!
Now are we bound toward mockery and scorn.
Our corn is stolen, folk will call us fools,
The warden and the fellows at the schools,
And specially this miller. Weladay!"

   Thus John complained as he went on his way
Toward the mill, with Bayard once more bound.
The miller sitting by the fire he found,
For it was night, and farther could they not;
But, for the love of God, they him besought
For shelter and for supper, for their penny.

The miller said to them: "If there be any,
Such as it is, why you shall have your part.
My house is small, but you have learned your art;
You can, by metaphysics, make a place
A full mile wide in twenty feet of space.
Let us see now if this place will suffice,
Or make more room with speech, by some device."
    "Now, Simon," said John, "by Saint Cuthbert's beard,
You're always merry and have well answered.
As I've heard, man shall take one of two things:
Such as he finds, or take such as he brings.
But specially, I pray you, mine host dear,
Give us some meat and drink and some good cheer,
And we will pay you, truly, to the full.
With empty hand no man takes hawk or gull;
Well, here's our silver, ready to be spent."
    This miller to the town his daughter sent
For ale and bread, and roasted them a goose,
And tied their horse, that it might not go loose;
And then in his own chamber made a bed,
With sheets and with good blankets fairly spread,
Not from his bed more than twelve feet, or ten.
The daughter made her lone bed near the men,
In the same chamber with them, by and by;
It could not well be bettered, and for why?
There was no larger room in all the place.
They supped and talked, and gained some small solace,
And drank strong ale, that evening, of the best.
Then about midnight all they went to rest.
    Well had this miller varnished his bald head,
    For pale he was with drinking, and not red.
He hiccoughed and he mumbled through his nose,
As he were chilled, with humours lachrymose.
To bed he went, and with him went his wife.
As any jay she was with laughter rife,
So copiously was her gay whistle wet.
The cradle near her bed's footboard was set,
Handy for rocking and for giving suck.
And when they'd drunk up all there was in crock,

To bed went miller's daughter, and anon
To bed went Alain and to bed went John.
There was no more; they did not need a dwale.
This miller had so roundly bibbed his ale
That, like a horse, he snorted in his sleep,
While of his tail behind he kept no keep.
His wife joined in his chorus, and so strong,
Men might have heard her snores a full furlong;
And the girl snored, as well, for company.
Alain the clerk, who heard this melody,
He poked at John and said: "Asleep? But how?
Did you hear ever such a song ere now?
Lo, what a compline is among them all!
Now may the wildfire on their bodies fall!
Who ever heard so outlandish a thing?
But they shall have the flour of ill ending.
Through this long night there'll be for me no rest;
But never mind, 'twill all be for the best.
For, John," said he, "so may I ever thrive,
As, if I can, that very wench I'll swive.
Some recompense the law allows to us;
For, John, there is a statute which says thus,
That if a man in one point be aggrieved,
Yet in another shall he be relieved.
Our corn is stolen, to that there's no nay,
And we have had an evil time this day.
But since I may not have amending, now,
Against my loss I'll set some fun—and how!
By God's great soul it shan't be otherwise!"
This John replied: "Alain, let me advise.
The miller is a dangerous man," he said,
"And if he be awakened, I'm afraid
He may well do us both an injury."
But Alain said: "I count him not a fly."
And up he rose and to the girl he crept.
This wench lay on her back and soundly slept,
Until he'd come so near, ere she might spy,
It was too late to struggle, then, or cry;
And, to be brief, these two were soon at one.

Now play, Alain! For I will speak of John.
 This John lay still a quarter hour, or so,
Pitied himself and wept for all his woe.
"Alas," said he, "this is a wicked jape!
Now may I say that I am but an ape.
Yet has my friend, there, something for his harm;
He has the miller's daughter on his arm.
He ventured, and his pains are now all fled,
While I lie like a sack of chaff in bed;
And when this jape is told, another day,
I shall be held an ass, a milksop, yea!
I will arise and chance it, by my fay!
'Unhardy is unhappy,' as they say."
 And up he rose, and softly then he went
To find the cradle for expedient,
And bore it over to his own foot-board.
 Soon after this the wife no longer snored,
But woke and rose and went outside to piss,
And came again and did the cradle miss,
And groped round, here and there, but found it not.
"Alas!" thought she, "my way I have forgot.
I nearly found myself in the clerks' bed.
Eh, ben'cite, but that were wrong!" she said.
And on, until by cradle she did stand.
And, groping a bit farther with her hand,
She found the bed, and thought of naught but good,
Because her baby's cradle by it stood,
And knew not where she was, for it was dark;
But calmly then she crept in by the clerk,
And lay right still, and would have gone to sleep.
But presently this John the clerk did leap,
And over on this goodwife did he lie.
No such gay time she'd known in years gone by.
He pricked her hard and deep, like one gone mad.
And so a jolly life these two clerks had
Till the third cock began to crow and sing.
 Alain grew weary in the grey dawning,
For he had laboured hard through all the night;
And said: "Farewell, now, Maudy, sweet delight!

The day is come, I may no longer bide;
But evermore, whether I walk or ride,
I am your own clerk, so may I have weal."
    "Now, sweetheart," said she, "go and fare you well!
But ere you go, there's one thing I must tell.
When you go walking homeward past the mill,
Right at the entrance, just the door behind,
You shall a loaf of half a bushel find
That was baked up of your own flour, a deal
Of which I helped my father for to steal.
And, darling, may God save you now and keep!"
And with that word she almost had to weep.
    Alain arose and thought: "Ere it be dawn,
I will go creep in softly by friend John."
And found the cradle with his hand, anon.
"By God!" thought he, "all wrong I must have gone;
My head is dizzy from my work tonight,
And that's why I have failed to go aright.
I know well, by this cradle, I am wrong,
For here the miller and his wife belong."
And on he went, and on the devil's way,
Unto the bed wherein the miller lay.
He thought to have crept in by comrade John,
So, to the miller, in he got anon,
And caught him round the neck, and softly spake,
Saying: "You, John, you old swine's head, awake,
For Christ's own soul, and hear a noble work,
For by Saint James, and as I am a clerk,
I have, three times in this short night, no lack,
Swived that old miller's daughter on her back,
While you, like any coward, were aghast.'
    "You scoundrel," cried the miller, "you trespassed?
Ah, traitor false and treacherous clerk!" cried he,
"You shall be killed, by God's own dignity!
Who dares be bold enough to bring to shame
My daughter, who is born of such a name?"
    And by the gullet, then, he caught Alain.
And pitilessly he handled him amain,
And on the nose he smote him with his fist.

Down ran the bloody stream upon his breast;
And on the floor, with nose and mouth a-soak,
They wallowed as two pigs do in a poke.
And up they came, and down they both went, prone,
Until the miller stumbled on a stone,
And reeled and fell down backwards on his wife,
Who nothing knew of all this silly strife;
For she had fallen into slumber tight
With John the clerk, who'd been awake all night.
But at the fall, from sleep she started out.
"Help, holy Cross of Bromholm!" did she shout,
"In manus tuas, Lord, to Thee I call!
Simon, awake, the Fiend is on us all!
My heart is broken, help, I am but dead!
There lies one on my womb, one on my head!
Help, Simpkin, for these treacherous clerks do fight!"
    John started up, as fast as well he might,
And searched along the wall, and to and fro,
To find a staff; and she arose also,
And knowing the room better than did John,
She found a staff against the wall, anon;
And then she saw a little ray of light,
For through a hole the moon was shining bright;
And by that light she saw the struggling two,
But certainly she knew not who was who,
Except she saw a white thing with her eye.
And when she did this same white thing espy,
She thought the clerk had worn a nightcap here.
And with the staff she nearer drew, and near,
And, thinking to hit Alain on his poll,
She fetched the miller on his bald white skull,
And down he went, crying out, "Help, help, I die!"
The two clerks beat him well and let him lie;
And clothed themselves, and took their horse anon,
And got their flour, and on their way were gone.
And at the mill they found the well-made cake
Which of their meal the miller's wife did bake.
    Thus is the haughty miller soundly beat,
And thus he's lost his pay for grinding wheat,

And paid for the two suppers, let me tell,
Of Alain and of John, who've tricked him well,
His wife is taken, also his daughter sweet;
Thus it befalls a miller who's a cheat.
And therefore is this proverb said with truth,
"An evil end to evil man, forsooth."
The cheater shall himself well cheated be.
And God, Who sits on high in majesty,
Save all this company, both strong and frail!
Thus have I paid this miller with my tale.

The Sailor's Tale

The Sailor's Prologue

Our host upon his stirrups stood, anon,
And said: "Good men, now hearken, every one;
This was a useful story, for the nonce!
Sir parish priest," quoth he, "for God His bones.
Tell us a tale, as you agreed before.
I see well that you learned men of lore
Have learned much good, by God's great dignity!"
    The parson answered: "*Benedicite!*
What ails the man, so sinfully to swear?"
    Our host replied: "Ho, Jenkin, are you there?
I smell a Lollard in the wind," quoth he.
"Ho, good men!" said our host, "now hearken me;
Wait but a bit, for God's high passion do,
For we shall have a sermon ere we're through;
This Lollard here will preach to us somewhat."
    "Nay, by my father's soul, that shall he not!"
Replied the sailor; "Here he shall not preach,
Nor comment on the gospels here, nor teach.
We all believe in the great God," said he,
"But he would sow among us difficulty,
Or sprinkle cockles in our good clean corn;
And therefore, host, beforehand now, I warn
My jolly body shall a story tell
And I will clink for you so merry a bell
That it shall waken all this company;
But it shall not be of philosophy,
Nor yet of physics, nor quaint terms of law;
There is but little Latin in my maw."

The Sailor's Tale

A merchant, dwelling, once, at Saint-Denis,
Was rich, for which men held him wise, and he
Had got a wife of excellent beauty,
And very sociable and gay was she,
Which is a thing that causes more expense
Than all the good cheer and the deference
That men observe at festivals and dances;
Such salutations and masked countenances
Pass by as does a shadow on the wall;
But woe to him that must pay for it all.
The foolish husband, always he must pay;
He must buy clothes and other fine array,
And all for his own worship, wealthily,
In which, indeed, women dance jollily.
And if he cannot thus, peradventure,
Or cares not such expenses to endure,
But thinks his money wasted or quite lost,
Why then another man must pay the cost,
Or else lend gold, and that is dangerous.
    This noble merchant had a worthy house,
To which, each day, so many did repair,
Since he was generous and his wife was fair,
'Twas to be wondered at; but hear my tale.
Among his many guests of great and small
There was a monk, a handsome man and bold,
I think that he was thirty winters old,
Who was for ever coming to that place.
This youthful monk, who was so fair of face,
Was so far intimate with the worthy man,
And had been since their friendship first began,
That in the house familiar was he
As it is possible for friend to be.
    And in as much as this same goodly man
And too, this monk of whom I first began,
Were both born in the village they'd lived in,
The monk claimed him for cousin, or such kin;
And he again, he never said him nay,
But was as glad thereof as bird of day;

For to his heart it was a great pleasance.
Thus they were knit by endless alliance,
And each of them did other one assure
Of brotherhood the while their lives endure.
    Free was Dan John with money and expense
When in that house; and full of diligence
To please all there, whatever be his age.
He ne'er forgot to tip the humblest page
In all that house; according to degree
He gave the master, then the company,
Whene'er he came, some kind of honest thing;
For which they were as glad of his coming
As bird is glad when the new sun uprises.
No more of all this now, for it suffices.
    It so befell, this merchant, on a day,
Prepared to make all ready his array,
Since to the town of Bruges he was to fare
To purchase there a quantity of ware;
To which end he'd to Paris sent someone
With messages, and he had prayed Dan John
That he should come to Saint-Denis to pay
Him and his wife a visit for a day,
Said 'twas a thing he certainly must do.
    This noble monk, whereof I'm telling you,
Had from his abbot, when he wished, license,
Because he was a man of great prudence,
An officer, indeed, who out did ride
To see to barns and granges, far and wide;
And now to Saint-Denis he came anon.
Who was so welcome as my lord Dan John,
Our cousin dear, so full of courtesy?
With him he brought a jug of rare malmsey,
And still another full of fine vernage,
And wild fowls, too, as was his long usage.
And so I let them eat and drink and play,
This monk and merchant, for a night and day.
    Upon the third day this good trader rises,
And on his needs discreetly he advises;
And up into his countinghouse goes he
To reckon up his books, as well may be,

For the past year, to learn how matters stood
And what he'd spent, and whether it were good,
And whether he were wealthier than before.
His books and bags, all that he had in store,
He put before him on his counting board;
He was right rich in goods and rich in hoard,
For the which cause he bolted fast his door;
He'd have no one disturb him while before
Him stood his books and monies at that time;
And thus he sat till it was well past prime.

   Dan John had risen with the dawn, also,
And in the garden wandered to and fro,
Having said all his prayers full reverently.

   Then came this goodwife, walking secretly
Into the garden, walking slow and soft.
And kissed him in salute, as she'd done oft.
A little girl came walking at her side,
Was in her charge to govern and to guide,
For yet beneath the rod was this small maid.

   "O my dear cousin, O Dan John," she said,
"What ails you that so early you arise?"

   "Dear niece," said he, "surely it should suffice
To sleep for five full hours of any night,
Unless 'twere for some old and languid wight,
As are these married men, who doze and dare
About as in the form the weary hare,
Worn all distraught by hounds both great and small.
But, my dear niece, just why are you so pale?
I must suppose of course that our good man
Has you belaboured since the night began,
And you were forced to sleep but scantily."

   And with that word he laughed right merrily,
And, what of his own thoughts, he blushed all red.

   This pretty wife began to shake her head,
And answered thus: "Aye, God knows all!" said she:
"Nay, cousin mine, it stands not so with me.
For by that God Who gave me soul and life,
In all the realm of France there is no wife
Who has less lust for that same sorry play.
For I may sing 'Alas!' and 'Welaway

That I was born!' but to no man," said she,
"Dare I to tell how this thing stands with me.
Wherefore I'm thinking from this land to wend,
Or else of my own life to make an end,
I am so fearful and so full of care."
    This monk began, then, at the wife to stare,
And said: "Alas, my niece, may God forbid
That you, for any care or fear morbid,
Destroy yourself! But tell me of your grief;
Perhaps I may, whatever the mischief,
Counsel or help, and therefore do tell me
All the annoyance, for 'twill secret be;
For on my breviary I make oath
That never in my life, though lief or loath,
Shall I your secret whisper or betray."
    "The same to you again," said she, "I say;
By God and by this breviary, I swear,
Though men this body of mine apieces tear,
No I will never, though I go to Hell,
Betray a single word that you may tell,
And this, not for our kinship and alliance,
But verily for love and true reliance."
    Thus are they sworn, and thereupon they kissed,
And each told other such things as they list.
"Cousin," said she, "if I had time and space,
As I have not, and specially in this place,
Then would I tell a legend of my life,
What I have suffered since I've been a wife,
From my husband, though he is your cousin."
    "Nay," quoth the monk, "by God and Saint Martin,
He is no more a cousin unto me
Than is this leaf a-hanging on the tree!
I call him so, by Saint-Denis of France,
To have but better reason to advance
With you, whom I have loved especially
Above all other women, and truly;
I swear this to you on the faith I own.
Tell me your grief before your man comes down,
Come, hasten now, and go your way anon."
    "My dearest love," said she, "O my Dan John,

Right glad I were this counsel for to hide,
But it must out, I can't it more abide.
To me my husband is the poorest man
That ever was, since first the world began.
But since I am a wife, becomes not me
To tell a living soul our privity,
Either abed or in some other place;
God guard that I should tell it, of His grace!
For wife must never talk of her husband,
Save to his honour, as I understand.
But now to you thus much I can and shall:
So help me God, he is not worth, at all,
In any wise, the value of a fly.
But yet this grieves me most—he's niggardly;
And well you know that women naturally
Desire six things, and even so do I.
For women all would have their husbands be
Hardy, and wise, and rich, and therewith free,
Obedient to the wife, and fresh in bed.
But by that very Lord Who for us bled,
Though in his honour, myself to array
On Sunday next, I must yet go and pay
A hundred francs, or else be but forlorn.
Yet would I rather never have been born
Than have a scandal or disgrace, say I.
And if my husband such a thing should spy,
I were but lost, and therefore do I pray,
Lend me this sum, or else I perish, yea!
Dan John, I say, lend me these hundred francs;
By gad, I will not fail to give you thanks,
If only you will do the thing I pray.
For on a certain day I will repay,
And give to you what pleasure and service
I can give, aye, just as you may devise.
And if I don't, God take on me vengeance
As foul as once on Ganelon of France!"
    This gentle monk replied as you shall hear:
"Now truthfully, my own sweet lady dear,
I have," said he, "on you so great a ruth
That I do swear and promise you, in truth,

That when your husband goes to Flanders there,
I will deliver you from all this care;
For I will bring to you a hundred francs."
   And with that word he caught her by the flanks
And hugged her to him hard and kissed her oft.
"Go now your way," he said, "all still and soft,
And let us dine as soon as ever we may,
For by my dial it's the prime of day.
Go now, and be as true as I shall be."
"Now all else God forbid, sir," then said she.
And in she went as jolly as a pie,
And bade the cooks that they to kitchen hie,
So that her men might dine, and that anon.
Up to her husband is this wife then gone,
And knocked upon his counting room boldly.
   "*Qui est là?*" asked he.
   "Peter! It is I,"
Said she; "What, sir, and how long will you fast?
How long time will you reckon up and cast
Your sums and books and other tiresome things?
The devil take away such reckonings!
You have enough, by gad, of God's mercy;
Come down today, and let your gold bags be.
Why, are you not ashamed that our Dan John
Has fasted miserably all morning gone?
What! Let us hear a Mass and then go dine."
   "Wife," said this man, "little can you divine
The curious businesses that merchants have.
As for us traders, as may God me save,
And by that lord that all we call Saint Yve,
Among twelve merchants scarcely two shall thrive
Continually, and lasting into age.
We must keep open house and blithe visage,
While goes the world as it may chance to be,
And hold all our affairs in secrecy
Till we are dead; or else we must go play
At pilgrimage, or else go clean away.
And therefore have I great necessity
That on this curious world advised I be;
For evermore we merchants stand in dread

Of chance and mishap as our ways we tread.
"To Flanders go I at the break of day,
And I'll come back as soon as ever I may.
For which, my dearest wife, your aid I seek
To be, to all, both courteous and meek,
And to maintain our wealth be studious,
And govern honourably and well our house.
You have enough in every sort of wise
That, to a thrifty household, should suffice.
You've clothes and food, I've seen to each detail,
And silver in your purse shall never fail."
      And with that word his counting door he shut
And down he went, no longer tarrying, but
Right hastily a Mass for them was said,
And speedily the tables there were spread,
And to the dinner swiftly all they sped;
And richly then the monk this merchant fed.
      After the dinner Dan John soberly
This merchant took aside, and privately
He said to him, "Cousin, it stands just so,
For I see well that you to Bruges will go.
God and good Saint Augustine speed and guide!
I pray you, cousin, that you'll wisely ride;
Guard your health well, and govern your diet
Temperately, especially in this heat.
Neither of us requires outlandish fare;
Farewell, dear cousin; God shield you from care.
If anything there be, by day or night,
If it lie in my power and my might,
That you would have me do, in any wise,
It shall be done, just as you may devise.
      "One thing, before you go, if it may be,
I pray you do, and that is, to lend me
A hundred francs, for but a week or two,
For certain cattle I must buy, to do
The stocking of a little place of ours.
So help me God, I would that it were yours!
I will not fail you, come next settling day,
Not for a thousand francs, a mile away.
But let this thing be secret, pray, for I,

Even tonight, must go these beasts to buy;
And farewell now, my own good cousin dear.
And many thanks for entertainment here."
   This noble merchant, civilly, anon,
Answered and said: "O cousin mine, Dan John,
Now surely this is but a small request;
My gold is yours and aye at your behest.
And not gold only, no but all my ware;
Take what you like, God shield that you should spare.
   "There's but one thing, which you know well enow
Of traders, for their money is their plow.
We may on credit trade, while we've a name,
But to be goldless is to lose the game.
Pay it again when you are at your ease;
In all I can, full fain am I to please."
   These hundred francs he went and got anon,
And privately he gave them to Dan John.
No one in all the world knew of this loan,
Saving this merchant and Dan John alone.
They drink, and talk, and walk awhile, and play,
Until Dan John sets out for his abbey.
   The morrow came and forth this merchant rides
Toward Flanders; and his apprentice guides
Until he came to Bruges all happily.
Now went this merchant fast and busily
About his trade, and bought, and borrowed gold;
He neither played at dice nor danced, I'm told,
But like a merchant, briefly here to tell,
He led his life, and there I let him dwell.
   On the first Sunday after he was gone,
To Saint-Denis is come again Dan John,
With face and tonsure shining from a shave.
In all the house was not so small a knave,
Nor any other, but was right glad, then,
Because my lord Dan John was come again.
And coming briefly to the point, anon
This lovely wife agreed with her Dan John
That for these hundred francs he should, all night,
Have her within his arms and bolt upright;
And this agreement was performed in bed.

In mirth all night a busy life they led
Till it was dawn, when Dan John went his way,
Bidding the household "Farewell!" and "Good-day!"
For none of them, nor any in the town,
Had of Dan John the least suspicion shown.
So forth he rode, home to his own abbey,
Or where he wished; no more of him I say.

   This merchant, when all ended was the fair,
To Saint-Denis made ready to repair;
And with his wife he feasted and made cheer,
And told her that, since goods were very dear,
He needs must get more cash at his command,
For he was bound by his own note of hand
To pay some twenty thousand crowns anon.
For which this merchant is to Paris gone
To borrow there, from certain friends he had,
Some certain francs unto his own to add.
And when he'd come at length into the town,
Out of great friendship never yet outgrown,
Unto Dan John he went first, there to play,
Not to talk business, nor ask money, nay,
But to inquire and see to his welfare,
And, too, to tell about his Flemish ware,
As friends are wont when come from far or near.
Dan John made him a feast and merry cheer;
And he told him again, and specially,
How he had purchased well and luckily—
Thanks be to God!—all of his merchandise.
Save that he must, nor fail in any wise,
Obtain a loan, at least it would be best,
And then he'd have some time for joy and rest.

   Dan John replied: "No gladness do I feign
That sound in health you are come home again.
And if I were but rich, as I have bliss,
These twenty thousand crowns you should not miss,
Since you so kindly, but the other day,
Lent me some gold; and as I can and may,
I thank you, by the Lord and by Saint James!
Nevertheless, to no hand but our dame's,
Your wife at home, I gave the gold again

Upon your counter; she'll remember when
By certain tokens that I gave to her.
Now, by your leave, I must get up and stir,
Our abbot will be leaving town anon;
And in his company I must be gone.
Greet well our dame, your wife and my niece sweet,
And farewell, cousin dear, until we meet."
　　This merchant, being a man full wary-wise,
Has got his loan and paid there in Paris,
To certain Lombards, ready in their hand,
The sum of gold, and got his note back, and
Now home he goes as merry as a jay.
For well he knew he stood in such array
That now he needs must make, with nothing lost,
A thousand francs above his total cost.
　　His wife, all ready, met him at the gate,
As she was wont, though he came soon or late,
And all that night with pleasure did they pet,
For he was rich and cleanly out of debt.
When it was day, this merchant did embrace
His wife anew, and kissed her on her face,
And up he goes and makes it rather tough.
　　"No more," cried she, "by God, you've had enough!"
　　And wantonly again with him she played,
Till, at the last, this merchant sighed and said:
"By God," said he, "I am a little wroth
With you, my wife, though to be so I'm loath.
And know you why? By God, and as I guess,
You've been the causing of some small strangeness
Between me and my cousin, dear Dan John.
You should have warned me, really, ere I'd gone,
That he to you a hundred francs had paid
In cash; he was put out, I am afraid,
Because I spoke to him of loans, by chance,
At least I judged so by his countenance.
Nevertheless, by God our Heavenly King,
I never thought to ask him such a thing.
I pray you, wife, never again do so;
But always tell me, ere away I go,
If any debtor has, in my absence,

Repaid to you, lest through your negligence
I might demand a sum already paid."
    This wife was not astounded nor afraid,
But boldly she spoke up and that anon:
"Marry, I challenge that false monk, Dan John!
I kept, of all his coins, not one to tell.
He brought me certain gold—that know I well!
What! Ill success upon his friar's snout!
For God knows that I thought, with never a doubt.
That he had given it me because of you,
To advance thus my honour, and yours too,
In cousinhood, and for the merry cheer
That he has found so many a time right here.
But since I see our peace is thus disjoint,
I'll answer you but briefly, to the point.
You have far slacker debtors than am I!
For I will pay you well and readily
From day to day; and if it be I fail,
I am your wife, tally it on my tail,
And I will pay as soon as ever I may.
For by my truth I have, on new array,
And not on rubbish, spent it, every sou.
And since so well I've spent it, all for you,
All for your honour, for God's sake, I say,
Do not be angry, but let's laugh and play.
My jolly body's yours in pledge," she said,
"By God, I will not pay you, save in bed!
Forgive me, then, my own sweet husband dear;
Let us be happy now—turn over here!"
    This merchant saw there was no remedy,
And, thought he, chiding were but great folly,
Since that the thing might not amended be.
    "Now wife," he said, "I do forgive, you see;
But on your life, don't run so far at large;
Conserve our wealth hereafter, so I charge."
    Thus ends my tale, and may the good God send
Tales fair enough until our lives shall end! Amen.

The Prioress's Tale

The Prioress's Prologue

Well said, by *corpus dominus*," said our host,
"Now long time may you sail along the coast,
Sir gentle master, gentle mariner!
God give this monk a thousand years bitter!
Aha, comrades, beware of such a jape!
The monk put into that man's hood an ape,
And in the wife's too, by Saint Augustine!
Invite no more monks to your house or inn.
   "But let that pass, and let us look about
To see who shall be next, of all this rout,
          To tell a tale."
   And after that he said,
As courteously as it had been a maid:
"My lady prioress, and by your leave,
So that I knew I should in no way grieve,
I would opine that tell a tale you should,
The one that follows next if you but would.
Now will you please vouchsafe it, lady dear?"
   "Gladly," said she, and spoke as you shall hear.
                    Explicit

The Prioress's Invocation

                Domine, dominus noster.
O Lord, Our Lord, Thy name how marvelous
Is spread through all this mighty world," said she;
"For not alone Thy praise so glorious
Is given by men of worth and dignity,

But from the mouths of children Thy bounty
Is hymned, yea, even sucklings at the breast
Do sometimes Thy laudation manifest.

"Wherefore in praise, as best I can or may,
Of Thee and of that pure white Lily flower
Who bore Thee, and is yet a maid alway,
I tell a tale as best is in my power,
Not that I may increase Her heavenly dower,
For She Herself is honour and the one
From Whom spring wealth and goodness, next Her Son.

"O Mother Maid! O Maiden Mother free!
O bush unburnt, burning in Moses' sight,
Who ravished so the Soul of Deity,
With Thy meekness, the Spirit of the Light,
That His virtue, which was Thy soul's delight,
Conceived in Thee the Father's wise Essence,
Help me to speak now with all reverence!

"Lady, Thy goodness and Thy generous grace,
Thy virtue and Thy great humility—
No tongue may say, no pen may fully trace;
For sometimes, Lady, ere men pray to Thee,
Thou goest before, of Thy benignity,
And givest us the true light, by Thy prayer,
To guide us all unto Thy Son so dear.

"I cannot bear the burden, blessed Queen,
Of fitly praising all Thy worthiness,
My wisdom and my knowledge are too mean;
But as a child of twelve months old, or less,
That scarcely any word can well express,
So fare I now, and therefore do I pray,
Guide Thou that song of Thee which I shall say!"
                                          Explicit

The Prioress's Tale

In Asia, in a city rich and great
There was a Jewry set amidst the town,

Established by a rich lord of the state
For usury and gain of ill renown,
Hateful to Christ and those who are His own;
And through that street a man might ride or wend,
For it was free and open at each end.

A little school for Christian folk there stood,
Down at the farther end, in which there were
A many children born of Christian blood,
Who learned in that same school, year after year,
Such teachings as with men were current there,
Which is to say, to sing well and to read,
As children do of whatsoever creed.

Among these children was a widow's son,
A little choir boy, seven years of age,
Who went to school as days passed one by one,
And who, whenever saw he the image
Of Jesus' Mother, it was his usage,
As he'd been taught, to kneel down there and say
Ave Maria, ere he went his way.

Thus had this widow her small son well taught
Our Blessed Lady, Jesus' Mother dear,
To worship always, and he ne'er forgot,
For simple child learns easily and clear;
But ever, when I muse on matters here,
Saint Nicholas stands aye in my presence,
For he, when young, did do Christ reverence.

This little child, his little lesson learning,
Sat at his primer in the school, and there,
While boys were taught the antiphons, kept turning,
And heard the *Alma redemptoris* fair,
And drew as near as ever he did dare,
Marking the words, remembering every note,
Until the first verse he could sing by rote.

He knew not what this Latin meant to say,
Being so young and of such tender age,
But once a young school comrade did he pray

To expound to him the song in his language,
Or tell him why the song was in usage;
Asking the boy the meaning of the song,
On his bare knees he begged him well and long.

His fellow was an older lad than he,
And answered thus: "This song, as I've heard say,
Was made to praise Our Blessed Lady free,
Her to salute and ever Her to pray
To be our help when comes our dying day.
I can expound to you only so far;
I've learned the song; I know but small grammar."

"And is this song made in all reverence
Of Jesus' Mother?" asked this innocent;
"Now truly I will work with diligence
To learn it all ere Christmas sacrament,
Though for my primer I take punishment
And though I'm beaten thrice within the hour,
Yet will I learn it by Our Lady's power!"

His fellow taught him on their homeward way
Until he learned the antiphon by rote.
Then clear and bold he sang it day by day,
Each word according with its proper note;
And twice each day it welled from out his throat,
As schoolward went he and as homeward went;
On Jesus' Mother was his fixed intent.

As I have said, as through the Jewry went
This little schoolboy, out the song would ring,
And joyously the notes he upward sent;
O *Alma redemptoris* would he sing;
To his heart's core it did the sweetness bring
Of Christ's dear Mother, and, to Her to pray,
He could not keep from singing on his way.

Our primal foe, the serpent Sathanas,
Who has in Jewish heart his hornets' nest,
Swelled arrogantly: "O Jewish folk, alas!

Is it to you a good thing, and the best,
That such a boy walks here, without protest,
In your despite and doing such offense
Against the teachings that you reverence?"

From that time forth the Jewish folk conspired
Out of the world this innocent to chase;
A murderer they found, and thereto hired,
Who in an alley had a hiding place;
And as the child went by at sober pace,
This cursed Jew did seize and hold him fast,
And cut his throat, and in a pit him cast.

I say, that in a cesspool him they threw,
Wherein these Jews did empty their entrails.
O cursed folk of Herod, born anew,
How can you think your ill intent avails?
Murder will out, 'tis sure, nor ever fails,
And chiefly when God's honour vengeance needs,
The blood cries out upon your cursed deeds.

"O martyr firm in thy virginity,
Now mayest thou sing, and ever follow on
The pure white Lamb Celestial"—quoth she—
"Whereof the great evangelist, Saint John,
In Patmos wrote, saying that they are gone
Before the Lamb, singing a song that's new,
And virgins all, who never woman knew."

This widow poor awaited all that night
Her child's return to her, but he came not;
For which, so soon as it was full daylight,
With pale face full of dread, and busy thought,
At school she sought and everywhere she sought,
Until, at last, from all her questioning she
Learned that he last was seen in the Jewry.

With mother's pity in her breast enclosed
She ran, as she were half out of her mind,
To every place where it might be supposed,

In likelihood, that she her son should find;
And ever on Christ's Mother meek and kind
She called until, at last, Our Lady wrought
That amongst the cursed Jews the widow sought.

She asked and she implored, all piteously,
Of every Jew who dwelt in that foul place,
To tell her where her little child could be.
They answered "Nay." But Jesus, of His grace,
Put in her mind, within a little space,
That after him in that same spot she cried
Where he'd been cast in pit, or near beside.

O Thou great God, Who innocents hast called
To give Thee praise, now shown is Thy great might!
This gem of chastity, this emerald,
Of martyrdom the ruby clear and bright,
Began, though slain and hidden there from sight,
The *Alma redemptoris* loud to sing,
So clear that all the neighbourhood did ring.

The Christian folk that through the ghetto went
Came running for the wonder of this thing,
And hastily they for the provost sent;
He also came without long tarrying,
And gave Christ thanks, Who is of Heaven King,
And, too, His Mother, honour of mankind;
And after that the Jews there did he bind.

This child, with piteous lamentation, then
Was taken up, singing his song alway;
And, honoured by a great concourse of men,
Carried within an abbey near, that day.
Swooning, his mother by the black bier lay,
Nor easily could people who were there
This second Rachel carry from the bier.

With torture and with shameful death, each one,
The provost did these cursed Hebrews serve
Who of the murder knew, and that anon;

From justice to the villains he'd not swerve.
Evil shall have what evil does deserve.
And therefore, with wild horses, did he draw,
And after hang, their bodies, all by law.

Upon the bier lay this poor innocent
Before the altar, while the mass did last,
And after that the abbot and monks went
About the coffin for to close it fast;
But when the holy water they did cast,
Then spoke the child, at touch of holy water,
And sang, "O Alma redemptoris mater!"

This abbot, who was a right holy man,
As all monks are, or as they ought to be,
The dead young boy to conjure then began,
Saying: "O dear child, I do beg of thee,
By virtue of the Holy Trinity,
Tell me how it can be that thou dost sing
After thy throat is cut, to all seeming?"

"My throat is cut unto the spinal bone,"
Replied the child. "By nature of my kind
I should have died, aye, many hours agone,
But Jesus Christ, as you in books shall find,
Wills that His glory last in human mind;
Thus for the honour of His Mother dear,
Still may I sing 'O Alma' loud and clear.

"This well of mercy, Jesus' Mother sweet,
I always loved, after my poor knowing;
And when came time that I my death must meet,
She came to me and bade me only sing
This anthem in the pain of my dying,
As you have heard, and after I had sung,
She laid a precious pearl upon my tongue.

"Wherefore I sing, and sing I must, 'tis plain,
In honour of that blessed Maiden free,
Till from my tongue is taken away the grain;

And afterward she said thus unto me:
'My little child, soon will I come for thee,
When from thy tongue the little bead they take;
Be not afraid, thee I will not forsake.'"

The holy monk, this abbot, so say I,
The tongue caught out and took away the grain,
And he gave up the ghost, then, easily,
And when the abbot saw this wonder plain,
The salt tears trickled down his cheeks like rain,
And humbly he fell prone upon the ground,
Lying there still as if he had been bound.

And all the monks lay there on the pavement,
Weeping and praising Jesus' Mother dear,
And after that they rose and forth they went,
Taking away this martyr from his bier,
And in a tomb of marble, carved and clear,
Did they enclose his little body sweet;
Where he is now—God grant us him to meet!

O you young Hugh of Lincoln, slain also
By cursed Jews, as is well known to all,
Since it was but a little while ago,
Pray you for us, sinful and weak, who call,
That, of His mercy, God will still let fall
Something of grace, and mercy multiply,
For reverence of His Mother dear on high. Amen.

Sir Thopas

The Merry Words of the Host to Chaucer

Sir Thopas's Prologue

When told was all this miracle, every man
So sober fell 'twas wonderful to see,
Until our host in jesting wise began,
And for the first time did he glance at me,
Saying, "What man are you?"—'twas thus quoth he—
"You look as if you tried to find a hare,
For always on the ground I see you stare.

"Come near me then, and look up merrily.
Now make way, sirs, and let this man have place;
He in the waist is shaped as well as I;
This were a puppet in an arm's embrace
For any woman, small and fair of face.
Why, he seems absent, by his countenance,
And gossips with no one for dalliance.

"Since other folk have spoken, it's your turn;
Tell us a mirthful tale, and that anon."
"Mine host," said I, "don't be, I beg, too stern,
For of good tales, indeed, sir, have I none,
Save a long rhyme I learned in years agone."
"Well, that is good," said he; "now shall we hear
It seems to me, a thing to bring us cheer."
                              Explicit

Sir Thopas's Tale

The First Fit

Listen, lords, with good intent,
I truly will a tale present
Of mirth and of solace;
All of a knight was fair and gent
In battle and in tournament.
    His name was Sir Thopas.

Born he was in a far country,
In Flanders, all beyond the sea,
    And Poperinghe the place;
His father was a man full free,
And lord he was of that countree,
    As chanced to be God's grace.

Sir Thopas was a doughty swain,
White was his brow as paindemaine,
    His lips red as a rose;
His cheeks were like poppies in grain,
And I tell you, and will maintain,
    He had a comely nose.

His hair and beard were like saffron
And to his girdle reached adown,
    His shoes were of cordwain;
From Bruges were come his long hose brown,
His rich robe was of ciclatoun—
    And cost full many a jane.

Well could he hunt the dim wild deer
And ride a-hawking by river,
    With grey goshawk on hand;
Therewith he was a good archer,
At wrestling was there none his peer
    Where any ram did stand.

Full many a maiden, bright in bower,
Did long for him for paramour
  When they were best asleep;
But chaste he was, no lecher sure,
And sweet as is the bramble flower
  That bears a rich red hepe.

And so befell, upon a day,
In truth, as I can tell or may,
  Sir Thopas out would ride;
He mounted on his stallion grey,
And held in hand a lance, I say,
  With longsword by his side.

He spurred throughout a fair forest
Wherein was many a dim wild beast,
  Aye, both the buck and hare;
And as he spurred on, north and east,
I tell you now he had, in breast,
  A melancholy care.

There herbs were springing, great and small,
The licorice blue and white setwall,
  And many a gillyflower,
And nutmeg for to put in ale,
All whether it be fresh or stale,
  Or lay in chest in bower.

The birds they sang, upon that day,
The sparrow hawk and popinjay,
  Till it was joy to hear;
The missel thrush he made his lay,
The tender stockdove on the spray,
  She sang full loud and clear.

Sir Thopas fell to love-longing
All when he heard the throstle sing,
  And spurred as madman would:

His stallion fair, for this spurring,
Did sweat till men his coat might wring,
  His two flanks were all blood.

Sir Thopas grown so weary was
With spurring on the yielding grass,
  So fierce had been his speed,
That down he laid him in that place
To give the stallion some solace
  And let him find his feed.

"O holy Mary, ben'cite!
What ails my heart that love in me
  Should bind me now so sore?
For dreamed I all last night, pardie,
An elf-queen shall my darling be,
  And sleep beneath my gore.

"An elf-queen will I love, ywis,
For in this world no woman is
  Worthy to be my make
    In town;
All other women I forsake,
And to an elf-queen I'll betake
  Myself, by dale and down!"

Into his saddle he climbed anon
And spurred then over stile and stone,
  An elf-queen for to see,
Till he so far had ridden on
He found a secret place and won
  The land of Faëry
    So wild;
For in that country was there none
That unto him dared come, not one,
  Not either wife or child.

Until there came a great giant,
Whose name it was Sir Oliphant,
  A dangerous man indeed;

He said: "O Childe, by Termagant,
Save thou dost spur from out my haunt,
 Anon I'll slay thy steed
  With mace.
For here the queen of Faëry,
With harp and pipe and harmony,
 Is dwelling in this place."

The Childe said: "As I hope to thrive,
We'll fight the morn, as I'm alive,
 When I have my armour;
For well I hope, and *par ma fay*,
That thou shalt by this lance well pay,
 And suffer strokes full sore;
  Thy maw
Shall I pierce through, and if I may,
Ere it be fully prime of day,
 Thou'lt die of wounds most raw."

Sir Thopas drew aback full fast;
This giant at him stones did cast
 Out of a fell staff-sling;
 But soon escaped was Childe Thopas,
And all it was by God's own grace,
 And by his brave bearing.

And listen yet, lords, to my tale,
Merrier than the nightingale,
 Whispered to all and some,
How Sir Thopas, with pride grown pale,
Hard spurring over hill and dale,
 Came back to his own home.

His merry men commanded he
To make for him both game and glee,
 For needs now must he fight
With a great giant of heads three,
For love in the society
 Of one who shone full bright.

"Do come," he said, "my minstrels all,
And jesters, tell me tales in hall
     Anon in mine arming;
Of old romances right royal,
Of pope and king and cardinal,
     And e'en of love-liking."

They brought him, first, the sweet, sweet wine,
And mead within a maselyn,
     And royal spicery
Of gingerbread that was full fine,
Cumin and licorice, I opine,
     And sugar so dainty.

He drew on, next his white skin clear,
Of finest linen, clean and sheer,
     His breeches and a shirt;
And next the shirt a stuffed acton,
And over that a habergeon
     'Gainst piercing of his heart.

And over that a fine hauberk
That was wrought all of Jewish work
     And reinforced with plate;
And over that his coat of arms,
As white as lily flower that charms,
     Wherein he will debate.

His shield was all of gold so red,
And thereon was a wild boar's head
     A carbuncle beside;
And now he swore, by ale and bread,
That soon "this giant shall be dead,
     Betide what may betide!"

His jambeaux were of cuir-bouilli,
His sword sheath was of ivory,
     His helm of latten bright,
His saddle was of rewel bone,

And as the sun his bridle shone,
   Or as the full moonlight.

His spear was of fine cypress wood,
That boded war, not brotherhood,
   The head full sharply ground;
His steed was all a dapple grey
Whose gait was ambling, on the way,
   Full easily and round
     In land.
Behold, my lords, here is a fit!
If you'll have any more of it,
   You have but to command.

The Second Fit

Now hold your peace, *par charitee,*
Both knight and lady fair and free,
   And hearken to my spell;
Of battle and of chivalry
And all of ladies' love-drury
   Anon I will you tell.

Romances men recount of price,
Of King Horn and of Hypotis,
   Of Bevis and Sir Guy,
Of Sir Libeaux and Plain-d'Amour;
But Sir Thopas is flower sure
   Of regal chivalry.

His good horse all he then bestrode,
And forth upon his way he rode
   Like spark out of a brand;
Upon his crest he bore a tower,
Wherein was thrust a lily flower;
   God grant he may withstand!

He was a knight adventurous,
Wherefore he'd sleep within no house,
   But lay down in his hood;

His pillow was his helmet bright,
And by him browsed his steed all night
   On forage fine and good.

Himself drank water of the well,
As did the knight Sir Percival,
   So worthy in his weeds,
Till on a day . . .

The Nun's Priest's Tale

The Prologue to the Nun's Priest's Tale

"Hold!" cried the knight. "Good sir, no more of this,
What you have said is right enough, and is
Very much more; a little heaviness
Is plenty for the most of us, I guess.
For me, I say it's saddening, if you please,
As to men who've enjoyed great wealth and ease,
To hear about their sudden fall, alas!
But the contrary's joy and great solace,
As when a man has been in poor estate
And he climbs up and waxes fortunate,
And there abides in all prosperity.
Such things are gladsome, as it seems to me,
And of such things it would be good to tell."
    "Yea," quoth our host, "and by Saint Paul's great bell,
You say the truth; this monk, his clapper's loud.
He spoke how 'Fortune covered with a cloud'
I know not what, and of a 'tragedy,'
As now you heard, and gad! no remedy
It is to wail and wonder and complain
That certain things have happened, and it's pain,
As you have said, to hear of wretchedness.
Sir monk, no more of this, so God you bless!
Your tale annoys the entire company;
Such talking is not worth a butterfly;
For in it is no sport nor any game.
Wherefore, sir monk, Don Peter by your name,
I pray you heartily tell us something else,
For truly, but for clinking of the bells
That from your bridle hang on either side,
By Heaven's king, Who for us all has died,
I should, ere this, have fallen down for sleep,
Although the mud had never been so deep;

Then had your story all been told in vain.
For certainly, as all these clerks complain,
'Whenas a man has none for audience,
It's little help to speak his evidence.'
And well I know the substance is in me
To judge of things that well reported be.
Sir, tell a tale of hunting now, I pray."
    "Nay," said this monk, "I have no wish to play;
Now let another tell, as I have told."
    Then spoke our host out, in rude speech and bold,
And said he unto the nun's priest anon:
"Come near, you priest, come hither, you Sir John,
Tell us a thing to make our hearts all glad;
Be blithe, although you ride upon a jade.
What though your horse may be both foul and lean?
If he but serves you, why, don't care a bean;
Just see your heart is always merry. So."
    "Yes, sir," said he, "yes, host, so may I go,
For, save I'm merry, I know I'll be blamed."
    And right away his story has he framed,
And thus he said unto us, every one,
This dainty priest, this goodly man, Sir John.

Explicit

The Nun's Priest's Tale

                    Of the Cock and Hen, Chanticleer and Pertelote
A widow poor, somewhat advanced in age,
Lived, on a time, within a small cottage
Beside a grove and standing down a dale.
This widow, now, of whom I tell my tale,
Since that same day when she'd been last a wife
Had led, with patience, her strait simple life,
For she'd small goods and little income-rent;
By husbanding of such as God had sent
She kept herself and her young daughters twain.
Three large sows had she, and no more, 'tis plain,
Three cows and a lone sheep that she called Moll.
Right sooty was her bedroom and her hall,

Wherein she'd eaten many a slender meal.
Of sharp sauce, why she needed no great deal,
For dainty morsel never passed her throat;
Her diet well accorded with her coat.
Repletion never made this woman sick;
A temperate diet was her whole physic,
And exercise, and her heart's sustenance.
The gout, it hindered her nowise to dance,
Nor apoplexy spun within her head;
And no wine drank she, either white or red;
Her board was mostly garnished, white and black,
With milk and brown bread, whereof she'd no lack,
Broiled bacon and sometimes an egg or two,
For a small dairy business did she do.
    A yard she had, enclosed all roundabout
With pales, and there was a dry ditch without,
And in the yard a cock called Chanticleer.
In all the land, for crowing, he'd no peer.
His voice was merrier than the organ gay
On Mass days, which in church begins to play;
More regular was his crowing in his lodge
Than is a clock or abbey horologe.
By instinct he'd marked each ascension down
Of equinoctial value in that town;
For when fifteen degrees had been ascended,
Then crew he so it might not be amended.
His comb was redder than a fine coral,
And battlemented like a castle wall.
His bill was black and just like jet it shone;
Like azure were his legs and toes, each one;
His spurs were whiter than the lily flower;
And plumage of the burnished gold his dower.
This noble cock had in his governance
Seven hens to give him pride and all pleasance,
Which were his sisters and his paramours
And wondrously like him as to colours,
Whereof the fairest hued upon her throat
Was called the winsome Mistress Pertelote.
Courteous she was, discreet and debonnaire,
Companionable, and she had been so fair

Since that same day when she was seven nights old,
That truly she had taken the heart to hold
Of Chanticleer, locked in her every limb;
He loved her so that all was well with him.
But such a joy it was to hear them sing,
Whenever the bright sun began to spring,
In sweet accord, "My love walks through the land."
For at that time, and as I understand,
The beasts and all the birds could speak and sing.
　　So it befell that, in a bright dawning,
As Chanticleer 'midst wives and sisters all
Sat on his perch, the which was in the hall,
And next him sat the winsome Pertelote,
This Chanticleer he groaned within his throat
Like man that in his dreams is troubled sore.
And when fair Pertelote thus heard him roar,
She was aghast and said: "O sweetheart dear,
What ails you that you groan so? Do you hear?
You are a sleepy herald. Fie, for shame!"
　　And he replied to her thus: "Ah, madame,
I pray you that you take it not in grief:
By God, I dreamed I'd come to such mischief,
Just now, my heart yet jumps with sore affright.
Now God," cried he, "my vision read aright
And keep my body out of foul prison!
I dreamed, that while I wandered up and down
Within our yard, I saw there a strange beast
Was like a dog, and he'd have made a feast
Upon my body, and have had me dead.
His colour yellow was and somewhat red;
And tipped his tail was, as were both his ears,
With black, unlike the rest, as it appears;
His snout was small and gleaming was each eye.
Remembering how he looked, almost I die;
And all this caused my groaning, I confess."
　　"Aha," said she, "fie on you, spiritless!
Alas!" cried she, "for by that God above,
Now have you lost my heart and all my love;
I cannot love a coward, by my faith.
For truly, whatsoever woman saith,

We all desire, if only it may be,
To have a husband hardy, wise, and free,
And trustworthy, no niggard, and no fool,
Nor one that is afraid of every tool,
Nor yet a braggart, by that God above!
How dare you say, for shame, unto your love
That there is anything that you have feared?
Have you not man's heart, and yet have a beard?
Alas! And are you frightened by a vision?
Dreams are, God knows, a matter for derision.
Visions are generated by repletions
And vapours and the body's bad secretions
Of humours overabundant in a wight.
Surely this dream, which you have had tonight,
Comes only of the superfluity
Of your bilious irascibility,
Which causes folk to shiver in their dreams
For arrows and for flames with long red gleams,
For great beasts in the fear that they will bite,
For quarrels and for wolf whelps great and slight;
Just as the humour of melancholy
Causes full many a man, in sleep, to cry,
For fear of black bears or of bulls all black,
Or lest black devils put them in a sack.
Of other humours could I tell also,
That bring, to many a sleeping man, great woe;
But I'll pass on as lightly as I can.
　　"Lo, Cato, and he was a full wise man,
Said he not, we should trouble not for dreams?
Now, sir," said she, "when we fly from the beams,
For God's love go and take some laxative;
On peril of my soul, and as I live,
I counsel you the best, I will not lie,
That both for choler and for melancholy
You purge yourself; and since you shouldn't tarry,
And on this farm there's no apothecary,
I will myself go find some herbs for you
That will be good for health and pecker too;
And in our own yard all these herbs I'll find,
The which have properties of proper kind

To purge you underneath and up above.
Forget this not, now, for God's very love!
You are so very choleric of complexion.
Beware the mounting sun and all dejection,
Nor get yourself with sudden humours hot;
For if you do, I dare well lay a groat
That you shall have the tertian fever's pain,
Or some ague that may well be your bane.
A day or two you shall have digestives
Of worms before you take your laxatives
Of laurel, centuary, and fumitory,
Or else of hellebore purificatory,
Or caper spurge, or else of dogwood berry,
Or herb ivy, all in our yard so merry;
Peck them just as they grow and gulp them in.
Be merry, husband, for your father's kin!
Dread no more dreams. And I can say no more."
   "Madam," said he, "gramercy for your lore.
Nevertheless, not running Cato down,
Who had for wisdom such a high renown,
And though he says to hold no dreams in dread,
By God, men have, in many old books, read
Of many a man more an authority
That ever Cato was, pray pardon me,
Who say just the reverse of his sentence,
And have found out by long experience
That dreams, indeed, are good significations,
As much of joys as of all tribulations
That folk endure here in this life present.
There is no need to make an argument;
The very proof of this is shown indeed.
   "One of the greatest authors that men read
Says thus: That on a time two comrades went
On pilgrimage, and all in good intent;
And it so chanced they came into a town
Where there was such a crowding, up and down,
Of people, and so little harbourage,
That they found not so much as one cottage
Wherein the two of them might sheltered be.
Wherefore they must, as of necessity,

For that one night at least, part company;
And each went to a different hostelry
And took such lodgment as to him did fall.
Now one of them was lodged within a stall,
Far in a yard, with oxen of the plow;
That other man found shelter fair enow,
As was his luck, or was his good fortune,
Whatever 'tis that governs us, each one.
    "So it befell that, long ere it was day,
This last man dreamed in bed, as there he lay,
That his poor fellow did unto him call,
Saying: 'Alas! For in an ox's stall
This night shall I be murdered where I lie.
Now help me, brother dear, before I die.
Come in all haste to me.' 'Twas thus he said.
This man woke out of sleep, then, all afraid;
But when he'd wakened fully from his sleep,
He turned upon his pillow, yawning deep,
Thinking his dream was but a fantasy.
And then again, while sleeping, thus dreamed he.
And then a third time came a voice that said
(Or so he thought): 'Now, comrade, I am dead;
Behold my bloody wounds, so wide and deep!
Early arise tomorrow from your sleep,
And at the west gate of the town,' said he,
A wagon full of dung there shall you see,
Wherein is hid my body craftily;
Do you arrest this wagon right boldly.
They killed me for what money they could gain.
And told in every point how he'd been slain,
With a most pitiful face and pale of hue.
And trust me well, this dream did all come true;
For on the morrow, soon as it was day,
Unto his comrade's inn he took the way;
And when he'd come into that ox's stall,
Upon his fellow he began to call.
    "The keeper of the place replied anon,
And said he: 'Sir, your friend is up and gone;
As soon as day broke he went out of town.'
This man, then, felt suspicion in him grown,

Remembering the dream that he had had,
And forth he went, no longer tarrying, sad,
Unto the west gate of the town, and found
A dung cart on its way to dumping ground,
And it was just the same in every wise
As you have heard the dead man advertise;
And with a hardy heart he then did cry
Vengeance and justice on this felony:
'My comrade has been murdered in the night,
And in this very cart lies, face upright.
I cry to all the officers,' said he.
'That ought to keep the peace in this city.
Alas, alas, here lies my comrade slain!'
     "Why should I longer with this tale detain?
The people rose and turned the cart to ground,
And in the center of the dung they found
The dead man, lately murdered in his sleep.
     "O Blessed God, Who art so true and deep!
Lo, how Thou dost turn murder out alway!
Murder will out, we see it every day.
Murder's so hateful and abominable
To God, Who is so just and reasonable,
That He'll not suffer that it hidden be;
Though it may skulk a year, or two, or three,
Murder will out, and I conclude thereon.
Immediately the rulers of that town,
They took the carter and so sore they racked
Him and the host, until their bones were cracked,
That they confessed their wickedness anon,
And hanged they both were by the neck, and soon.
     "Here may men see that dreams are things to dread.
And certainly, in that same book I read,
Right in the very chapter after this
(I spoof not, as I may have joy and bliss),
Of two men who would voyage oversea,
For some cause, and unto a far country,
If but the winds had not been all contrary,
Causing them both within a town to tarry,
Which town was builded near the haven-side.
But then, one day, along toward eventide,

The wind did change and blow as suited best.
Jolly and glad they went unto their rest.
And were prepared right early for to sail;
But unto one was told a marvelous tale.
For one of them, a-sleeping as he lay,
Did dream a wondrous dream ere it was day.
He thought a strange man stood by his bedside
And did command him, he should there abide,
And said to him: 'If you tomorrow wend,
You shall be drowned; my tale is at an end.'
He woke and told his fellow what he'd met
And prayed him quit the voyage and forget;
For just one day he prayed him there to bide.
His comrade, who was lying there beside,
Began to laugh and scorned him long and fast.
'No dream,' said he, 'may make my heart aghast,
So that I'll quit my business for such things.
I do not care a straw for your dreamings,
For visions are but fantasies and japes.
Men dream, why, every day, of owls and apes,
And many a wild phantasm therewithal;
Men dream of what has never been, nor shall.
But since I see that you will here abide,
And thus forgo this fair wind and this tide,
God knows I'm sorry; nevertheless, good day!'
    "And thus he took his leave and went his way.
But long before the half his course he'd sailed,
I know not why, nor what it was that failed,
But casually the vessel's bottom rent,
And ship and men under the water went,
In sight of other ships were there beside,
The which had sailed with that same wind and tide.
    "And therefore, pretty Pertelote, my dear,
By such old-time examples may you hear
And learn that no man should be too reckless
Of dreams, for I can tell you, fair mistress,
That many a dream is something well to dread.
    "Why in the 'Life' of Saint Kenelm I read
(Who was Kenelphus' son, the noble king
Of Mercia), how Kenelm dreamed a thing;

A while ere he was murdered, so they say,
His own death in a vision saw, one day.
His nurse interpreted, as records tell,
That vision, bidding him to guard him well
From treason; but he was but seven years old,
And therefore 'twas but little he'd been told
Of any dream, so holy was his heart.
By God! I'd rather than retain my shirt
That you had read this legend, as have I.
Dame Pertelote, I tell you verily,
Macrobius, who wrote of Scipio
The African a vision long ago,
He holds by dreams, saying that they have been
Warnings of things that men have later seen.
   "And furthermore, I pray you to look well
In the Old Testament at Daniel,
Whether he held dreams for mere vanity.
Read, too, of Joseph, and you there shall see
Where dreams have sometimes been (I say not all)
Warnings of things that after did befall.
Consider Egypt's king, Dan Pharaoh,
His baker and his butler, these also,
Whether they knew of no effect from dreams.
Whoso will read of sundry realms the themes
May learn of dreams full many a wondrous thing.
Lo, Croesus, who was once of Lydia king,
Dreamed he not that he sat upon a tree,
Which signified that hanged high he should be?
Lo, how Andromache, great Hector's wife,
On that same day when Hector lost his life,
She dreamed upon the very night before
That Hector's life should be lost evermore,
If on that day he battled, without fail.
She warned him, but no warning could avail;
He went to fight, despite all auspices,
And so was shortly slain by Achilles.
But that same tale is all too long to tell,
And, too, it's nearly day, I must not dwell
Upon this; I but say, concluding here,
That from this vision I have cause to fear

Adversity; and I say, furthermore,
That I do set by laxatives no store,
For they are poisonous, I know it well.
Them I defy and love not, truth to tell.
    "But let us speak of mirth and stop all this;
My lady Pertelote, on hope of bliss,
In one respect God's given me much grace;
For when I see the beauty of your face,
You are so rosy red beneath each eye,
It makes my dreadful terror wholly die.
For there is truth in *In principio*
Mulier est hominis confusio
(Madam, the meaning of this Latin is,
Woman is man's delight and all his bliss).
For when I feel at night your tender side,
Although I cannot then upon you ride,
Because our perch so narrow is, alas!
I am so full of joy and all solace
That I defy, then, vision, aye and dream."
    And with that word he flew down from the beam,
For it was day, and down went his hens all;
And with a cluck he them began to call,
For he had found some corn within the yard.
Regal he was, and fears he did discard.
He feathered Pertelote full many a time
And twenty times he trod her ere 'twas prime.
He looked as if he were a grim lion
As on his toes he strutted up and down;
He deigned not set his foot upon the ground.
He clucked when any grain of corn he found,
And all his wives came running at his call.
Thus regal, as a prince is in his hall,
I'll now leave busy Chanticleer to feed,
And with events that followed I'll proceed.
    When that same month wherein the world began,
Which is called March, wherein God first made man,
Was ended, and were passed of days also,
Since March began, full thirty days and two,
It fell that Chanticleer, in all his pride,
His seven wives a-walking by his side,

Cast up his two eyes toward the great bright sun
(Which through the sign of Taurus now had run
Twenty degrees and one, and somewhat more),
And knew by instinct and no other lore
That it was prime, and joyfully he crew,
"The sun, my love," he said, "has climbed anew
Forty degrees and one, and somewhat more.
My lady Pertelote, whom I adore,
Mark now these happy birds, hear how they sing,
And see all these fresh flowers, how they spring;
Full is my heart of revelry and grace."
    But suddenly he fell in grievous case;
For ever the latter end of joy is woe.
God knows that worldly joys do swiftly go;
And if a rhetorician could but write,
He in some chronicle might well indite
And mark it down as sovereign in degree.
Now every wise man, let him hark to me:
This tale is just as true, I undertake,
As is the book of *Launcelot of the Lake,*
Which women always hold in such esteem.
But now I must take up my proper theme.
    A brant-fox, full of sly iniquity,
That in the grove had lived two years, or three,
Now by a fine premeditated plot
That same night, breaking through the hedge, had got
Into the yard where Chanticleer the fair
Was wont, and all his wives too, to repair;
And in a bed of greenery still he lay
Till it was past the quarter of the day,
Waiting his chance on Chanticleer to fall,
As gladly do these killers one and all
Who lie in ambush for to murder men.
O murderer false, there lurking in your den!
O new Iscariot, O new Ganelon!
O false dissimulator, Greek Sinon
That brought down Troy all utterly to sorrow!
O Chanticleer, accursed be that morrow
When you into that yard flew from the beams!
You were well warned, and fully, by your dreams

That this day should hold peril damnably.
But that which God foreknows, it needs must be,
So says the best opinion of the clerks.
Witness some cleric perfect for his works,
That in the schools there's a great altercation
In this regard, and much high disputation
That has involved a hundred thousand men.
But I can't sift it to the bran with pen,
As can the holy Doctor Augustine,
Or Boethius, or Bishop Bradwardine,
Whether the fact of God's great foreknowing
Makes it right needful that I do a thing
(By needful, I mean, of necessity);
Or else, if a free choice he granted me,
To do that same thing, or to do it not,
Though God foreknew before the thing was wrought;
Or if His knowing constrains never at all,
Save by necessity conditional.
I have no part in matters so austere;
My tale is of a cock, as you shall hear,
That took the counsel of his wife, with sorrow,
To walk within the yard upon that morrow
After he'd had the dream whereof I told.
Now women's counsels oft are ill to hold;
A woman's counsel brought us first to woe,
And Adam caused from Paradise to go,
Wherein he was right merry and at ease.
But since I know not whom it may displease
If woman's counsel I hold up to blame,
Pass over, I but said it in my game.
Read authors where such matters do appear,
And what they say of women, you may hear.
These are the cock's words, they are none of mine;
No harm in women can I e'er divine.
    All in the sand, a-bathing merrily,
Lay Pertelote, with all her sisters by,
There in the sun; and Chanticleer so free
Sang merrier than a mermaid in the sea
(For Physiologus says certainly
That they do sing, both well and merrily).

And so befell that, as he cast his eye
Among the herbs and on a butterfly,
He saw this fox that lay there, crouching low.
Nothing of urge was in him, then, to crow;
But he cried "Cock-cock-cock" and did so start
As man who has a sudden fear at heart.
For naturally a beast desires to flee
From any enemy that he may see,
Though never yet he's clapped on such his eye.
   When Chanticleer the fox did then espy,
He would have fled but that the fox anon
Said: "Gentle sir, alas! Why be thus gone?
Are you afraid of me, who am your friend?
Now, surely, I were worse than any fiend
If I should do you harm or villainy.
I came not here upon your deeds to spy;
But, certainly, the cause of my coming
Was only just to listen to you sing.
For truly, you have quite as fine a voice
As angels have that Heaven's choirs rejoice;
Boethius to music could not bring
Such feeling, nor do others who can sing.
My lord your father (God his soul pray bless!)
And too your mother, of her gentleness,
Have been in my abode, to my great ease;
And truly, sir, right fain am I to please.
But since men speak of singing, I will say
(As I still have my eyesight day by day),
Save you, I never heard a man so sing
As did your father in the grey dawning;
Truly 'twas from the heart, his every song.
And that his voice might ever be more strong,
He took such pains that, with his either eye,
He had to blink, so loudly would he cry,
A-standing on his tiptoes therewithal,
Stretching his neck till it grew long and small.
And such discretion, too, by him was shown,
There was no man in any region known
That him in song or wisdom could surpass.
I have well read, in *Dan Burnell the Ass,*

Among his verses, how there was a cock,
Because a priest's son gave to him a knock
Upon the leg, while young and not yet wise,
He caused the boy to lose his benefice.
But, truly, there is no comparison
With the great wisdom and the discretion
Your father had, or with his subtlety.
Now sing, dear sir, for holy charity,
See if you can your father counterfeit."
   This Chanticleer his wings began to beat,
As one that could no treason there espy,
So was he ravished by this flattery.
Alas, you lords! Full many a flatterer
Is in your courts, and many a cozener,
That please your honours much more, by my fay,
Than he that truth and justice dares to say.
Go read the Ecclesiast on flattery;
Beware, my lords, of all their treachery!
   This Chanticleer stood high upon his toes,
Stretching his neck, and both his eyes did close,
And so did crow right loudly, for the nonce;
And Russel Fox, he started up at once,
And by the gorget grabbed our Chanticleer,
Flung him on back, and toward the wood did steer,
For there was no man who as yet pursued.
O destiny, you cannot be eschewed!
Alas, that Chanticleer flew from the beams!
Alas, his wife recked nothing of his dreams!
And on a Friday fell all this mischance.
O Venus, who art goddess of pleasance,
Since he did serve thee well, this Chanticleer,
And to the utmost of his power here,
More for delight than cocks to multiply,
Why would'st thou suffer him that day to die?
O Gaufred, my dear master sovereign,
Who, when King Richard Lionheart was slain
By arrow, sang his death with sorrow sore,
Why have I not your faculty and lore
To chide Friday, as you did worthily?
(For truly, on a Friday slain was he).

Then would I prove how well I could complain
For Chanticleer's great fear and all his pain.
    Certainly no such cry and lamentation
Were made by ladies at Troy's desolation,
When Pyrrhus with his terrible bared sword
Had taken old King Priam by the beard
And slain him (as the Aeneid tells to us),
As made then all those hens in one chorus
When they had caught a sight of Chanticleer.
But fair Dame Pertelote assailed the ear
Far louder than did Hasdrubal's good wife
When that her husband bold had lost his life,
And Roman legionaries burned Carthage;
For she so full of torment was, and rage,
She voluntarily to the fire did start
And burned herself there with a steadfast heart.
And you, O woeful hens, just so you cried
As when base Nero burned the city wide
Of Rome, and wept the senators' stern wives
Because their husbands all had lost their lives,
For though not guilty, Nero had them slain.
Now will I turn back to my tale again.
    This simple widow and her daughters two
Heard these hens cry and make so great ado,
And out of doors they started on the run
And saw the fox into the grove just gone,
Bearing upon his back the cock away.
And then they cried, "Alas, and weladay!
Oh, oh, the fox!" and after him they ran,
And after them, with staves, went many a man;
Ran Coll, our dog, ran Talbot and Garland,
And Malkin with a distaff in her hand;
Ran cow and calf and even the very hogs,
So were they scared by barking of the dogs
And shouting men and women all did make,
They all ran so they thought their hearts would break.
They yelled as very fiends do down in Hell;
The ducks they cried as at the butcher fell;
The frightened geese flew up above the trees;
Out of the hive there came the swarm of bees;

So terrible was the noise, ah *ben'cite!*
Certainly old Jack Straw and his army
Never raised shouting half so loud and shrill
When they were chasing Flemings for to kill,
As on that day was raised upon the fox.
They brought forth trumpets made of brass, of box,
Of horn, of bone, wherein they blew and pooped,
And therewithal they screamed and shrieked and whooped;
It seemed as if the heaven itself should fall!
     And now, good men, I pray you hearken all.
Behold how Fortune turns all suddenly
The hope and pride of even her enemy!
This cock, which lay across the fox's back,
In all his fear unto the fox did clack
And say: "Sir, were I you, as I should be,
Then would I say (as God may now help me!),
'Turn back again, presumptuous peasants all!
A very pestilence upon you fall!
Now that I've gained here to this dark wood's side,
In spite of you this cock shall here abide.
I'll eat him, by my faith, and that anon!'"
     The fox replied: "In faith, it shall be done!"
And as he spoke that word, all suddenly
This cock broke from his mouth, full cleverly,
And high upon a tree he flew anon.
And when the fox saw well that he was gone,
"Alas," quoth he, "O Chanticleer, alas!
I have against you done a base trespass
In that I frightened you, my dear old pard,
When you I seized and brought from out that yard;
But, sir, I did it with no foul intent;
Come down, and I will tell you what I meant.
I'll tell the truth to you, God help me so!"
"Nay then," said he, "beshrew us both, you know,
But first, beshrew myself, both blood and bones,
If you beguile me, having done so once,
You shall no more, with any flattery,
Cause me to sing and close up either eye.
For he who shuts his eyes when he should see,
And wilfully, God let him ne'er be free!"

"Nay," said the fox, "but God give him mischance
Who is so indiscreet in governance
He chatters when he ought to hold his peace."
   Lo, such it is when watch and ward do cease,
And one grows negligent with flattery.
But you that hold this tale a foolery,
As but about a fox, a cock, a hen,
Yet do not miss the moral, my good men.
For Saint Paul says that all that's written well
Is written down some useful truth to tell.
Then take the wheat and let the chaff lie still.
   And now, good God, and if it be Thy will,
As says Lord Christ, so make us all good men
And bring us into His high bliss. Amen.

The Wife of Bath

The Wife of Bath's Prologue

Experience, though no authority
Were in this world, were good enough for me,
To speak of woe that is in all marriage;
For, masters, since I was twelve years of age,
Thanks be to God Who is for aye alive,
Of husbands at church door have I had five;
For men so many times have wedded me;
And all were worthy men in their degree.
But someone told me not so long ago
That since Our Lord, save once, would never go
To wedding (that at Cana in Galilee),
Thus, by this same example, showed He me
I never should have married more than once.
Lo and behold! What sharp words, for the nonce,
Beside a well Lord Jesus, God, and man,
Spoke in reproving the Samaritan:
'For thou hast had five husbands,' thus said He,
'And he whom thou hast now to be with thee
Is not thine husband.' Thus He said that day,
But what He meant thereby I cannot say;
And I would ask now why that same fifth man
Was not husband to the Samaritan?
How many might she have, then, in marriage?
For I have never heard, in all my age,
Clear exposition of this number shown,
Though men may guess and argue up and down.
But well I know and say, and do not lie,
God bade us to increase and multiply;
That worthy text can I well understand.
And well I know He said, too, my husband
Should father leave, and mother, and cleave to me;
But no specific number mentioned He,

Whether of bigamy or octogamy;
Why should men speak of it reproachfully?
  Lo, there's the wise old king Dan Solomon;
I understand he had more wives than one;
And now would God it were permitted me
To be refreshed one half as oft as he!
Which gift of God he had for all his wives!
No man has such that in this world now lives.
God knows, this noble king, it strikes my wit,
The first night he had many a merry fit
With each of them, so much he was alive!
Praise be to God that I have wedded five!
Of whom I did pick out and choose the best
Both for their nether purse and for their chest.
Different schools make divers perfect clerks,
Different methods learned in sundry works
Make the good workman perfect, certainly.
Of full five husbands tutoring am I.
Welcome the sixth whenever come he shall.
Forsooth, I'll not keep chaste for good and all;
When my good husband from the world is gone,
Some Christian man shall marry me anon;
For then, the apostle says that I am free
To wed, in God's name, where it pleases me.
He says that to be wedded is no sin;
Better to marry than to burn within.
What care I though folk speak reproachfully
Of wicked Lamech and his bigamy?
I know well Abraham was holy man,
And Jacob, too, as far as know I can;
And each of them had spouses more than two;
And many another holy man also.
Or can you say that you have ever heard
That God has ever by His express word
Marriage forbidden? Pray you, now, tell me;
Or where commanded He virginity?
I read as well as you no doubt have read
The apostle when he speaks of maidenhead;
He said, commandment of the Lord he'd none.
Men may advise a woman to be one,

But such advice is not commandment, no;
He left the thing to our own judgment so.
For had Lord God commanded maidenhood,
He'd have condemned all marriage as not good;
And certainly, if there were no seed sown,
Virginity—where then should it be grown?
Paul dared not to forbid us, at the least,
A thing whereof his Master'd no behest.
The dart is set up for virginity;
Catch it who can; who runs best let us see.

  "But this word is not meant for every wight,
But where God wills to give it, of His might.
I know well that the apostle was a maid;
Nevertheless, and though he wrote and said
He would that everyone were such as he,
All is not counsel to virginity;
And so to be a wife he gave me leave
Out of permission; there's no shame should grieve
In marrying me, if that my mate should die,
Without exception, too, of bigamy.
And though 'twere good no woman's flesh to touch,
He meant, in his own bed or on his couch;
For peril 'tis fire and tow to assemble;
You know what this example may resemble.
This is the sum: he held virginity
Nearer perfection than marriage for frailty.
And frailty's all, I say, save he and she
Would lead their lives throughout in chastity.

  "I grant this well, I have no great envy
Though maidenhood's preferred to bigamy;
Let those who will be clean, body and ghost,
Of my condition I will make no boast.
For well you know, a lord in his household,
He has not every vessel all of gold;
Some are of wood and serve well all their days.
God calls folk unto Him in sundry ways,
And each one has from God a proper gift,
Some this, some that, as pleases Him to shift.

  "Virginity is great perfection known,
And continence e'en with devotion shown.

But Christ, Who of perfection is the well,
Bade not each separate man he should go sell
All that he had and give it to the poor
And follow Him in such wise going before.
He spoke to those that would live perfectly;
And, masters, by your leave, such am not I.
I will devote the flower of all my age
To all the acts and harvests of marriage.
"Tell me also, to what purpose or end
The genitals were made, that I defend,
And for what benefit was man first wrought?
Trust you right well, they were not made for naught.
Explain who will and argue up and down
That they were made for passing out, as known,
Of urine, and our two belongings small
Were just to tell a female from a male,
And for no other cause—ah, say you no?
Experience knows well it is not so;
And, so the clerics be not with me wroth,
I say now that they have been made for both,
That is to say, for duty and for ease
In getting, when we do not God displease.
Why should men otherwise in their books set
That man shall pay unto his wife his debt?
Now wherewith should he ever make payment,
Except he used his blessed instrument?
Then on a creature were devised these things
For urination and engenderings.
   "But I say not that every one is bound,
Who's fitted out and furnished as I've found,
To go and use it to beget an heir;
Then men would have for chastity no care.
Christ was a maid, and yet shaped like a man,
And many a saint, since this old world began,
Yet has lived ever in perfect chastity.
I bear no malice to virginity;
Let such be bread of purest white wheat seed,
And let us wives be called but barley bread;
And yet with barley bread (if Mark you scan)
Jesus Our Lord refreshed full many a man.

In such condition as God places us
I'll persevere, I'm not fastidious.
In wifehood I will use my instrument
As freely as my Maker has it sent.
If I be niggardly, God give me sorrow!
My husband he shall have it, eve and morrow,
When he's pleased to come forth and pay his debt.
I'll not delay, a husband I will get
Who shall be both my debtor and my thrall
And have his tribulations therewithal
Upon his flesh, the while I am his wife.
I have the power during all my life
Over his own good body, and not he.
For thus the apostle told it unto me;
And bade our husbands that they love us well.
And all this pleases me whereof I tell."

   Up rose the pardoner, and that anon.
"Now dame," said he, "by God and by Saint John,
You are a noble preacher in this case!
I was about to wed a wife, alas!
Why should I buy this on my flesh so dear?
No, I would rather wed no wife this year."

   "But wait," said she, "my tale is not begun;
Nay, you shall drink from out another tun
Before I cease, and savour worse than ale.
And when I shall have told you all my tale
Of tribulation that is in marriage,
Whereof I've been an expert all my age,
That is to say, myself have been the whip,
Then may you choose whether you will go sip
Out of that very tun which I shall broach.
Beware of it ere you too near approach;
For I shall give examples more than ten.
Whoso will not be warned by other men
By him shall other men corrected be.
The self-same words has written Ptolemy;
Read in his Almagest and find it there."

   "Lady, I pray you, if your will it were,"
Spoke up this pardoner, "as you began,
Tell forth your tale, nor spare for any man,

And teach us younger men of your technique."
   "Gladly," said she, 'since it may please, not pique.
But yet I pray of all this company
That if I speak from my own phantasy,
They will not take amiss the things I say;
For my intention's only but to play.
   "Now, sirs, now will I tell you forth my tale.
And as I may drink ever wine and ale,
I will tell truth of husbands that I've had,
For three of them were good and two were bad.
The three were good men and were rich and old;
Not easily could they the promise hold
Whereby they had been bound to cherish me.
You know well what I mean by that, pardie!
So help me God, I laugh now when I think
How pitifully by night I made them swink;
And by my faith I set by it no store.
They'd given me their gold, and treasure more;
I needed not do longer diligence
To win their love, or show them reverence.
They all loved me so well, by God above,
I never did set value on their love!
A woman wise will strive continually
To get herself loved, when she's not, you see.
But since I had them wholly in my hand,
And since to me they'd given all their land,
Why should I take heed, then, that I should please,
Save it were for my profit or my ease?
I set them so to work, that, by my fay,
Full many a night they sighed out 'Welaway!'
The bacon was not brought them home, I trow,
That some men have in Essex at Dunmowe.
I governed them so well, by my own law,
That each of them was happy as a daw,
And fain to bring me fine things from the fair.
And they were right glad when I spoke them fair;
For God knows that I nagged them mercilessly.
   "Now hearken how I bore me properly,
All you wise wives that well can understand.
   "Thus shall you speak and wrongfully demand;

For half so brazenfacedly can no man
Swear to his lying as a woman can.
I say not this to wives who may be wise,
Except when they themselves do misadvise.
A wise wife, if she knows what's for her good,
Will swear the crow is mad, and in this mood
Call up for witness to it her own maid;
But hear me now, for this is what I said.
  "'Sir Dotard, is it thus you stand today?
Why is my neighbour's wife so fine and gay?
She's honoured over all where'er she goes;
I sit at home, I have no decent clo'es.
What do you do there at my neighbour's house?
Is she so fair? Are you so amorous?
Why whisper to our maid? *Benedicite!*
Sir Lecher old, let your seductions be!
And if I have a gossip or a friend,
Innocently, you blame me like a fiend
If I but walk, for company, to his house!
You come home here as drunken as a mouse,
And preach there on your bench, a curse on you!
You tell me it's a great misfortune, too,
To wed a girl who costs more than she's worth;
And if she's rich and of a higher birth,
You say it's torment to abide her folly
And put up with her pride and melancholy.
And if she be right fair, you utter knave,
You say that every lecher will her have;
She may no while in chastity abide
That is assailed by all and on each side.
  "'You say, some men desire us for our gold,
Some for our shape and some for fairness told;
And some, that she can either sing or dance,
And some, for courtesy and dalliance;
Some for her hands and for her arms so small;
Thus all goes to the devil in your tale.
You say men cannot keep a castle wall
That's long assailed on all sides, and by all.
  "'And if that she be foul, you say that she
Hankers for every man that she may see;

For like a spaniel will she leap on him
Until she finds a man to be victim;
And not a grey goose swims there in the lake
But finds a gander willing her to take.
You say, it is a hard thing to enfold
Her whom no man will in his own arms hold.
This say you, worthless, when you go to bed;
And that no wise man needs thus to be wed,
No, nor a man that hearkens unto Heaven.
With furious thunder claps and fiery levin
May your thin, withered, wrinkled neck be broke!
　"'You say that dripping eaves, and also smoke,
And wives contentious, will make men to flee
Out of their houses; ah, *benedicite!*
What ails such an old fellow so to chide?
　"'You say that all we wives our vices hide
Till we are married, then we show them well;
That is a scoundrel's proverb, let me tell!
　"'You say that oxen, asses, horses, hounds
Are tried out variously, and on good grounds;
Basins and bowls, before men will them buy,
And spoons and stools and all such goods you try,
And so with pots and clothes and all array;
But of their wives men get no trial, you say,
Till they are married, base old dotard you!
And then we show what evil we can do.
　"'You say also that it displeases me
Unless you praise and flatter my beauty,
And save you gaze always upon my face
And call me "lovely lady" every place;
And save you make a feast upon that day
When I was born, and give me garments gay;
And save due honour to my nurse is paid
As well as to my faithful chambermaid,
And to my father's folk and his allies—
Thus you go on, old barrel full of lies!
　"'And yet of our apprentice, young Jenkin,
　For his crisp hair, showing like gold so fine,
Because he squires me walking up and down,
A false suspicion in your mind is sown;

I'd give him naught, though you were dead tomorrow.
"'But tell me this, why do you hide, with sorrow,
The keys to your strongbox away from me?
It is my gold as well as yours, pardie.
Why would you make an idiot of your dame?
Now by Saint James, but you shall miss your aim,
You shall not be, although like mad you scold,
Master of both my body and my gold;
One you'll forgo in spite of both your eyes;
Why need you seek me out or set on spies?
I think you'd like to lock me in your chest!
You should say: "Dear wife, go where you like best,
Amuse yourself, I will believe no tales;
You're my wife Alis true, and truth prevails."
We love no man that guards us or gives charge
Of where we go, for we will be at large.
"'Of all men the most blessed may he be,
That wise astrologer, Dan Ptolemy,
Who says this proverb in his Almagest:
"Of all men he's in wisdom the highest
That nothing cares who has the world in hand."
And by this proverb shall you understand:
Since you've enough, why do you reck or care
How merrily all other folks may fare?
For certainly, old dotard, by your leave,
You shall have cunt all right enough at eve.
He is too much a niggard who's so tight
That from his lantern he'll give none a light.
For he'll have never the less light, by gad;
Since you've enough, you need not be so sad.
"'You say, also, that if we make us gay
With clothing, all in costliest array,
That it's a danger to our chastity;
And you must back the saying up, pardie!
Repeating these words in the apostle's name:
"In habits meet for chastity, not shame,
Your women shall be garmented," said he,
"And not with broidered hair, or jewellery,
Or pearls, or gold, or costly gowns and chic";
After your text and after your rubric

I will not follow more than would a gnat.
You said this, too, that I was like a cat;
For if one care to singe a cat's furred skin,
Then would the cat remain the house within;
And if the cat's coat be all sleek and gay,
She will not keep in house a half a day,
But out she'll go, ere dawn of any day,
To show her skin and caterwaul and play.
This is to say, if I'm a little gay,
To show my rags I'll gad about all day.
    "'Sir Ancient Fool, what ails you with your spies?
Though you pray Argus, with his hundred eyes,
To be my bodyguard and do his best,
Faith, he sha'n't hold me, save I am modest;
I could delude him easily—trust me!
    "'You said, also, that there are three things— three—
The which things are a trouble on this earth,
And that no man may ever endure the fourth:
O dear Sir Rogue, may Christ cut short your life!
Yet do you preach and say a hateful wife
Is to be reckoned one of these mischances.
Are there no other kinds of resemblances
That you may liken thus your parables to,
But must a hapless wife be made to do?
    "'You liken woman's love to very Hell,
To desert land where waters do not well.
You liken it, also, unto wildfire;
The more it burns, the more it has desire
To consume everything that burned may be.
You say that just as worms destroy a tree,
Just so a wife destroys her own husband;
Men know this who are bound in marriage band.'
    "Masters, like this, as you must understand,
Did I my old men charge and censure, and
Claim that they said these things in drunkenness;
And all was false, but yet I took witness
Of Jenkin and of my dear niece also.
O Lord, the pain I gave them and the woe,
All guiltless, too, by God's grief exquisite!
For like a stallion could I neigh and bite.

I could complain, though mine was all the guilt,
Or else, full many a time, I'd lost the tilt.
Whoso comes first to mill first gets meal ground;
I whimpered first and so did them confound.
They were right glad to hasten to excuse
Things they had never done, save in my ruse.

  "With wenches would I charge him, by this hand,
When, for some illness, he could hardly stand.
Yet tickled this the heart of him, for he
Deemed it was love produced such jealousy.
I swore that all my walking out at night
Was but to spy on girls he kept outright;
And under cover of that I had much mirth.
For all such wit is given us at birth;
Deceit, weeping, and spinning, does God give
To women, naturally, the while they live.
And thus of one thing I speak boastfully,
I got the best of each one, finally,
By trick, or force, or by some kind of thing,
As by continual growls or murmuring;
Especially in bed had they mischance,
There would I chide and give them no pleasance;
I would no longer in the bed abide
If I but felt his arm across my side,
Till he had paid his ransom unto me;
Then would I let him do his nicety.
And therefore to all men this tale I tell,
Let gain who may, for everything's to sell.
With empty hand men may no falcons lure;
For profit would I all his lust endure,
And make for him a well-feigned appetite;
Yet I in bacon never had delight;
And that is why I used so much to chide.
For if the pope were seated there beside
I'd not have spared them, no, at their own board.
For by my truth, I paid them, word for word.
So help me the True God Omnipotent,
Though I right now should make my testament,
I owe them not a word that was not quit.
I brought it so about, and by my wit,

That they must give it up, as for the best,
Or otherwise we'd never have had rest.
For though he glared and scowled like lion mad,
Yet failed he of the end he wished he had.
    "Then would I say: 'Good dearie, see you keep
In mind how meek is Wilkin, our old sheep;
Come near, my spouse, come let me kiss your cheek!
You should be always patient, aye, and meek,
And have a sweetly scrupulous tenderness,
Since you so preach of old Job's patience, yes.
Suffer always, since you so well can preach;
And, save you do, be sure that we will teach
That it is well to leave a wife in peace.
One of us two must bow, to be at ease;
And since a man's more reasonable, they say,
Than woman is, you must have patience aye.
What ails you that you grumble thus and groan?
Is it because you'd have my cunt alone?
Why take it all, lo, have it every bit;
Peter! Beshrew you but you're fond of it!
For if I would go peddle my *belle chose*,
I could walk out as fresh as is a rose;
But I will keep it for your own sweet tooth.
You are to blame, by God I tell the truth.'
    "Such were the words I had at my command.
Now will I tell you of my fourth husband.
    "My fourth husband, he was a reveller,
That is to say, he kept a paramour;
And young and full of passion then was I,
Stubborn and strong and jolly as a pie.
Well could I dance to tune of harp, nor fail
To sing as well as any nightingale
When I had drunk a good draught of sweet wine.
Metellius, the foul churl and the swine,
Did with a staff deprive his wife of life
Because she drank wine; had I been his wife
He never should have frightened me from drink;
For after wine, of Venus must I think:
For just as surely as cold produces hail,
A liquorish mouth must have a lickerish tail.

In women wine's no bar of impotence,
This know all lechers by experience.

"But Lord Christ! When I do remember me
Upon my youth and on my jollity,
It tickles me about my heart's deep root.
To this day does my heart sing in salute
That I have had my world in my own time.
But age, alas! that poisons every prime,
Has taken away my beauty and my pith;
Let go, farewell, the devil go therewith!
The flour is gone, there is no more to tell,
The bran, as best I may, must I now sell;
But yet to be right merry I'll try, and
Now will I tell you of my fourth husband.

"I say that in my heart I'd great despite
When he of any other had delight.
But he was quit, by God and by Saint Joce!
I made, of the same wood, a staff most gross;
Not with my body and in manner foul,
But certainly I showed so gay a soul
That in his own thick grease I made him fry
For anger and for utter jealousy.
By God, on earth I was his purgatory,
For which I hope his soul lives now in glory.
For God knows, many a time he sat and sung
When the shoe bitterly his foot had wrung.
There was no one, save God and he, that knew
How, in so many ways, I'd twist the screw.
He died when I came from Jerusalem,
And lies entombed beneath the great rood-beam,
Although his tomb is not so glorious
As was the sepulchre of Darius,
The which Apelles wrought full cleverly;
'Twas waste to bury him expensively.
Let him fare well. God give his soul good rest,
He now is in the grave and in his chest.

"And now of my fifth husband will I tell.
God grant his soul may never get to Hell!
And yet he was to me most brutal, too;
My ribs yet feel as they were black and blue,

And ever shall, until my dying day.
But in our bed he was so fresh and gay,
And therewithal he could so well impose,
What time he wanted use of my *belle chose*,
That though he'd beaten me on every bone,
He could re-win my love, and that full soon.
I guess I loved him best of all, for he
Gave of his love most sparingly to me.
We women have, if I am not to lie,
In this love matter, a quaint fantasy;
Look out a thing we may not lightly have,
And after that we'll cry all day and crave.
Forbid a thing, and that thing covet we;
Press hard upon us, then we turn and flee.
Sparingly offer we our goods, when fair;
Great crowds at market make for dearer ware,
And what's too common brings but little price;
All this knows every woman who is wise.
    "My fifth husband, may God his spirit bless!
Whom I took all for love, and not riches,
Had been sometime a student at Oxford,
And had left school and had come home to board
With my best gossip, dwelling in our town,
God save her soul! Her name was Alison.
She knew my heart and all my privity
Better than did our parish priest, s'help me!
To her confided I my secrets all.
For had my husband pissed against a wall,
Or done a thing that might have cost his life,
To her and to another worthy wife,
And to my niece whom I loved always well,
I would have told it—every bit I'd tell,
And did so, many and many a time, God wot,
Which made his face full often red and hot
For utter shame; he blamed himself that he
Had told me of so deep a privity.
    "So it befell that on a time, in Lent
(For oftentimes I to my gossip went,
Since I loved always to be glad and gay
And to walk out, in March, April, and May,

From house to house, to hear the latest malice),
Jenkin the clerk, and my gossip Dame Alis,
And I myself into the meadows went.
My husband was in London all that Lent;
I had the greater leisure, then, to play,
And to observe, and to be seen, I say,
By pleasant folk; what knew I where my face
Was destined to be loved, or in what place?
Therefore I made my visits round about
To vigils and processions of devout,
To preaching too, and shrines of pilgrimage,
To miracle plays, and always to each marriage,
And wore my scarlet skirt before all wights.
These worms and all these moths and all these mites,
I say it at my peril, never ate;
And know you why? I wore it early and late.
    "Now will I tell you what befell to me.
I say that in the meadows walked we three
Till, truly, we had come to such dalliance,
This clerk and I, that, of my vigilance,
I spoke to him and told him how that he,
Were I a widow, might well marry me.
For certainly I say it not to brag,
But I was never quite without a bag
Full of the needs of marriage that I seek.
I hold a mouse's heart not worth a leek
That has but one hole into which to run,
And if it fail of that, then all is done.
    "I made him think he had enchanted me;
My mother taught me all that subtlety.
And then I said I'd dreamed of him all night,
He would have slain me as I lay upright,
And all my bed was full of very blood;
But yet I hoped that he would do me good,
For blood betokens gold, as I was taught.
And all was false, I dreamed of him just—naught,
Save as I acted on my mother's lore,
As well in this thing as in many more.
    "But now, let's see, what was I going to say?
Aha, by God, I know! It goes this way.

"When my fourth husband lay upon his bier,
I wept enough and made but sorry cheer,
As wives must always, for it's custom's grace,
And with my kerchief covered up my face;
But since I was provided with a mate,
I really wept but little, I may state.
    "To church my man was borne upon the morrow
By neighbours, who for him made signs of sorrow;
And Jenkin, our good clerk, was one of them.
So help me God, when rang the requiem
After the bier, I thought he had a pair
Of legs and feet so clean-cut and so fair
That all my heart I gave to him to hold.
He was, I think, but twenty winters old,
And I was forty, if I tell the truth;
But then I always had a young colt's tooth.
Gap-toothed I was, and that became me well;
I had the print of holy Venus' seal.
So help me God, I was a healthy one,
And fair and rich and young and full of fun;
And truly, as my husbands all told me,
I had the silkiest *quoniam* that could be.
For truly, I am all Venusian
In feeling, and my brain is Martian.
Venus gave me my lust, my lickerishness,
And Mars gave me my sturdy hardiness.
Taurus was my ascendant, with Mars therein.
Alas, alas, that ever love was sin!
I followed always my own inclination
By virtue of my natal constellation;
Which wrought me so I never could withdraw
My Venus-chamber from a good fellow.
Yet have I Mars's mark upon my face,
And also in another private place.
For God so truly my salvation be
As I have never loved for policy,
But ever followed my own appetite,
Though he were short or tall, or black or white;
I took no heed, so that he cared for me,

How poor he was, nor even of what degree.
  "What should I say now, save, at the month's end,
This jolly, gentle, Jenkin clerk, my friend,
Had wedded me full ceremoniously,
And to him gave I all the land in fee
That ever had been given me before;
But later I repented me full sore.
He never suffered me to have my way.
By God, he smote me on the ear, one day,
Because I tore out of his book a leaf,
So that from this my ear is grown quite deaf.
Stubborn I was as is a lioness,
And with my tongue a very jay, I guess,
And walk I would, as I had done before,
From house to house, though I should not, he swore.
For which he oftentimes would sit and preach
And read old Roman tales to me and teach
How one Sulpicius Gallus left his wife
And her forsook for term of all his life
Because he saw her with bared head, I say,
Looking out from his door, upon a day.
  "Another Roman told he of by name
Who, since his wife was at a summer game
Without his knowing, he forsook her eke.
And then would he within his Bible seek
That proverb of the old Ecclesiast
Where he commands so freely and so fast
That man forbid his wife to gad about;
Then would he thus repeat, with never doubt:
  'Whoso would build his whole house out of sallows,
  And spur his blind horse to run over fallows,
  And let his wife alone go seeking hallows,
  Is worthy to be hanged upon the gallows.'
But all for naught, I didn't care a haw
For all his proverbs, nor for his old saw,
Nor yet would I by him corrected be.
I hate one that my vices tells to me,
And so do more of us—God knows!—than I.
This made him mad with me, and furiously,

That I'd not yield to him in any case.
   "Now will I tell you truth, by Saint Thomas,
Of why I tore from out his book a leaf,
For which he struck me so it made me deaf.
   "He had a book that gladly, night and day,
For his amusement he would read alway.
He called it 'Theophrastus' and 'Valerius',
At which book would he laugh, uproarious.
And, too, there sometime was a clerk at Rome,
A cardinal, that men called Saint Jerome,
Who made a book against Jovinian;
In which book, too, there was Tertullian,
Chrysippus, Trotula, and Heloïse
Who was abbess near Paris' diocese;
And too, the *Proverbs* of King Solomon,
And Ovid's *Art*, and books full many a one.
And all of these were bound in one volume.
And every night and day 'twas his custom,
When he had leisure and took some vacation
From all his other worldly occupation,
To read, within this book, of wicked wives.
He knew of them more legends and more lives
Than are of good wives written in the Bible.
For trust me, it's impossible, no libel,
That any cleric shall speak well of wives,
Unless it be of saints and holy lives,
But naught for other women will they do.
Who painted first the lion, tell me who?
By God, if women had but written stories,
As have these clerks within their oratories,
They would have written of men more wickedness
Than all the race of Adam could redress.
The children of Mercury and of Venus
Are in their lives antagonistic thus;
For Mercury loves wisdom and science,
And Venus loves but pleasure and expense.
Because they different dispositions own,
Each falls when other's in ascendant shown.
And God knows Mercury is desolate

In Pisces, wherein Venus rules in state;
And Venus falls when Mercury is raised;
Therefore no woman by a clerk is praised.
A clerk, when he is old and can naught do
Of Venus' labours worth his worn-out shoe,
Then sits he down and writes, in his dotage,
That women cannot keep vow of marriage!
"But now to tell you, as I started to,
Why I was beaten for a book, *pardieu*.
Upon a night Jenkin, who was our sire,
Read in his book, as he sat by the fire,
Of Mother Eve who, by her wickedness,
First brought mankind to all his wretchedness,
For which Lord Jesus Christ Himself was slain,
Who, with His heart's blood, saved us thus again.
Lo here, expressly of woman, may you find
That woman was the ruin of mankind.
"Then read he out how Samson lost his hairs,
Sleeping, his leman cut them with her shears;
And through this treason lost he either eye.
"Then read he out, if I am not to lie,
Of Hercules, and Deianira's desire
That caused him to go set himself on fire.
"Nothing escaped him of the pain and woe
That Socrates had with his spouses two;
How Xantippe threw piss upon his head;
This hapless man sat still, as he were dead;
He wiped his head, no more durst he complain
Than 'Ere the thunder ceases comes the rain.'
"Then of Pasiphaë, the queen of Crete,
For cursedness he thought the story sweet;
Fie! Say no more—it is an awful thing—
Of her so horrible lust and love-liking.
"Of Clytemnestra, for her lechery,
Who caused her husband's death by treachery,
He read all this with greatest zest, I vow.
"He told me, too, just when it was and how
Amphiaraus at Thebes lost his life;
My husband had a legend of his wife

Eriphyle who, for a brooch of gold,
In secrecy to hostile Greeks had told
Whereat her husband had his hiding place,
For which he found at Thebes but sorry grace.
   "Of Livia and Lucia told he me,
For both of them their husbands killed, you see,
The one for love, the other killed for hate;
Livia her husband, on an evening late,
Made drink some poison, for she was his foe.
Lucia, lecherous, loved her husband so
That, to the end he'd always of her think,
She gave him such a philtre, for love-drink,
That he was dead or ever it was morrow;
And husbands thus, by same means, came to sorrow.
   "Then did he tell how one Latumius
Complained unto his comrade Arrius
That in his garden grew a baleful tree
Whereon, he said, his wives, and they were three,
Had hanged themselves for wretchedness and woe.
'O brother,' Arrius said, 'and did they so?
Give me a graft of that same blessed tree
And in my garden planted it shall be!'
   "Of wives of later date he also read,
How some had slain their husbands in their bed
And let their lovers shag them all the night
While corpses lay upon the floor upright.
And some had driven nails into the brain
While husbands slept and in such wise were slain.
And some had given them poison in their drink.
He told more evil than the mind can think.
And therewithal he knew of more proverbs
Than in this world there grows of grass or herbs.
'Better,' he said, 'your habitation be
With lion wild or dragon foul,' said he,
'Than with a woman who will nag and chide.'
'Better,' he said, 'on the housetop abide
Than with a brawling wife down in the house;
Such are so wicked and contrarious
They hate the thing their husband loves, for aye.'

He said, 'a woman throws her shame away
When she throws off her smock,' and further, too:
'A woman fair, save she be chaste also,
Is like a ring of gold in a sow's nose.'
Who would imagine or who would suppose
What grief and pain were in this heart of mine?
    "And when I saw he'd never cease, in fine,
His reading in this cursed book at night,
Three leaves of it I snatched and tore outright
Out of his book, as he read on; and eke
I with my fist so took him on the cheek
That in our fire he reeled and fell right down.
Then he got up as does a wild lion,
And with his fist he struck me on the head,
And on the floor I lay as I were dead.
And when he saw how limp and still I lay,
He was afraid and would have run away,
Until at last out of my swoon I made:
'Oh, have you slain me, you false thief?' I said,
'And for my land have you thus murdered me?
Kiss me before I die, and let me be.'
    "He came to me and near me he knelt down,
And said: 'O my dear sister Alison,
So help me God, I'll never strike you more;
What I have done, you are to blame therefor.
But all the same forgiveness now I seek!'
And thereupon I hit him on the cheek,
And said: "Thief, so much vengeance do I wreak!
Now will I die, I can no longer speak!'
But at the last, and with much care and woe,
We made it up between ourselves. And so
He put the bridle reins within my hand
To have the governing of house and land;
And of his tongue and of his hand, also;
And made him burn his book, right then, oho!
And when I had thus gathered unto me
Masterfully, the entire sovereignty,
And he had said: 'My own true wedded wife,
Do as you please the term of all your life,

Guard your own honour and keep fair my state'—
After that day we never had debate.
God help me now, I was to him as kind
As any wife from Denmark unto Ind,
And also true, and so was he to me.
I pray to God, Who sits in majesty,
To bless his soul, out of His mercy dear!
Now will I tell my tale, if you will hear."

Behold the Words Between the Summoner and the Friar

The friar laughed when he had heard all this.
"Now dame," said he, "so have I joy or bliss,
This is a long preamble to a tale!"
    And when the summoner heard this friar's hail,
"Lo," said the summoner, "by God's arms two!
A friar will always interfere, mark you.
Behold, good men, a housefly, and a friar
Will fall in every dish and matters higher.
Why speak of preambling, you in your gown?
What! Amble, trot, hold peace, or go sit down;
You hinder our diversion thus to inquire."
    "Aye, say you so, sir summoner?" said the friar,
"Now by my faith I will, before I go,
Tell of a summoner such a tale, or so,
That all the folk shall laugh who're in this place."
    "Otherwise, friar, I beshrew your face,"
Replied this summoner, "and beshrew me
If I do not tell tales here, two or three,
Of friars ere I come to Sittingbourne,
That certainly will give you cause to mourn,
For well I know your patience will be gone.'
    Our host cried out, "Now peace, and that anon!"
And said he: "Let the woman tell her tale.
You act like people who are drunk with ale.
Do, lady, tell your tale, and that is best."
    "All ready, sir," said she, "as you request,
If I have license of this worthy friar."
    "Yes, dame," said he, "to hear you's my desire."

The Tale of the Wife of Bath

Now in the olden days of King Arthur,
Of whom the Britons speak with great honour,
All this wide land was land of faëry.
The elf-queen, with her jolly company,
Danced oftentimes on many a green mead;
This was the old opinion, as I read.
I speak of many hundred years ago;
But now no man can see the elves, you know.
For now the so-great charity and prayers
Of limiters and other holy friars
That do infest each land and every stream
As thick as motes are in a bright sunbeam,
Blessing halls, chambers, kitchens, ladies' bowers,
Cities and towns and castles and high towers,
Manors and barns and stables, aye and dairies—
This causes it that there are now no fairies.
For where was wont to walk full many an elf,
Right there walks now the limiter himself
In noons and afternoons and in mornings,
Saying his matins and such holy things,
As he goes round his district in his gown.
Women may now go safely up and down,
In every copse or under every tree;
There is no other incubus than he,
And would do them nothing but dishonour.
   And so befell it that this King Arthur
Had at his court a lusty bachelor
Who, on a day, came riding from river;
And happened that, alone as she was born,
He saw a maiden walking through the corn,
From whom, in spite of all she did and said,
Straightway by force he took her maidenhead;
for which violation was there such clamour,
And such appealing unto King Arthur,
That soon condemned was this knight to be dead
By course of law, and should have lost his head,
Peradventure, such being the statute then;
But that the other ladies and the queen

So long prayed of the king to show him grace,
He granted life, at last, in the law's place,
And gave him to the queen, as she should will,
Whether she'd save him, or his blood should spill.
   The queen she thanked the king with all her might,
And after this, thus spoke she to the knight,
When she'd an opportunity, one day:
"You stand yet," said she, "in such poor a way
That for your life you've no security.
I'll grant you life if you can tell to me
What thing it is that women most desire.
Be wise, and keep your neck from iron dire!
And if you cannot tell it me anon,
Then will I give you license to be gone
A twelvemonth and a day, to search and learn
Sufficient answer in this grave concern.
And your knight's word I'll have, ere forth you pace,
To yield your body to me in this place."
   Grieved was this knight, and sorrowfully he sighed;
But there! he could not do as pleased his pride.
And at the last he chose that he would wend,
And come again upon the twelvemonth's end,
With such an answer as God might purvey;
And so he took his leave and went his way.
   He sought out every house and every place
Wherein he hoped to find that he had grace
To learn what women love the most of all;
But nowhere ever did it him befall
To find, upon the question stated here,
Two persons who agreed with statement clear.
   Some said that women all loved best riches,
Some said, fair fame, and some said, prettiness;
Some, rich array, some said 'twas lust abed
And often to be widowed and re-wed.
   Some said that our poor hearts are aye most eased
When we have been most flattered and thus pleased.
And he went near the truth, I will not lie;
A man may win us best with flattery;
And with attentions and with busyness
We're often limed, the greater and the less.

And some say, too, that we do love the best
To be quite free to do our own behest,
And that no man reprove us for our vice,
But saying we are wise, take our advice.
For truly there is no one of us all,
If anyone shall rub us on a gall,
That will not kick because he tells the truth.
Try, and he'll find, who does so, I say sooth.
No matter how much vice we have within,
We would be held for wise and clean of sin.

And some folk say that great delight have we
To be held constant, also trustworthy,
And on one purpose steadfastly to dwell,
And not betray a thing that men may tell.
But that tale is not worth a rake's handle;
By God, we women can no thing conceal,
As witness Midas. Would you hear the tale?

Ovid, among some other matters small,
Said Midas had beneath his long curled hair,
Two ass's ears that grew in secret there,
The which defect he hid, as best he might,
Full cunningly from every person's sight,
And, save his wife, no one knew of it, no.
He loved her most, and trusted her also;
And he prayed of her that to no creature
She'd tell of his disfigurement impure.

She swore him: Nay, for all this world to win
She would do no such villainy or sin
And cause her husband have so foul a name;
Nor would she tell it for her own deep shame.
Nevertheless, she thought she would have died
Because so long the secret must she hide;
It seemed to swell so big about her heart
That some word from her mouth must surely start;
And since she dared to tell it to no man,
Down to a marsh, that lay hard by, she ran;
Till she came there her heart was all afire,
And as a bittern booms in the quagmire,
She laid her mouth low to the water down:
"Betray me not, you sounding water blown,"

Said she, "I tell it to none else but you:
Long ears like asses' has my husband two!
Now is my heart at ease, since that is out:
I could no longer keep it, there's no doubt."
Here may you see, though for a while we bide,
Yet out it must; no secret can we hide.
The rest of all this tale, if you would hear,
Read Ovid: in his book does it appear.

   This knight my tale is chiefly told about
When what he went for he could not find out,
That is, the thing that women love the best,
Most saddened was the spirit in his breast;
But home he goes, he could no more delay.
The day was come when home he turned his way;
And on his way it chanced that he should ride
In all his care, beneath a forest's side,
And there he saw, a-dancing him before,
Full four and twenty ladies, maybe more;
Toward which dance eagerly did he turn
In hope that there some wisdom he should learn.
But truly, ere he came upon them there,
The dancers vanished all, he knew not where.
No creature saw he that gave sign of life,
Save, on the greensward sitting, an old wife;
A fouler person could no man devise.
Before the knight this old wife did arise,
And said: "Sir knight, hence lies no travelled way.
Tell me what thing you seek, and by your fay.
Perchance you'll find it may the better be;
These ancient folk know many things," said she.

   "Dear mother," said this knight assuredly,
"I am but dead, save I can tell, truly,
What thing it is that women most desire;
Could you inform me, I'd pay well your hire."

   "Plight me your troth here, hand in hand," said she,
"That you will do, whatever it may be,
The thing I ask if it lie in your might;
And I'll give you your answer ere the night."

   "Have here my word," said he. "That thing I grant."

   "Then," said the crone, "of this I make my vaunt,

Your life is safe; and I will stand thereby,
Upon my life, the queen will say as I.
Let's see which is the proudest of them all
That wears upon her hair kerchief or caul,
Shall dare say no to that which I shall teach;
Let us go now and without longer speech."
    Then whispered she a sentence in his ear,
And bade him to be glad and have no fear.
    When they were come unto the court, this knight
Said he had kept his promise as was right,
And ready was his answer, as he said.
Full many a noble wife, and many a maid,
And many a widow, since they are so wise,
The queen herself sitting as high justice,
Assembled were, his answer there to hear;
And then the knight was bidden to appear.
    Command was given for silence in the hall,
And that the knight should tell before them all
What thing all worldly women love the best.
This knight did not stand dumb, as does a beast,
But to this question presently answered
With manly voice, so that the whole court heard:
"My liege lady, generally," said he,
"Women desire to have the sovereignty
As well upon their husband as their love,
And to have mastery their man above;
This thing you most desire, though me you kill
Do as you please, I am here at your will."
    In all the court there was no wife or maid
Or widow that denied the thing he said,
But all held, he was worthy to have life.
    And with that word up started the old wife
Whom he had seen a-sitting on the green.
"Mercy," cried she, "my sovereign lady queen!
Before the court's dismissed, give me my right.
'Twas I who taught the answer to this knight;
For which he did plight troth to me, out there,
That the first thing I should of him require
He would do that, if it lay in his might.
Before the court, now, pray I you, sir knight,"

Said she, "that you will take me for your wife;
For well you know that I have saved your life.
If this be false, say nay, upon your fay!"

   This knight replied: "Alas and welaway!
That I so promised I will not protest.
But for God's love pray make a new request,
Take all my wealth and let my body go."

   "Nay then," said she, "beshrew us if I do!
For though I may be foul and old and poor,
I will not, for all metal and all ore
That from the earth is dug or lies above,
Be aught except your wife and your true love."

   "My love?" cried he, "nay, rather my damnation!
Alas! that any of my race and station
Should ever so dishonoured foully be!"

   But all for naught; the end was this, that he
Was so constrained he needs must go and wed,
And take his ancient wife and go to bed.

   Now, peradventure, would some men say here,
That, of my negligence, I take no care
To tell you of the joy and all the array
That at the wedding feast were seen that day.
Make a brief answer to this thing I shall;
I say, there was no joy or feast at all;
There was but heaviness and grievous sorrow;
For privately he wedded on the morrow,
And all day, then, he hid him like an owl;
So sad he was, his old wife looked so foul.

   Great was the woe the knight had in his thought
When he, with her, to marriage bed was brought;
He rolled about and turned him to and fro.
His old wife lay there, always smiling so,
And said: "O my dear husband, ben'cite!
Fares every knight with wife as you with me?
Is this the custom in King Arthur's house?
Are knights of his all so fastidious?
I am your own true love and, more, your wife;
And I am she who saved your very life;
And truly, since I've never done you wrong,
Why do you treat me so, this first night long?

You act as does a man who's lost his wit;
What is my fault? For God's love tell me it,
And it shall be amended, if I may."
    "Amended!" cried this knight, "Alas, nay, nay!
It will not be amended ever, no!
You are so loathsome, and so old also,
And therewith of so low a race were born,
It's little wonder that I toss and turn.
Would God my heart would break within my breast!"
    "Is this," asked she, "the cause of your unrest?"
    "Yes, truly," said he, "and no wonder 'tis."
    "Now, sir," said she, "I could amend all this,
If I but would, and that within days three,
If you would bear yourself well towards me.

    "But since you speak of such gentility
As is descended from old wealth, till ye
Claim that for that you should be gentlemen,
I hold such arrogance not worth a hen.
Find him who is most virtuous alway,
Alone or publicly, and most tries aye
To do whatever noble deeds he can,
And take him for the greatest gentleman.
Christ wills we claim from Him gentility,
Not from ancestors of landocracy.
For though they give us all their heritage,
For which we claim to be of high lineage,
Yet can they not bequeath, in anything,
To any of us, their virtuous living,
That made men say they had gentility,
And bade us follow them in like degree.

    "Well does that poet wise of great Florence,
Called Dante, speak his mind in this sentence;
Somewhat like this may it translated be:
'Rarely unto the branches of the tree
Doth human worth mount up: and so ordains
He Who bestows it; to Him it pertains.'
For of our fathers may we nothing claim
But temporal things, that man may hurt and maim.

    "And everyone knows this as well as I,
If nobleness were implanted naturally

Within a certain lineage, down the line,
In private and in public, I opine,
The ways of gentleness they'd alway show
And never fall to vice and conduct low.
    "Take fire and carry it in the darkest house
Between here and the Mount of Caucasus,
And let men shut the doors and from them turn;
Yet will the fire as fairly blaze and burn
As twenty thousand men did it behold;
Its nature and its office it will hold,
On peril of my life, until it die.
    "From this you see that true gentility
Is not allied to wealth a man may own,
Since folk do not their deeds, as may be shown,
As does the fire, according to its kind.
For God knows that men may full often find
A lord's son doing shame and villainy;
And he that prizes his gentility
In being born of some old noble house,
With ancestors both noble and virtuous,
But will himself do naught of noble deeds
Nor follow him to whose name he succeeds,
He is not gentle, be he duke or earl;
For acting churlish makes a man a churl.
Gentility is not just the renown
Of ancestors who have some greatness shown,
In which you have no portion of your own.
Your own gentility comes from God alone;
Thence comes our true nobility by grace,
It was not willed us with our rank and place
    "Think how noble, as says Valerius,
Was that same Tullius Hostilius,
Who out of poverty rose to high estate.
Seneca and Boethius inculcate,
Expressly (and no doubt it thus proceeds),
That he is noble who does noble deeds;
And therefore, husband dear, I thus conclude:
Although my ancestors mayhap were rude,
Yet may the High Lord God, and so hope I,
Grant me the grace to live right virtuously.

Then I'll be gentle when I do begin
To live in virtue and to do no sin.
"And when you me reproach for poverty,
The High God, in Whom we believe, say I,
In voluntary poverty lived His life.
And surely every man, or maid, or wife
May understand that Jesus, Heaven's King,
Would not have chosen vileness of living.
Glad poverty's an honest thing, that's plain,
Which Seneca and other clerks maintain.
Whoso will be content with poverty,
I hold him rich, though not a shirt has he.
And he that covets much is a poor wight,
For he would gain what's all beyond his might.
But he that has not, nor desires to have,
Is rich, although you hold him but a knave.
    "True poverty, it sings right naturally;
Juvenal gaily says of poverty:
'The poor man, when he walks along the way,
Before the robbers he may sing and play.'
Poverty's odious good, and, as I guess,
It is a stimulant to busyness;
A great improver, too, of sapience
In him that takes it all with due patience.
Poverty's this, though it seem misery—
Its quality may none dispute, say I.
Poverty often, when a man is low,
Makes him his God and even himself to know.
And poverty's an eyeglass, seems to me,
Through which a man his loyal friends may see.
Since you've received no injury from me,
Then why reproach me for my poverty.
    "Now, sir, with age you have upbraided me;
And truly, sir, though no authority
Were in a book, you gentles of honour
Say that men should the aged show favour,
And call him father, of your gentleness;
And authors could I find for this, I guess.
    "Now since you say that I am foul and old,
Then fear you not to be made a cuckold;

For dirt and age, as prosperous I may be,
Are mighty wardens over chastity.
Nevertheless, since I know your delight,
I'll satisfy your worldly appetite.
   "Choose, now," said she, "one of these two things, aye,
To have me foul and old until I die,
And be to you a true and humble wife,
And never anger you in all my life;
Or else to have me young and very fair
And take your chance with those who will repair
Unto your house, and all because of me,
Or in some other place, as well may be.
Now choose which you like better and reply."
   This knight considered, and did sorely sigh,
But at the last replied as you shall hear:
"My lady and my love, and wife so dear,
I put myself in your wise governing;
Do you choose which may be the more pleasing,
And bring most honour to you, and me also.
I care not which it be of these things two;
For if you like it, that suffices me."
   "Then have I got of you the mastery,
Since I may choose and govern, in earnest?"
   "Yes, truly, wife," said he, "I hold that best."
   "Kiss me," said she, "we'll be no longer wroth,
For by my truth, to you I will be both;
That is to say, I'll be both good and fair.
I pray God I go mad, and so declare,
If I be not to you as good and true
As ever wife was since the world was new.
And, save I be, at dawn, as fairly seen
As any lady, empress, or great queen
That is between the east and the far west,
Do with my life and death as you like best.
Throw back the curtain and see how it is."
   And when the knight saw verily all this,
That she so very fair was, and young too,
For joy he clasped her in his strong arms two,
His heart bathed in a bath of utter bliss;
A thousand times, all in a row, he'd kiss.

And she obeyed his wish in everything
That might give pleasure to his love-liking.
   And thus they lived unto their lives' fair end,
In perfect joy; and Jesus to us send
Meek husbands, and young ones, and fresh in bed,
And good luck to outlive them that we wed.
And I pray Jesus to cut short the lives
Of those who'll not be governed by their wives;
And old and querulous niggards with their pence,
And send them soon a mortal pestilence!

The Clerk's Tale

The Clerk's Prologue

"Sir clerk of Oxford," our good host then said,
"You ride as quiet and still as is a maid
But newly wedded, sitting at the board;
This day I've heard not from your tongue a word.
Perhaps you mull a sophism that's prime,
But Solomon says, each thing to its own time.
  "For God's sake, smile and be of better cheer,
It is no time to think and study here.
  Tell us some merry story, if you may;
For whatsoever man will join in play,
He needs must to the play give his consent.
But do not preach, as friars do in Lent,
To make us, for our old sins, wail and weep,
And see your tale shall put us not to sleep.
"Tell us some merry thing of adventures.
Your terms, your colours, and your speech-figures,
Keep them in store till so be you indite
High style, as when men unto kings do write.
Speak you so plainly, for this time, I pray,
That we can understand what things you say."
  This worthy clerk, benignly he answered.
"Good host," said he, "I am under your yard;
You have of us, for now, the governance,
And therefore do I make you obeisance
As far as reason asks it, readily.
I will relate to you a tale that I
Learned once, at Padua, of a worthy clerk,
As he proved by his words and by his work.
He's dead, now, and nailed down within his chest,
And I pray God to give his soul good rest!
  "Francis Petrarch, the laureate poet,
Was this clerk's name, whose rhetoric so sweet

Illumed all Italy with poetry,
As did Lignano with philosophy,
Or law, or other art particular;
But Death, that suffers us not very far,
Nor more, as 'twere, than twinkling of an eye,
Has slain them both, as all of us shall die.

"But forth, to tell you of this worthy man,
Who taught this tale to me, as I began,
I say that first, with high style he indites,
Before the body of his tale he writes,
A proem to describe those lands renowned,
Saluzzo, Piedmont, and the region round,
And speaks of Apennines, those hills so high
That form the boundary of West Lombardy,
And of Mount Viso, specially, the tall,
Whereat the Po, out of a fountain small,
Takes its first springing and its tiny source
That eastward ever increases in its course
Toward Emilia, Ferrara, and Venice;
The which is a long story to devise.
And truly, in my judgment reluctant
It is a thing not wholly relevant,
Save that he introduces thus his gear:
But this is his tale, which you now may hear."

The Clerk's Tale

There is, in the west side of Italy,
Down at the foot of Mount Viso the cold,
A pleasant plain that yields abundantly,
Where many a tower and town one may behold,
That were there founded in the times of old,
With many another fair delightful sight;
Saluzzo is this noble region bright.

A marquis once was lord of all that land,
As were his noble ancestors before;
Obedient and ready to his hand
Were all his lieges, both the less and more.

Thus in delight he lived, and had of yore,
Beloved and feared, through favour of Fortune,
Both by his lords and by the common run.

Therewith he was, to speak of lineage,
Born of the noblest blood of Lombardy,
With person fair, and strong, and young of age,
And full of honour and of courtesy;
Discreet enough to lead his nation, he,
Save in some things wherein he was to blame,
And Walter was this young lord's Christian name.

I blame him thus, that he considered naught
Of what in coming time might him betide,
But on his present wish was all his thought,
As, he would hunt and hawk on every side;
Well-nigh all other cares would he let slide,
And would not, and this was the worst of all,
Marry a wife, for aught that might befall.

That point alone his people felt so sore
That in a flock one day to him they went,
And one of them, the wisest in all lore,
Or else because the lord would best consent
That he should tell him what the people meant,
Or else that he could make the matter clear,
He to the marquis spoke as you shall hear.

"O noble marquis, your humanity
Assures us, aye, and gives us hardiness
As often as there is necessity
That we to you may tell our heaviness.
Accept, lord, now of your great nobleness
That we with sincere hearts may here complain,
Nor let your ears my humble voice disdain.

"Though I have naught to do in this matter
More than another man has in this place,
Yet for as much as you, most honoured sir,
Have always showed me favour and much grace,

I dare the more to ask of you a space
Of audience, to set forth our request,
And you, my lord, will do as you like best.

"For truly, lord, so well do we like you
And all your works (and ever have), that we—
We could not, of ourselves, think what to do
To make us live in more felicity,
Save one thing, lord, and if your will it be,
That to be wedded man you hold it best,
Then were your people's hearts at utter rest.

"But bow your neck beneath that blessed yoke
Of sovereignty and not of hard service,
The which men call espousal or wedlock;
And pray think, lord, among your thoughts so wise,
How our days pass and each in different guise;
For though we sleep or wake or roam or ride,
Time flies, and for no man will it abide.

"And though your time of green youth flower as yet,
Age creeps in always, silent as a stone;
Death threatens every age, nor will forget
For any state, and there escapes him none:
And just as surely as we know, each one,
That we shall die, uncertain are we all
What day it is when death shall on us fall.

"Accept then of us, lord, the true intent,
That never yet refused you your behest,
And we will, lord, if you will give consent,
Choose you a wife without delay, at least,
Born of the noblest blood and the greatest
Of all this land, so that it ought to seem
Honour to God and you, as we shall deem.

"Deliver us from all our constant dread
And take yourself a wife, for High God's sake;
For if it so befell, which God forbid,
That by your death your noble line should break

And that a strange successor should come take
Your heritage, woe that we were alive!
Wherefore we pray you speedily to wive."

Their humble prayer and their so earnest cheer
Roused in the marquis' heart great sympathy.
"You'd have me," he replied, "my people dear,
Do what I've never yet thought necessary.
I have rejoiced in my fond liberty,
That men so seldom find in their marriage;
Where I was free, I must be in bondage.

"Nevertheless, I see your true intent,
And know there's always sense in what you say;
Wherefore of my free will will I consent
To wed a wife, as soon as ever I may.
But whereas you have offered here today
To choose a wife for me, I you release
From that, and pray that you thereof will cease.

"For God knows well that children oft retain
Naught of their worthy elders gone before;
Goodness comes all from God, not of the strain
Whereof they were engendered; furthermore
I trust in God's great goodness, and therefore
My marriage and my state and all my ease
I leave to Him to do with as He please.

"Let me alone in choosing of my wife,
That burden on my own back I'll endure;
But I pray you, and charge you on your life,
That what wife I may take, me you'll assure
You'll honour her throughout her life's tenure,
In word and deed, both here and everywhere,
As if she were an emperor's daughter fair.

"And furthermore, this shall you swear, that you
Against my choice shall neither grouse nor strive;
Since I'm forgoing liberty, and woo

At your request, so may I ever thrive
As, where my heart is set, there will I wive;
And save you give consent in such manner,
I pray you speak no more of this matter."

With hearty will they swore and gave assent
To all this, and no one of them said nay;
Praying him, of his grace, before they went,
That he would set for them a certain day
For his espousal, soon as might be; yea,
For still the people had a little dread
Lest that the marquis would no woman wed.

He granted them the day that pleased him best
Whereon he would be married, certainly,
And said he did all this at their request;
And they with humble hearts, obediently,
Kneeling upon their knees full reverently,
All thanked him there, and thus they made an end
Of their design and homeward did they wend.

And thereupon he to his officers
Ordered that for the fête they should provide,
And to his household gentlemen and squires,
Such charges gave as pleased him to decide;
And all obeyed him: let him praise or chide,
And each of them did all his diligence
To show unto the fête his reverence.

> *Explicit prima pars.*
> *Incipit secunda pars.*

Not far from that same honoured palace where
This marquis planned his marriage, at this tide,
There stood a hamlet, on a site most fair,
Wherein the poor folk of the countryside
Stabled their cattle and did all abide,
And where their labour gave them sustenance
After the earth had yielded abundance.

Amongst these humble folk there dwelt a man
Who was considered poorest of them all;
But the High God of Heaven sometimes can
Send His grace to a little ox's stall;
Janicula men did this poor man call.
A daughter had he, fair enough to sight;
Griselda was this young maid's name, the bright.

If one should speak of virtuous beauty,
Then was she of the fairest under sun;
Since fostered in dire poverty was she,
No lust luxurious in her heart had run;
More often from the well than from the tun
She drank, and since she would chaste virtue please,
She knew work well, but knew not idle ease.

But though this maiden tender was of age,
Yet in the breast of her virginity
There was enclosed a ripe and grave courage;
And in great reverence and charity
Her poor old father fed and fostered she;
A few sheep grazing in a field she kept,
For she would not be idle till she slept.

And when she homeward came, why she would bring
Roots and green herbs, full many times and oft,
The which she'd shred and boil for her living,
And made her bed a hard one and not soft;
Her father kept she in their humble croft
With what obedience and diligence
A child may do for father's reverence.

Upon Griselda, humble daughter pure,
The marquis oft had looked in passing by,
As he a-hunting rode at adventure;
And when it chanced that her he did espy,
Not with the glances of a wanton eye
He gazed at her, but all in sober guise,
And pondered on her deeply in this wise:

Commending to his heart her womanhood,
And virtue passing that of any wight,
Of so young age in face and habitude.
For though the people have no deep insight
In virtue, he considered all aright
Her goodness, and decided that he would
Wed only her, if ever wed he should.

The day of wedding came, but no one can
Tell who the woman is that bride shall be;
At which strange thing they wondered, many a man,
And they said, marvelling, in privacy:
"Will not our lord yet leave his vanity?
Will he not wed? Alas, alas, the while!
Why will he thus himself and us beguile?"

Nevertheless, this marquis has bade make,
Of jewels set in gold and in rich azure,
Brooches and rings, all for Griselda's sake,
And for her garments took he then the measure
By a young maiden of her form and stature,
And found all other ornaments as well
That for such wedding would be meet to tell.

The time of mid-morn of that very day
Approached when this lord's marriage was to be;
And all the palace was bedecked and gay,
Both hall and chambers, each in its degree;
With kitchens stuffed with food in great plenty,
There might one see the last and least dainty
That could be found in all of Italy.

This regal marquis, splendidly arrayed,
With lords and ladies in his company
(Who to attend the feasting had been prayed),
And of his retinue the bachelory,
With many a sound of sundry melody,
Unto the village whereof I have told,
In this array the nearest way did hold.

Griselda who, God knows, was innocent
That for her sake was all this fine array,
To fetch some water, to a fountain went,
Yet she returned soon, did this lovely may,
For she had heard it said that on this day
The marquis was to wed, and if she might,
She was full fain to see the glorious sight.

She thought: "With other maidens I will stand
(Who are my friends) within our door, and see
The marchioness, and therefore I'll turn hand
To do at home, as soon as it may be,
The household work that's waiting there for me;
And then I'll be at leisure to behold
Her, if they this way to the castle hold."

And as across her threshold she'd have gone,
The marquis came, and for her did he call;
And she set down her water jar anon
Beside the threshold, in an ox's stall,
And down upon her two knees did she fall
And, kneeling, with grave countenance, was still
Till she had heard what was his lordship's will.

This thoughtful marquis spoke unto this maid
Full soberly, and said in this manner:
"Griselda, where's your father?" so he said.
And she, with reverence and with humble cheer,
Answered: "My lord, he is but inside here."
And in she went without more tarrying
And to the marquis did her father bring.

He by the hand then took this ancient man
And said, when he had led him well aside:
"Janicula, I neither will nor can
Conceal my love, nor my heart's longing hide,
If you but acquiesce, whate'er betide,
Your daughter will I take, before I wend,
To be my wife until her life's dear end.

"You love me, and I know it well today,
And are my faithful liege, and were of yore;
And all that pleases me, I dare well say,
Pleases you too; especially therefore
Assure me on the point I made before—
Can we together in this compact draw,
And will you take me as your son-in-law?"

This sudden word the man astonished so
That red he grew, abashed, and all quaking
He stood; nor could he answer further, no,
Than but to say: "O Lord, I am willing
To do your will; but against your liking
I'll do no thing; you are my lord so dear
That what you wish governs this matter here."

"Then I will," said this marquis, quietly,
"That in your chamber you and I and she
Have consultation, and do you know why?
Because I'd ask her if her will it be
To be my wife and so be ruled by me;
And all this shall be done in your presence,
I will not speak without your audience."

And while in chamber they three were about
Their business, whereof you'll hereafter hear,
The people crowded through the house without
And wondered by what honest method there
So carefully she'd kept her father dear.
But more Griselda wondered, as she might,
For never before that saw she such a sight.

No wonder, though, astonishment she felt
At seeing so great a guest within that place;
With people of his sort she'd never dealt,
Wherefore she looked on with a pallid face.
But briefly through the matter now to race,
These are the very words the marquis said
To this most modest, truly constant maid.

"Griselda," said he, "you shall understand
It's pleasing to your father and to me
That I wed you, and even it may stand,
As I suppose, that you would have it be.
But these demands must I first make," said he,
"And since it shall be done in hasty wise,
Will you consent, or will you more advise?"

"I say this: Are you ready with good heart
To grant my wish, and that I freely may,
As I shall think best, make you laugh or smart,
And you to grumble never, night or day?
And too, when I say 'yea' you say not 'nay'
By word or frown to what I have designed.
Swear this, and here I will our contract bind."

Wondering upon this word, quaking for fear,
She said: "My lord, unsuited, unworthy
Am I to take the honour you give me here;
But what you'd have, that very thing would I.
And here I swear that never willingly,
In deed or thought, will I you disobey,
To save my life, and I love life, I say."

"This is enough, Griselda mine," cried he.
And forth he went then with full sober cheer
Out at the door, and after him came she,
And to the people who were waiting near,
"This is my wife," he said, "who's standing here.
Honour her, all, and love her, all, I pray,
Who love me; and there is no more to say."

And so that nothing of her former gear
She should take with her to his house, he bade
That women strip her naked then and there;
Whereat these ladies were not overglad
To handle clothes wherein she had been clad.
Nevertheless, this maiden bright of hue
From head to foot they clothed her all anew.

Her hair they combed and brushed, which fell untressed
All artlessly, and placed a coronal
With their small fingers on her head, and dressed
Her robes with many jewels great and small;
Of her array how shall I tell withal?
Scarcely the people knew her for fairness,
So transformed was she in her splendid dress.

This marquis her has married with a ring
Brought for the purpose there; and then has set
Upon a horse, snow-white and well ambling,
And to his palace, without longer let,
With happy following folk and more they met,
Convoyed her home, and thus the day they spent
In revelry until the sun's descent.

And briefly forth throughout this tale to chase,
I say that unto this new marchioness
God has such favour sent her, of His grace,
It seemed in no way true, by likeliness,
That she was born and bred in humbleness,
As in a hovel or an ox's stall,
But rather nurtured in an emperor's hall.

To everyone she soon became so dear
And worshipful, that folk where she had dwelt
And from her birth had known her, year by year,
Although they could have sworn it, scarcely felt
That to Janicula, with whom I've dealt,
She really was a daughter, for she seemed
Another creature now, or so they deemed.

For though she ever had been virtuous,
She was augmented by such excellence
Of manners based on noble goodness thus,
And so discreet and wise of eloquence,
So gentle and so worthy reverence,
And she could so the people's hearts embrace,
That each her loved that looked upon her face.

Not only in Saluzzo, in the town,
Was published wide the goodness of her name,
But throughout many a land where she'd renown
If one said well, another said the same;
So widespread of her goodness was the fame
That men and women came; the young and old
Went to Saluzzo, her but to behold.

Thus Walter lowly, nay, but royally,
Wedded, by Fortune's grace, right honourably,
In the good peace of God lived easily
At home, and outward grace enough had he;
And since he saw that under low degree
Is virtue often hid, the people fairly
Held him a prudent man, and that's done rarely.

Not only this Griselda through her wit
Knew how with wifely arts her home to bless,
But also, when there was a need for it,
The people's wrongs she knew how to redress.
There was no discord, rancour, heaviness
In all that land that she could not appease,
And wisely bring them all to rest and ease.

Although her husband from the court were gone,
If gentlemen, or less, of her country
Were angered, she would bring them all at one;
So wise and so mature of speech was she,
And judgments gave of so great equity,
Men felt that God from Heaven her did send
People to save and every wrong to amend.

Not long Griselda had, it seems, been wed
Before a daughter to her lord she bore,
Though of a son she'd rather have gone to bed.
Glad were the marquis and the folk therefor;
For though a girl-child came thus all before,
She might well to a boy-child yet attain,
Since barren she was not, it now was plain.

Explicit secunda pars.
Incipit tercia pars.

It happened, as it has sometimes before,
That when this child had sucked a month or so,
This marquis in his heart such longing bore
To test his wife, her patience thus to know,
He could not in his heart the chance forgo
This marvelous desire his wife to try;
'Twas needless, God knows, thus to peek and pry.

He had sufficiently tried her before
And found her ever good; what needed it
That he should test her ever more and more?
Though some men praise it for a subtle wit,
Yet I say that to him 'twas no credit
To try his wife when there was never need,
Putting her heart to anguish and to dread.

In doing which the marquis took this turn:
He came alone by night to where she lay
And with a troubled look and features stern
He said to her: "Griselda mine, that day
When I removed you from your poor array
And placed you in a state of nobleness—
You have not all forgotten that, I guess.

"I say, Griselda, this your dignity
Wherein I have so placed you, as I trow,
Has not made you forgetful now to be
That I raised you from poor estate and low
For any good you might then have or know.
Take heed of every word that now I say,
There's no one else shall hear it, by my fay.

"You know and well enough how you came here
Into this house, it is not long ago,
And though to me you are both lief and dear,
Unto my nobles you are not; and so

They say that unto them 'tis shame and woe
To be your subjects and compelled to serve
You who are village-born and naught deserve.

"And specially, since that girl-child you bore,
These things they've said—of this there is no doubt;
But I desire, as I have done before,
To live at peace with all the folk about;
I cannot in this matter leave them out.
I must do with your daughter what is best,
Not as I would, but under men's behest.

"And yet, God knows, the act is hard for me;
And only with your knowledge would I bring
The deed to pass, but this I would," said he,
"That you assent with me to this one thing.
Show now that patience in your life's dealing
You told me of and swore to in your village
The day that marked the making of our marriage."

When she had heard all this, this she received
With never a word or change of countenance;
For, as it seemed, she was in no way grieved.
She said: "Lord, all lies at your own pleasance;
My child and I, with hearty obeisance,
Are all yours, and you may save us or kill
That which is yours; do you what thing you will.

"There is no thing, and so God my soul save,
That you may like displeasing unto me;
I do not wish a single thing to have,
Nor dread a thing to lose, save only ye;
This will is in my heart and aye shall be,
Nor length of time nor death may this deface,
Nor turn my passion to another place."

Glad was this marquis of her answering,
And yet he feigned as if he were not so;
All dreary were his face and his bearing
When it came time from chamber he should go.

Soon after this, a quarter hour or so,
He privily told all of his intent
Unto a man, whom to his wife he sent.

A kind of sergeant was this serving man,
Who had proved often faithful, as he'd found,
In matters great, and such men often can
Do evil faithfully, as can a hound.
The lord knew this man loved him and was bound;
And when this sergeant learned his lordship's will
He stalked into the chamber, grim and still.

"Madam," said he, "you must forgive it me,
Though I do that to which I am constrained;
You are so wise you know well, it may be,
That a lord's orders may not well be feigned;
They may be much lamented or complained,
But men must needs their every wish obey,
And thus will I; there is no more to say.

"This child I am commanded now to take"—
And spoke no more, but seized that innocent
Pitilessly, and did a gesture make
As if he would have slain it ere he went,
Griselda, she must suffer and consent;
And so, meek as a lamb, she sat there, still,
And let this cruel sergeant do his will.

Suspicious of repute was this same man,
Suspect his face, suspect his word also,
Suspect the time when this thing he began,
Alas! Her daughter that she had loved so,
She thought he'd slay it right there, whether or no.
Nevertheless, she neither wept nor sighed,
Doing the marquis' liking though she died.

At last she found her voice and thus began
And meekly to the sergeant then she prayed
That, as he was a worthy, gentle man,
She might kiss her child once before his blade;

And on her breast this little child she laid,
With sad face, and so kissed it and did press
And lulled it and at last began to bless.

And thus she said in her benignant voice:
"Farewell, my child that I no more shall see;
But now I've crossed you thus, I will rejoice
That of the Father blessed may you be,
Who died for us upon the bitter tree.
Your soul, my little child, to Him I give;
This night you die for my sake—though I live."

I think that to a nurse in such a case
It had been hard this pitiful thing to see;
Well might a mother then have cried "Alas!"
But so steadfastly serious was she
That she endured all her adversity,
And to the sergeant she but meekly said:
"I give you now again your little maid."

"Go now," said she, "and do my lord's behest,
But one thing will I pray you, of your grace,
That, save my lord forbade you, at the least
Bury this little body in some place
Where beasts nor birds will tear its limbs and face."
But no word to that purpose would he say,
But took the child and went upon his way.

This sergeant went unto his lord again
And of Griselda's words and of her cheer
He told him point by point, all short and plain,
And so presented him his daughter dear.
A little pity felt the marquis here;
Nevertheless, he held his purpose still,
As great lords do when they will have their will;

And bade the sergeant that he privily
Should softly swaddle the young child and wrap
With all the necessaries, tenderly,

And in a coffer or some garment lap;
But upon pain his head should meet mishap
No man should know the least of his intent,
Nor whence he came, nor whither that he went;

But to Bologna, to his sister dear
Who then was of Panago the countess,
He should take it, and tell of matters here,
Asking of her she do her busyness
This child to foster in all nobleness;
And whose the child was, that he bade her hide
From everyone, for aught that might betide.

The sergeant goes and has fulfilled this thing;
But to this marquis now return must we;
For soon he went to see her, wondering
If by his wife's demeanour he might see,
Or by her conversation learn that she
Were changed in aught; but her he could not find
Other than ever serious and kind.

As glad, as humble, as busy in service,
And even in love, as she was wont to be,
Was she to him at all times in each wise;
And of her daughter not a word spoke she.
No strange nor odd look of adversity
Was seen in her, and her dear daughter's name
She never named in earnest nor in game.

> *Explicit tercia pars.*
> *Sequitur pars quarta.*

In this way over them there passed four years
Ere she with child was; but as High God would,
A boy-child then she bore, as it appears,
By Walter, fair and pleasing to behold.
And when folk this word to the father told,
Not only he but all the people raised
Their joyous hymns to God and His grace praised.

When he was two years old and from the breast
Weaned by his nurse, it chanced upon a day
This marquis had another wish to test
And try his wife yet further, so they say.
Oh, needless her temptation in this way!
But wedded men no measure can observe
When they've a wife who's patient and will serve.

"Wife," said this marquis, "you have heard berore,
My people bear our marriage with ill will;
Particularly since my son you bore
Now it is worse than ever, all this ill.
Their murmurs all my heart and courage kill,
For to my ears come words so aimed to smart
That they have well-nigh broken all my heart.

"Now they say this: 'When Walter's dead and gone,
Then shall Janicula's base blood succeed
And be our lord, for other have we none!'
Such words my people say, 'tis true, indeed!
Well ought I of such murmurs to take heed;
For truly do I fear the populace,
Though they say nothing plainly to my face.

"I would exist in peace, if that I might;
Wherefore I am determined utterly
That as his sister served I, and by night,
Just so will I serve him full secretly;
And thus I warn you, that not suddenly
Out of yourself for woe you start or stray;
Be patient in this sorrow, so I pray."

"I have," said she, "said thus, and ever shall:
I'll have no thing, or not have, that's certain,
Save as you wish; nothing grieves me at all,
Even though my daughter and my son are slain
At your command, and that, I think, is plain.
I have had no part in my children twain
But sickness first, and after, woe and pain.

"You are our master; do with your own thing
Just as you like; no counsel ask of me.
For, as I left at home all my clothing
When first I came to you, just so," said she,
"Left I my will and all my liberty,
And took your clothing; wherefore do I pray
You'll do your pleasure, I'll your wish obey.

"For certainly, if I had prescience
Your will to know ere you your wish had told,
I would perform it without negligence;
But now I know the wish that you unfold,
To do your pleasure firmly will I hold;
For knew I that my death would give you ease,
Right gladly would I die, lord, you to please.

"For death can offer no loss that is known
Compared to your love's loss." And when, I say,
He saw his wife's great constancy, then down
He cast his eyes, and wondered at the way
She would in patience all his will obey;
And forth he went with dreary countenance,
But in his heart he knew a great pleasance.

This ugly sergeant in the very wise
That he her daughter took away, so he
(Or worse, if worse than this men could devise)
Has taken her son, the child of such beauty.
And always yet so all-patient was she
That she no sign gave forth of heaviness,
But kissed her son and so began to bless;

Save this: She prayed him that, and if he might,
Her son he'd bury in an earthen grave,
His tender limbs, so delicate to sight,
From ravenous birds and from all beasts to save.
But she no answer out of him could have.
He went his way as if he cared nor thought,
But to Bologna tenderly 'twas brought.

This marquis wondered ever more and more
Upon her patience; and indeed if he
Had not known truly in her years before
That she had loved her children perfectly,
He would have thought that out of subtlety
And malice, or from some urge more savage
She suffered this with calm face and courage.

But well he knew that, next himself, 'twas plain
She loved her children best in every wise.
But now to ask of women I am fain,
Whether these trials should not the man suffice?
What could an obdurate husband more devise
To prove her wifehood and her faithfulness,
And he continuing in his stubbornness?

But there are folk to such condition grown
That, when they do a certain purpose take,
They cannot quit the intent they thus own,
But just as they were bound unto a stake
They will not from that first hard purpose shake.
Just so this marquis fully was purposed
To test his wife, as he was first disposed.

He watched her, if by word or countenance
She show a change toward him, or in courage;
But never could he find a variance.
She was aye one in heart and in visage;
And aye the farther that she went in age,
The more true, if such thing were possible,
She was in love, and painstaking, as well.

From which it seemed that, as between those two,
There was but one will, for, to Walter's quest,
The same thing was her sole desire also,
And—God be thanked!—all fell out for the best.
She showed well that, in all this world's unrest,
A wife, of her volition, nothing should
Will to be done, save as her husband would.

The scandal of this Walter widely spread,
That, of his cruel heart, he'd wickedly
(Because a humble woman he had wed)
Murdered his two young children secretly.
Such murmurs went among them commonly.
No wonder, either, for to people's ear
There came no word but they'd been murdered there.

For which, whereas the people theretofore
Had loved him, now the scandal of such shame
Caused them to hate where they had loved before;
To be a murderer brings a hateful name.
Nevertheless, in earnest nor in game
Would he from this his cruel plan be bent;
To test his wife was all his fixed intent.

Now when his daughter was twelve years of age,
He to the court of Rome (in subtle wise
Informed of his design) sent his message,
Commanding them such bulls they should devise
As for his cruel purpose would suffice,
How that the pope, for Walter's people's rest,
Bade him to wed another, and the best.

I say, he ordered they should counterfeit
A papal bull and set it forth therein
That he had leave his first wife now to quit,
By papal dispensation, with no sin,
To stop all such dissension as did win
Between his folk and him; thus said the bull,
The which thing they did publish to the full.

The ignorant people, as no wonder is,
Supposed of course that things were even so;
But when Griselda's ears caught word of this,
I judge that then her heart was filled with woe.
But she, for ever steadfast, still did show
Herself disposed, this humble meek creature,
The adversity of Fortune to endure.

Abiding ever his wish and pleasure still,
To whom she had been given, heart and all,
He was her worldly hope, for good or ill;
But to tell all this briefly, if I shall,
This marquis wrote, in letter personal,
The devious working of his whole intent
And secretly 'twas to Bologna sent.

Unto Panago's count, who had, we know,
Wedded his sister, prayed he specially
To bring him home again his children two,
In honourable estate, all openly.
But one more thing he prayed him, utterly,
That he to no one, whoso should inquire,
Would tell who was their mother or their sire,

But say: The maiden married was to be
Unto Saluzzo's marquis, and anon.
And as this count was asked, so then did he;
For on day set he on his way was gone
Toward Saluzzo, with lords many a one,
In rich array, this maiden there to guide,
With her young brother riding at her side.

So toward her marriage went this fresh young maid,
Clad richly and bedecked with jewels clear;
Her brother with her, boyishly arrayed,
And all anew, was now in his eighth year.
And thus in great pomp and with merry cheer,
Toward Saluzzo went they on their way,
And rode along together day by day.

    Explicit quarta pars.
    Sequitur pars quinta.

Meanwhile, according to his wicked way,
This marquis, still to test his wife once more,
Even to the final proof of her, I say,
Fully to have experience to the core
If she were yet as steadfast as before,

He on a day in open audience
Loudly said unto her this rude sentence:

"Truly, Griselda, I'd much joy, perchance,
When you I took for wife, for your goodness
And for your truth and your obedience,
Not for your lineage nor your wealth, I guess;
But now I know, in utter certainness,
That in great lordship, if I well advise,
There is great servitude in sundry wise.

"I may not act as every plowman may;
My people have constrained me that I take
Another wife, and this they ask each day;
And now the pope, hot rancour thus to slake,
Consents, I dare the thing to undertake;
And truly now this much to you I'll say,
My new wife journeys hither on her way.

"Be strong of heart and leave at once her place,
And that same dower that you brought to me,
Take it again, I grant it of my grace;
Return you to your father's house." said he;
"No man may always have prosperity;
With a calm heart I urge you to endure
The stroke of Fortune or of adventure."

And she replied again, of her patience:
"My lord," said she, "I know, and knew alway,
How that between your own magnificence
And my poor state, no person can or may
Make a comparison in an equal way.
I never held me worthy or of grade
To be your wife, no, nor your chambermaid.

"And in this house, where lady you made me
(The High God do I take now to witness,
And as He truly may my soul's joy be),
I never held me lady nor mistress,
But only servant to your worthiness;

And ever shall, while my life may endure,
Beyond all worldly beings, that is sure.

"That you so long, of your benignity,
Have held me here in honour in this way,
Where I was never worthy, once, to be,
For that, thank God and you—to God I pray
He will reward you. There's no more to say.
Unto my father gladly will I wend
And dwell with him until my life shall end.

"Where I was fostered when an infant small,
There will I lead my life till I be dead,
A widow, clean in body, heart, and all.
For, since I gave to you my maidenhead,
And am your true and lawful wife, wedded,
May God forbid such a lord's wife to take
Another man for husband or love's sake.

"And of your new wife, may God of His grace
Grant you but joy and all prosperity:
For I will gladly yield to her my place,
Wherein so happy I was wont to be,
For since it pleases you, my lord," said she,
Who have been all my heart's ease and its rest,
That I shall go, I'll go when you request.

"But whereas now you proffer me such dower
As first I brought to you, it's in my mind
That 'twas my wretched clothes and nothing fair.
The which to me were hard now for to find.
O my good God! How noble and how kind
You seemed then, in your speech and in your face.
The day we married in that humble place.

"But truth is said—at least I find it true
For actually its proof is seen in me—
Old love is not the same as when it's new.
But truly, lord, for no adversity,
Though I should die of all this, shall it be

That ever in word or deed I shall repent
That I gave you my heart in whole intent.

"My lord, you know that, in my father's place,
You stripped from me my poor and humble weed
And clothed me richly, of your noble grace.
I brought you nothing else at all indeed,
Than faith and nakedness and maidenhead.
And here again my clothing I restore,
And, too, my wedding ring, for evermore.

"The rest of all your jewels, they will be
Within your chamber, as I dare maintain;
Naked out of my father's house," said she,
"I came, and naked I return again.
To follow aye your pleasure I am fain,
But yet I hope it is not your intent
That smockless from your palace I be sent.

"You could not do so base and shameful thing
That the same womb in which your children lay
Should, before all the folk, in my walking,
Be seen all bare; and therefore do I pray
Let me not like a worm go on my way.
Remember that, my own lord, always dear,
I was your wife, though I unworthy were.

"Wherefore, as guerdon for my maidenhead,
The which I brought, but shall not with me bear,
Let them but give me, for my only meed,
Such a poor smock as I was wont to wear,
That I therewith may hide the womb of her
Who was your wife; and here I take my leave
Of you, my own dear lord, lest you should grieve."

"The smock," said he, "that you have on your back,
Let it stay there and wear it forth," said he.
But firmness in so saying the man did lack;
But went his way for ruth and for pity.
Before the folk her body then stripped she

And in her smock, with head and feet all bare,
Toward her father's hovel did she fare.

The folk they followed, weeping and with cries,
And Fortune did they curse as they passed on;
But she with weeping did not wet her eyes,
And all this while of words she said not one.
Her father, who had heard this news anon,
Cursed then the day and hour when from the earth,
A living creature, nature gave him birth.

For, beyond any doubt, this poor old man
Had always feared the marquis soon would tire,
And doubted since the marriage first began,
If when the lord had satisfied desire,
He would not think a wife of station higher,
For one of his degree, had been more right,
And send her thence as soon as ever he might.

To meet his daughter hastily went he,
For he, by noise of folk, knew her coming;
And with her old coat, such as it might be,
He covered her, full sorrowfully weeping;
But the coat over her he could not bring,
For poor the cloth, and many days had passed
Since on her marriage day she wore it last.

Thus with her father, for a certain space,
Did dwell this flower of wifely meek patience,
Who neither by her words nor in her face,
Before the people nor in their absence,
Showed that she thought to her was done offense;
Nor of her high estate a remembrance
Had she, to judge by her calm countenance.

No wonder, though, for while in high estate,
Her soul kept ever full humility;
No mouth complaining, no heart delicate,
No pomp, no look of haughty royalty,
But full of patience and benignity,

Discreet and prideless, always honourable,
And to her husband meek and firm as well.

Men speak of Job and of his humbleness,
As clerks, when they so please, right well can write
Concerning men, but truth is, nevertheless,
Though clerks' praise of all women is but slight,
No man acquits himself in meekness quite
As women can, nor can be half so true
As women are, save this be something new.

   Explicit quinta pars.
   Sequitur pars sexta.

Now from Bologna is Panago come,
Whereof the word spread unto great and less,
And in the ears of people, all and some,
It was told, too, that a new marchioness
Came with him, in such pomp and such richness
That never had been seen with human eye
So noble array in all West Lombardy.

The marquis, who had planned and knew all this,
Before this count was come, a message sent
To poor Griselda, who had lost her bliss;
With humble heart and features glad she went
And on her knees before her lord she bent.
No pride of thought did her devotion dim;
She wisely and with reverence greeted him.

He said, "Griselda, hear what I shall say:
This maiden, who'll be wedded unto me,
Shall be received with splendour of array
As royally as in my house may be,
And, too, that everyone in his degree
Have his due rank in seating and service,
And high pleasance, as I can best devise.

"I have not serving women adequate
To set the rooms in order as I would,

And so I wish you here to regulate
All matters of the sort as mistress should.
You know of old the ways I think are good,
And though you're clothed in such a slattern's way,
Go do at least your duty as you may."

"Not only am I glad, my lord," said she,
"To do your wish, but I desire also
To serve you and to please in my degree;
This without wearying I'll always do.
And ever, lord, in happiness or woe,
The soul within my heart shall not forgo
To love you best with true intent, I know."

Then she began to put the house aright,
To set the tables and the beds to make;
And was at pains to do all that she might,
Praying the chambermaids, for good God's sake,
To make all haste and sweep hard and to shake;
And she, who was most serviceable of all,
Did every room array, and his wide hall.

About mid-morning did this count alight,
Who brought with him these noble children twain,
Whereat the people ran to see the sight
Of their array, so rich was all the train;
And for the first time did they not complain,
But said that Walter was no fool, at least,
To change his wife, for it was for the best.

For she was fairer far, so thought they all,
Than was Griselda, and of younger age,
And fairer fruit betwixt the two should fall,
And pleasing more, for her high lineage;
Her brother, too, so fair was of visage,
That, seeing them, the people all were glad,
Commending now the sense the marquis had.

"O storm-torn people! Unstable and untrue!
Aye indiscreet, and changing as a vane,

Delighting ever in rumour that is new,
For like the moon aye do you wax and wane;
Full of all chatter, dear at even a jane;
Your judgment's false, your constancy deceives,
A full great fool is he that you believes!"

Thus said the sober folk of that city,
Seeing the people staring up and down,
For they were glad, just for the novelty,
To have a young new lady of their town.
No more of this I'll mention or make known;
But to Griselda I'll myself address
To tell her constancy and busyness.

Full busy Griselda was in everything
That to the marquis' feast was pertinent;
Nothing was she confused by her clothing,
Though rude it was and somewhat badly rent.
But with a glad face to the gate she went,
With other folk, to greet the marchioness,
And afterward she did her busyness.

With so glad face his guests she did receive,
And with such tact, each one in his degree,
That no fault in it could a man perceive;
But all they wondered much who she might be
That in so poor array, as they could see,
Yet knew so much of rank and reverence;
And worthily they praised her high prudence.

In all this while she never once did cease
The maiden and her brother to commend
With kindness of a heart that was at peace,
So well that no man could her praise amend.
But at the last, when all these lords did wend
To seat themselves to dine, then did he call
Griselda, who was busy in his hall.

"Griselda," said he, as it were in play,
"How like you my new wife and her beauty?"

"Right well," said she, "my lord, for by my fay
A fairer saw I never than is she.
I pray that God give her prosperity;
And so I hope that to you both He'll send
Great happiness until your lives shall end.

"One thing I beg, my lord, and warn also,
That you prick not, with any tormenting,
This tender maid, as you've hurt others so;
For she's been nurtured in her up-bringing
More tenderly, and, to my own thinking,
She could not such adversity endure
As could one reared in circumstances poor."

And when this Walter thought of her patience,
Her glad face, with no malice there at all,
And how so oft he'd done to her offence,
And she aye firm and constant as a wall,
Remaining ever blameless through it all,
This cruel marquis did his heart address
To pity for her wifely steadfastness.

"This is enough, Griselda mine!" cried he,
"Be now no more ill pleased nor more afraid;
I have your faith and your benignity,
As straitly as ever woman's was, assayed
In high place and in poverty arrayed.
Now know I well, dear wife, your steadfastness."
And he began to kiss her and to press.

And she, for wonder, took of this no keep;
She heard not what the thing was he had cried;
She fared as if she'd started out of sleep,
Till from bewilderment she roused her pride.
"Griselda," said he, "by our God Who died,
You are my wife, no other one I have,
Nor ever had, as God my soul may save!

"This is your daughter, whom you have supposed
Should be my wife; the other child truly

Shall be my heir, as I have aye purposed;
You bore him in your body faithfully.
I've kept them at Bologna secretly;
Take them again, for now you cannot say
That you have lost your children twain for aye.

"And folk that otherwise have said of me,
I warn them well that I have done this deed
Neither for malice nor for cruelty,
But to make trial in you of virtue hid,
And not to slay my children, God forbid!
But just to keep them privily and still
Till I your purpose knew and all your will."

When she heard this, she swooned and down did fall
For pitiful joy, and after her swooning
Both her young children to her did she call,
And in her arms, full piteously weeping,
Embraced them, and all tenderly kissing,
As any mother would, with many a tear
She bathed their faces and their sunny hair.

Oh, what a pitiful thing it was to see
Her swooning, and her humble voice to hear!
"Thanks, lord, that I may thank you now," said she,
"That you have saved to me my children dear!
Now I am ready for my death right here;
Since I stand in your love and in your grace,
Death matters not, nor what my soul may face!

"O young, O dear, O tender children mine,
Your woeful mother thought for long, truly,
That cruel hounds, or birds, or foul vermin
Had eaten you; but God, of His mercy,
And your good father, all so tenderly,
Have kept you safely." And in swoon profound
Suddenly there she fell upon the ground.

And in her swoon so forcefully held she
Her children two, whom she'd had in embrace,

That it was hard from her to set them free,
Her arms about them gently to unlace.
Oh, many a tear on many a pitying face
Ran down, of those were standing there beside;
Scarcely, for sympathy, could they abide.

But Walter cheered her till her sorrow fled;
And she rose up, abashed, out of her trance;
All praised her now, and joyous words they said,
Till she regained her wonted countenance.
Walter so honoured her by word and glance
That it was pleasing to observe the cheer
Between them, now again together here.

These ladies, when they found a tactful way,
Withdrew her and to her own room were gone,
And stripped her out of her so rude array,
And in a cloth of gold that brightly shone,
Crowned with a crown of many a precious stone
Upon her head, once more to hall they brought
Her, where they honoured her as all they ought.

Thus had this heavy day a happy end,
For everyone did everything he might
The day in mirth and revelry to spend
Till in the heavens shone the stars' fair light.
For far more grand in every person's sight
This feast was, and of greater cost, 'twas said,
Than were the revels when they two were wed.

Full many a year in high prosperity
They lived, these two, in harmony and rest,
And splendidly his daughter married he
Unto a lord, one of the worthiest
In Italy; and then in peace, as best
His wife's old father at his court he kept
Until the soul out of his body crept.

His son succeeded to his heritage
In rest and peace, after the marquis' day,

And wedded happily at proper age,
Albeit he tried his wife not, so they say.
This world is not so harsh, deny who may,
As in old times that now are long since gone,
And hearken what this author says thereon.

This story's told here, not that all wives should
Follow Griselda in humility,
For this would be unbearable, though they would,
But just that everyone, in his degree,
Should be as constant in adversity
As was Griselda; for that Petrarch wrote
This tale, and in a high style, as you'll note.

For since a woman once was so patient
Before a mortal man, well more we ought
Receive in good part that which God has sent;
For cause he has to prove what He has wrought.
But He tempts no man that His blood has bought,
As James says, if you his epistle read;
Yet does He prove folk at all times, indeed,

And suffers us, for our good exercise,
With the sharp scourges of adversity
To be well beaten oft, in sundry wise;
Not just to learn our will; for truly He,
Ere we were born, did all our frailty see;
But for our good is all that He doth give.
So then in virtuous patience let us live.

But one word, masters, hearken ere I go:
One hardly can discover nowadays,
In all a town, Griseldas three or two;
For, if they should be put to such assays,
Their gold's so badly alloyed, in such ways,
With brass, that though the coin delight the eye,
'Twill rather break in two than bend, say I.

But now, for love of the good wife of Bath,
Whose life and all whose sex may God maintain

In mastery high, or else it were but scathe,
I will with joyous spirit fresh and green
Sing you a song to gladden you, I ween;
From all such serious matters let's be gone;
Hearken my song, which runs in this way on:

Envoy of Chaucer

Griselda's dead, and dead is her patience,
In Italy both lie buried, says the tale;
For which I cry in open audience,
That no man be so hardy as to assail
His own wife's patience, in a hope to find
Griselda, for 'tis certain he shall fail!

O noble wives, full of a high prudence,
Let not humility your free tongue nail,
Nor let some clerk have cause for diligence
To write of you so marvelous detail
As of Griselda, patient and so kind;
Lest Chichevache swallow you in her entrail!

Nay, follow Echo, that holds no silence,
But answers always like a countervail;
Be not befooled, for all your innocence,
But take the upper hand and you'll prevail.
And well impress this lesson on your mind,
For common profit, since it may avail.

Strong-minded women, stand at your defence,
Since you are strong as camel and don't ail,
Suffer no man to do to you offence;
And slender women in a contest frail,
Be savage as a tiger there in Ind;
Clatter like mill, say I, to beat the male.

Nay, fear them not, nor do them reverence;
For though your husband be all armed in mail,
The arrows of your shrewish eloquence
Shall pierce his breast and pierce his aventail.

In jealousy I counsel that you bind,
And you shall make him cower as does a quail.

If you are fair to see, in folks' presence.
Show them your face and with your clothes regale;
If you are foul, be lavish of expense,
To gain friends never cease to do travail;
Be lightsome as a linden leaf in wind,
And let him worry, weep, and wring, and wail!

The Merchant's Tale

The Merchant's Prologue

Of weeping and wailing, care and other sorrow
I know enough, at eventide and morrow,"
The merchant said, "and so do many more
Of married folk, I think, who this deplore,
For well I know that it is so with me.
I have a wife, the worst one that can be;
For though the foul Fiend to her wedded were,
She'd overmatch him, this I dare to swear.
How could I tell you anything special
Of her great malice? She is shrew in all.
There is a long and a large difference
Between Griselda's good and great patience
And my wife's more than common cruelty.
Were I unbound, as may I prosperous be!
I'd never another time fall in the snare.
We wedded men in sorrow live, and care;
Try it who will, and he shall truly find
I tell the truth, by Saint Thomas of Ind,
As for the greater part, I say not all.
Nay, God forbid that it should so befall!
   "Ah, good sir host! I have been married, lad,
These past two months, and no day more, by gad;
And yet I think that he whose days alive
Have been all wifeless, although men should rive
Him to the heart, he could in no wise clear
Tell you so much of sorrow as I here
Could tell you of my spouse's cursedness."
   "Now," said our host, "merchant, so God you bless,
Since you're so very learned in that art,
Full heartily, I pray you, tell us part."
   "Gladly," said he, "but of my own fresh sore,
For grief of heart I may not tell you more."

The Merchant's Tale

Once on a time there dwelt in Lombardy
One born in Pavia, a knight worthy,
And there he lived in great prosperity;
And sixty years a wifeless man was he,
And followed ever his bodily delight
In women, whereof was his appetite,
As these fool laymen will, so it appears.
And when he had so passed his sixty years,
Were it for piety or for dotage
I cannot say, but such a rapturous rage
Had this knight to become a wedded man
That day and night he did his best to scan
And spy a place where he might wedded be;
Praying Our Lord to grant to him that he
Might once know something of that blissful life
That is between a husband and his wife;
And so to live within that holy band
Wherein God first made man and woman stand.
"No other life," said he, "is worth a bean;
For wedlock is so easy and so clean
That in this world it is a paradise."
Thus said this ancient knight, who was so wise.
   And certainly, as sure as God is King,
To take a wife, it is a glorious thing,
Especially when a man is old and hoary;
Then is a wife the fruit of wealth and glory.
Then should he take a young wife and a fair,
On whom he may beget himself an heir,
And lead his life in joy and in solace,
Whereas these bachelors do but sing "Alas!"
When they fall into some adversity
In love, which is but childish vanity.
And truly, it is well that it is so
That bachelors have often pain and woe;
On shifting ground they build, and shiftiness
They find when they suppose they've certainness.
They live but as a bird does, or a beast,
In liberty and under no arrest,

Whereas a wedded man in his high state
Lives a life blissful, ordered, moderate,
Under the yoke of happy marriage bound;
Well may his heart in joy and bliss abound.
For who can be so docile as a wife?
Who is so true as she whose aim in life
Is comfort for him, sick or well, to make?
For weal or woe she will not him forsake.
She's ne'er too tired to love and serve, say I,
Though he may lie bedridden till he die.
And yet some writers say it is not so,
And Theophrastus is one such, I know.
What odds though Theophrastus chose to lie?
"Take not a wife," said he, "for husbandry,
If you would spare in household your expense;
A faithful servant does more diligence
To keep your goods than your own wedded wife.
For she will claim a half part all her life;
And if you should be sick, so God me save,
Your true friends or an honest serving knave
Will keep you better than she that waits, I say,
After your wealth, and has done, many a day.
And if you take a wife to have and hold,
Right easily may you become cuckold."
This judgment and a hundred such things worse
Did this man write, may God his dead bones curse?
But take no heed of all such vanity.
Defy old Theophrastus and hear me.
   A wife is God's own gift, aye verily;
All other kinds of gifts, most certainly,
As lands, rents, pasture, rights in common land,
Or moveables, in gift of Fortune stand,
And pass away like shadows on the wall.
But, without doubt, if plainly speak I shall,
A wife will last, and in your house endure
Longer than you would like, peradventure.
   But marriage is a solemn sacrament;
Who has no wife I hold on ruin bent;
He lives in helplessness, all desolate,
I speak of folk in secular estate.

And hearken why, I say not this for naught:
It's because woman was for man's help wrought.
The High God, when He'd Adam made, all rude,
And saw him so alone and belly-nude,
God of His goodness thus to speak began:
"Let us now make a help meet for this man,
Like to himself." And then he made him Eve.
Here may you see, and here prove, I believe,
A wife is a man's help and his comfort,
His earthly paradise and means of sport;
So docile and so virtuous is she
That they must needs live in all harmony.
One flesh they are, and one flesh, as I guess,
Has but one heart in weal and in distress.
   A wife! Ah, Holy Mary, *ben'cite!*
How may a man have any adversity
Who has a wife? Truly, I cannot say.
The bliss that is between such two, for aye,
No tongue can tell, nor any heart can think.
If he be poor, why, she helps him to swink;
She keeps his money and never wastes a deal;
All that her husband wishes she likes well;
She never once says "nay" when he says "yea."
"Do this," says he; "All ready, sir," she'll say.
O blissful state of wedlock, prized and dear,
So pleasant and so full of virtue clear,
So much approved and praised as fortune's peak,
That every man who holds him worth a leek
Upon his bare knees ought, through all his life,
To give God thanks, Who's sent to him a wife;
Or else he should pray God that He will send
A wife to him, to last till his life's end.
For then his life is set in certainness;
He cannot be deceived, as I may guess,
So that he act according as she's said;
Then may he boldly carry high his head,
They are so true and therewithal so wise;
Wherefore, if you will do as do the wise,
Then aye as women counsel be your deed.
   Lo, how young Jacob, as these clerics read,

About his hairless neck a kid's skin bound,
A trick that Dame Rebecca for him found,
By which his father's benison he won.

Lo, Judith, as the ancient stories run,
By her wise counsel she God's people kept,
And Holofernes slew, while yet he slept.

Lo, Abigail, by good advice how she
Did save her husband, Nabal, when that he
Should have been slain; and lo, Esther also
By good advice delivered out of woe
The people of God and got him, Mordecai,
By King Ahasuerus lifted high.

There is no pleasure so superlative
(Says Seneca) as a humble wife can give.

Suffer your wife's tongue, Cato bids, as fit;
She shall command, and you shall suffer it;
And yet she will obey, of courtesy.
A wife is keeper of your husbandry;
Well may the sick man wail and even weep
Who has no wife the house to clean and keep.
I warn you now, if wisely you would work,
Love well your wife, as Jesus loves His Kirk.
For if you love yourself, you love your wife;
No man hates his own flesh, but through his life
He fosters it, and so I bid you strive
To cherish her, or you shall never thrive.
Husband and wife, despite men's jape or play,
Of all the world's folk hold the safest way;
They are so knit there may no harm betide,
Especially upon the good wife's side.
For which this January, of whom I told,
Did well consider in his days grown old,
The pleasant life, the virtuous rest complete
That are in marriage, always honey-sweet;
And for his friends upon a day he sent
To tell them the effect of his intent.

With sober face his tale to them he's told;
He said to them: "My friends, I'm hoar and old,
And almost, God knows, come to my grave's brink;
About my soul, now, somewhat must I think.

I have my body foolishly expended;
Blessed be God, that thing shall be amended!
For I will be, truly, a wedded man,
And that anon, in all the haste I can,
Unto some maiden young in age and fair.
I pray you for my marriage all prepare,
And do so now, for I will not abide;
And I will try to find one, on my side,
To whom I may be wedded speedily.
But for as much as you are more than I,
It's better that you have the thing in mind
And try a proper mate for me to find.
     "But of one thing I warn you, my friends dear,
I will not have an old wife coming here.
She shan't have more than twenty years, that's plain;
Of old fish and young flesh I am full fain.
Better," said he, "a pike than pickerel;
And better than old beef is tender veal.
I'll have no woman thirty years of age,
It is but bean-straw and such rough forage.
And these old widows, God knows that, afloat,
They know so much of spells when on Wade's boat,
And do such petty harm, when they think best,
That with one should I never live at rest.
For several schools can make men clever clerks;
Woman in many schools learns clever works.
But certainly a young thing men may guide,
Just as warm wax may with one's hands be plied.
Wherefore I tell you plainly, in a clause,
I will not have an old wife, for that cause.
For if it chanced I made that sad mistake
And never in her could my pleasure take,
My life I'd lead then in adultery
And go straight to the devil when I die.
     No children should I then on her beget;
Yet would I rather hounds my flesh should fret
Than that my heritage descend and fall
Into strange hands, and this I tell you all.
I dote not, and I know the reason why
A man should marry, and furthermore know I

There speaks full many a man of all marriage
Who knows no more of it than knows my page,
Nor for what reasons man should take a wife.
If one may not live chastely all his life,
Let him take wife whose quality he's known
For lawful procreation of his own
Blood children, to the honour of God above,
And not alone for passion or for love;
And because lechery they should eschew
And do their family duty when it's due;
Or because each of them should help the other
In trouble, as a sister shall a brother;
And live in chastity full decently.
But, sirs, and by your leave, that is not I.
For, God be thanked, I dare to make a vaunt,
I feel my limbs are strong and fit to jaunt
In doing all man's are expected to;
I know myself and know what I can do.
Though I am hoar, I fare as does a tree
That blossoms ere the fruit be grown; you see
A blooming tree is neither dry nor dead.
And I feel nowhere hoary but on head;
My heart and all my limbs are still as green
As laurel through the year is to be seen.
And now that you have heard all my intent,
I pray that to my wish you will assent."
   Then divers men to him diversely told,
Of marriage, many an instance known of old.
Some blamed it and some praised it, that's certain,
But at the last, and briefly to make plain,
Since altercation follows soon or late
When friends begin such matters to debate,
There fell a strife between his brothers two,
Whereof the name of one was Placebo
And verily Justinus was that other.
   Placebo said: "O January, brother,
Full little need had you, my lord so dear,
Counsel to ask of anyone that's here;
Save that you are so full of sapience
That you like not, what of your high prudence,

To vary from the word of Solomon.
This word said he to each and every one:
'Do everything by counsel,' thus said he,
'And then thou hast no cause to repent thee.'
But although Solomon spoke such a word,
My own dear brother and my proper lord,
So truly may God bring my soul to rest
As I hold your own counsel is the best.
For, brother mine, of me take this one word,
I've been a courtier all my days, my lord.
And God knows well, though I unworthy be,
I have stood well, and in full great degree,
With many lords of very high estate;
Yet ne'er with one of them had I debate.
I never contradicted, certainly;
I know well that my lord knows more than I.
Whate'er he says, I hold it firm and stable;
I say the same, or nearly as I'm able.
A full great fool is any councillor
That serves a lord of any high honour
And dares presume to say, or else think it,
His counsel can surpass his lordship's wit.
Nay, lords are never fools, nay, by my fay;
You have yourself, sir, showed, and here today,
With such good sense and piety withal
That I assent to and confirm it all,
The words and the opinions you have shown.
By God, there is no man in all this town,
Or Italy, it better could have phrased;
And Christ Himself your counsel would have praised.
And truthfully, it argues high courage
In any man that is advanced in age
To take a young wife; by my father's kin,
A merry heart you've got beneath your skin!
Do in this matter at your own behest,
For, finally, I hold that for the best."
   Justinus, who sat still and calm, and heard,
Right in this wise Placebo he answered:
"Now, brother mine, be patient, so I pray;
Since you have spoken, hear what I shall say.

For Seneca, among his words so wise,
Says that a man ought well himself advise
To whom he'll give his chattels or his land.
And since I ought to know just where I stand
Before I give my wealth away from me,
How much more well advised I ought to be
To whom I give my body; for alway
I warn you well, that it is not child's play
To take a wife without much advisement.
Men must inquire, and this is my intent,
Whether she's wise, or sober, or drunkard,
Or proud, or else in other things froward,
Or shrewish, or a waster of what's had,
Or rich, or poor, or whether she's man-mad.
And be it true that no man finds, or shall,
One in this world that perfect is in all,
Of man or beast, such as men could devise;
Nevertheless, it ought enough suffice
With any wife, if so were that she had
More traits of virtue that her vices bad;
And all this leisure asks to see and hear.
For God knows I have wept full many a tear
In privity, since I have had a wife.
Praise whoso will a wedded man's good life,
Truly I find in it but cost and care
And many duties, of all blisses bare.
And yet, God knows, my neighbours round about,
Especially the women, many a rout,
Say that I've married the most steadfast wife,
Aye, and the meekest one there is in life.
But I know best where pinches me my shoe.
You may, for me, do as you please to do;
But take good heed, since you're a man of age,
How you shall enter into a marriage,
Especially with a young wife and a fair.
By Him Who made the water, earth, and air,
The youngest man there is in all this rout
Is busy enough to bring the thing about
That he alone shall have his wife, trust me.
You'll not be able to please her through years three,

That is to say, to give all she desires.
A wife attention all the while requires.
I pray you that you be not offended."
    "Well?" asked this January, "And have you said?
A straw for Seneca and your proverbs!
I value not a basketful of herbs
Your schoolmen's terms; for wiser men than you,
As you have heard, assent and bid me do
My purpose now. Placebo, what say ye?"
    "I say it is a wicked man," said he,
"That hinders matrimony, certainly."
    And with that word they rose up, suddenly,
Having assented fully that he should
Be wedded when he pleased and where he would.
    Imagination and his eagerness
Did in the soul of January press
As he considered marriage for a space.
Many fair shapes and many a lovely face
Passed through his amorous fancy, night by night.
As who might take a mirror polished bright
And set it in the common marketplace
And then should see full many a figure pace
Within the mirror; just in that same wise
Did January within his thought surmise
Of maidens whom he dwelt in town beside.
He knew not where his fancy might abide.
For if the one have beauty of her face,
Another stands so in the people's grace
For soberness and for benignity,
That all the people's choice she seems to be;
And some were rich and had an evil name.
Nevertheless, half earnest, half in game,
He fixed at last upon a certain one
And let all others from his heart be gone,
And chose her on his own authority;
For love is always blind and cannot see.
And when in bed at night, why then he wrought
To portray, in his heart and in his thought,
Her beauty fresh and her young age, so tender,
Her middle small, her two arms long and slender,

Her management full wise, her gentleness,
Her womanly bearing, and her seriousness.
And when to her at last his choice descended,
He thought that choice might never be amended.
For when he had concluded thus, egad,
He thought that other men had wits so bad
It were impossible to make reply
Against his choice, this was his fantasy.
His friends he sent to, at his own instance,
And prayed them give him, in this wise, pleasance,
That speedily they would set forth and come:
He would abridge their labour, all and some.
He need not more to walk about or ride,
For he'd determined where he would abide.

　　Placebo came, and all his friends came soon,
And first of all he asked of them the boon
That none of them an argument should make
Against the course he fully meant to take;
"Which purpose pleasing is to God," said he,
"And the true ground of my felicity."

　　He said there was a maiden in the town
Who had for beauty come to great renown,
Despite the fact she was of small degree;
Sufficed him well her youth and her beauty.
Which maid, he said, he wanted for his wife,
To lead in ease and decency his life.
And he thanked God that he might have her, all,
That none partook of his bliss now, nor shall.
And prayed them all to labour in this need
And so arrange that he'd fail not, indeed;
For then, he said, his soul should be at ease.

　　"And then," said he, "there's naught can me displease,
Save one lone thing that sticks in my conscience,
The which I will recite in your presence.

　　"I have," said he, "heard said, and long ago,
There may no man have perfect blisses two,
That is to say, on earth and then in Heaven.
For though he keep from sins the deadly seven,
And, too, from every branch of that same tree,
Yet is there so complete felicity

And such great pleasure in the married state
That I am fearful, since it comes so late,
That I shall lead so merry and fine a life,
And so delicious, without woe and strife,
That I shall have my heaven on earth here.
For since that other Heaven is bought so dear,
With tribulation and with great penance,
How should I then, who live in such pleasance,
As all these wedded men do with their wives,
Come to the bliss where Christ Eternal lives?
This is my fear, and you, my brothers, pray
Resolve for me this problem now, I say."
     Justinus, who so hated this folly,
Answered anon in jesting wise and free;
And since he would his longish tale abridge,
He would no old authority allege,
But said: "Sir, so there is no obstacle
Other than this, God, of high miracle
And of His mercy, may so for you work
That, ere you have your right of Holy Kirk,
You'll change your mind on wedded husband's life,
Wherein you say there is no woe or strife.
And otherwise, God grant that there be sent
To wedded man the fair grace to repent
Often, and sooner than a single man!
And therefore, sir, this is the best I can:
Despair not, but retain in memory,
Perhaps she may your purgatory be!
She may be God's tool, she may be God's whip;
Then shall your spirit up to Heaven skip
Swifter than does an arrow from the bow!
I hope to God, hereafter you shall know
That there is none so great felicity
In marriage, no nor ever shall there be,
To keep you from salvation that's your own,
So that you use, with reason that's well-known,
The charms of your wife's body temperately,
And that you please her not too amorously,
And that you keep as well from other sin.
My tale is done now, for my wit is thin.

Be not deterred hereby, my brother dear"—
   (But let us pass quite over what's said here.
The wife of Bath, if you have understood,
Has treated marriage, in its likelihood,
And spoken well of it in little space)—
"Fare you well now, God have you in His grace."
   And with that word this Justin and his brother
Did take their leave, and each of them from other.
For when they all saw that it must needs be,
They so arranged, by sly and wise treaty,
That she, this maiden, who was Maia hight,
As speedily indeed as ever she might,
Should wedded be unto this January.
I think it were too long a time to tarry
To tell of deed and bond between them, and
The way she was enfeoffed of all his land;
Or to hear tell of all her rich array.
But finally was come the happy day
When to the church together they two went,
There to receive the holy sacrament.
Forth came the priest with stole about his neck,
Saying of Rebecca and Sarah she should reck
For wisdom and for truth in her marriage;
And said his orisons, as is usage,
And crossed them, praying God that He should bless,
And made all tight enough with holiness.
   Thus are they wedded with solemnity,
And at the feast are sitting, he and she,
With other worthy folk upon the dais.
All full of joy and bliss the palace gay is,
And full of instruments and viandry,
The daintiest in all of Italy.
Before them played such instruments anon
That Orpheus or Theban Amphion
Never in life made such a melody.
   With every course there rose loud minstrelsy,
And never Joab sounded trump, to hear,
Nor did Theodomas, one half so clear
At Thebes, while yet the city hung in doubt.
Bacchus the wine poured out for all about,

And Venus gaily laughed for every wight.
For January had become her knight,
And would make trial of his amorous power
In liberty and in the bridal bower;
And with her firebrand in her hand, about
Danced she before the bride and all the rout.
And certainly I dare right well say this,
That Hymenaeus, god of wedded bliss,
Ne'er saw in life so merry a married man.
Hold thou thy peace, thou poet Marcian
Who tellest how Philology was wed
And how with Mercury she went to bed,
And of the sweet songs by the Muses sung.
Too slight are both thy pen and thy thin tongue
To show aright this wedding on thy page.
When tender youth has wedded stooping age,
There is such mirth that no one may it show;
Try it yourself, and then you well will know
Whether I lie or not in matters here.
    Maia, she sat there with so gentle cheer,
To look at her it seemed like faëry;
Queen Esther never looked with such an eye
Upon Ahasuerus, so meek was she.
I can't describe to you all her beauty;
But thus much of her beauty I can say,
That she was like the brightening morn of May,
Fulfilled of beauty and of all pleasance.
    January was rapt into a trance
With each time that he looked upon her face;
And in his heart her beauty he'd embrace,
And threatened in his arms to hold her tight,
Harder than Paris Helen did, that night.
But nonetheless great pity, too, had he
Because that night she must deflowered be;
And thought: "Alas! O tender young creature!
Now would God you may easily endure
All my desire, it is so sharp and keen.
I fear you can't sustain it long, my queen.
But God forbid that I do all I might!
And now would God that it were come to night,

And that the night would last for ever—oh,
I wish these people would arise and go."
And at the last he laboured all in all,
As best he might for manners there in hall,
To haste them from the feast in subtle wise.
    Time came when it was right that they should rise;
And after that men danced and drank right fast,
And spices all about the house they cast;
And full of bliss and joy was every man,
All but a squire, a youth called Damian,
Who'd carved before the knight full many a day.
He was so ravished by his Lady May
That for the very pain, as madman would,
Almost he fell down fainting where he stood.
So sore had Venus hurt him with her brand,
When she went dancing, bearing it in hand.
And to his bed he took him speedily;
No more of him just at this time say I.
I'll let him weep his fill, with woe complain,
Until fresh May have ruth upon his pain.
    O parlous fire that in the bedstraw breeds!
O foe familiar that his service speeds!
O treacherous servant, false domestic who
Is most like adder in bosom, sly, untrue,
God shield us all from knowing aught of you!
O January, drunk of pleasure's brew
In marriage, see how now your Damian,
Your own trained personal squire, born your man,
Wishes and means to do you villainy.
God grant that on this household foe you'll spy!
For in this world no pestilence is worse
Than foe domestic, constantly a curse.
    When traversed has the sun his arc of day,
No longer may the body of him stay
On the horizon, in that latitude.
Night with his mantle, which is dark and rude,
Did overspread the hemisphere about;
And so departed had this joyous rout
From January, with thanks on every side.
Home to their houses happily they ride,

Whereat they do what things may please them best,
And when they see the time come, go to rest.
Soon after that this hasty January
Would go to bed, he would no longer tarry.
He drank of claret, hippocras, vernage,
All spiced and hot to heighten his love's rage;
And many an aphrodisiac, full and fine,
Such as the wicked monk, Dan Constantine,
Has written in his book *De Coitu*;
Not one of all of them he did eschew.
And to his friends most intimate, said he:
"For God's love, and as soon as it may be,
Let all now leave this house in courteous wise."
And all they rose, just as he bade them rise.
They drank good-night, and curtains drew anon;
The bride was brought to bed, as still as stone;
And when the bed had been by priest well blessed,
Out of the chamber everyone progressed.
And January lay down close beside
His fresh young May, his paradise, his bride.
He soothed her, and he kissed her much and oft,
With the thick bristles of his beard, not soft,
But sharp as briars, like a dogfish skin,
For he'd been badly shaved ere he came in.
He stroked and rubbed her on her tender face,
And said: "Alas! I fear I'll do trespass
Against you here, my spouse, and much offend
Before the time when I will down descend.
But nonetheless, consider this," said he,
"There is no workman, whosoe'er he be,
That may work well, if he works hastily;
This will be done at leisure, perfectly.
It makes no difference how long we two play;
For in true wedlock were we tied today;
And blessed be the yoke that we are in,
For in our acts, now, we can do no sin.
A man can do no sin with his own wife,
Nor can he hurt himself with his own knife;
For we have leave most lawfully to play."
Thus laboured he till came the dawn of day;

And then he took in wine a sop of bread,
And upright sat within the marriage bed,
And after that he sang full loud and clear
And kissed his wife and made much wanton cheer.
He was all coltish, full of venery,
And full of chatter as a speckled pie.
The slackened skin about his neck did shake
The while he sang and chanted like a crake.
But God knows what thing May thought in her heart
When up she saw him sitting in his shirt,
In his nightcap, and with his neck so lean;
She valued not his playing worth a bean.
Then said he thus: "My rest now will I take;
Now day is come, I can no longer wake."
And down he laid his head and slept till prime.
And afterward, when saw he it was time,
Up rose this January; but fresh May,
She kept her chamber until the fourth day,
As custom is of wives, and for the best.
For every worker sometime must have rest,
Or else for long he'll certainly not thrive,
That is to say, no creature that's alive,
Be it of fish, or bird, or beast, or man.
     Now will I speak of woeful Damian,
Who languished for his love, as you shall hear;
I thus address him in this fashion here.
I say: "O hapless Damian, alas!
Answer to my demand in this your case,
How shall you to your lady, lovely May,
Tell all your woe? She would of course say 'Nay.'
And if you speak, she will your state betray;
God be your help! I can no better say."
     This lovesick Damian in Venus' fire
So burned, he almost perished for desire;
Which put his life in danger, I am sure;
Longer in this wise could he not endure;
But privily a pen-case did he borrow
And in a letter wrote he all his sorrow,
In form of a complaint or of a lay,
Unto his fair and blooming Lady May.

And in a purse of silk hung in his shirt,
He put the poem and laid it next his heart.
   The moon, which was at noon of that same day
Whereon this January wedded May
Half way through Taurus, had to Cancer glided,
So long had Maia in her chamber bided.
As is the custom among nobles all.
A bride shall not eat in the common hall
Until four days, or three days at the least,
Have fully passed; then let her go to feast.
On the fourth day, complete from noon to noon,
After the high Mass had been said and done,
In hall did January sit with May
As fresh as is the fair bright summer day.
And so befell it there that this good man
Recalled to mind his squire, this Damian,
And said: "Why holy Mary! How can it be
That Damian attends not here on me?
Is he sick always? How may this betide?"
His other squires, who waited there beside,
Made the excuse that he indeed was ill,
Which kept him from his proper duties still;
There was no other cause could make him tarry.
"That is a pity," said this January,
"He is a gentle squire, aye, by my truth!
If he should die, it were great harm and ruth;
As wise and secret, and discreet is he
As any man I know of his degree;
Therewith he's manly and he's serviceable,
And to become a useful man right able.
But after meat, as soon as ever I may,
I will myself go visit him, with May,
To give him all the comfort that I can."
And for that word they blessed him, every man,
Because, for goodness and his gentleness,
He would so go to comfort, in sickness,
His suffering squire, for 'twas a gentle deed.
"Dame," said this January, "take good heed
That after meat, you, with your women all,
When you have gone to chamber from this hall—

That all you go to see this Damian;
Cheer him a bit, for he's a gentleman;
And tell him that I'll come to visit him
After I've rested—a short interim;
And get this over quickly, for I'll bide
Awake until you sleep there at my side."
   And with that word he raised his voice to call
A squire, who served as marshal of his hall,
And certain things he wished arranged were told.
   This lovely May then did her straight way hold,
With all her women, unto Damian.
Down by his bed she sat, and so began
To comfort him with kindly word and glance.
This Damian, when once he'd found his chance,
In secret wise his purse and letter, too,
Wherein he'd said what he aspired to,
He put into her hand, with nothing more,
Save that he heaved a sigh both deep and sore,
And softly to her in this wise said he:
"Oh, mercy! Don't, I beg you, tell on me;
For I'm but dead if this thing be made known."
This purse she hid in bosom of her gown
And went her way; you get no more of me.
But unto January then came she,
Who on his bedside sat in mood full soft.
He took her in his arms and kissed her oft,
And laid him down to sleep, and that anon.
And she pretended that she must be gone
Where you know well that everyone has need.
And when she of this note had taken heed,
She tore it all to fragments at the last
And down the privy quietly it cast.
   Who's in brown study now but fair fresh May?
Down by old January's side she lay,
Who slept, until the cough awakened him;
He prayed her strip all naked for his whim;
He would have pleasure of her, so he said,
And clothes were an encumbrance when in bed,
And she obeyed him, whether lief or loath.
But lest these precious folk be with me wroth,

How there he worked, I dare not to you tell;
Nor whether she thought it paradise or hell;
But there I leave them working in their wise
Till vespers rang and they must needs arise.
   Were it by destiny or merely chance,
By nature or some other circumstance,
Or constellation's sign, that in such state
The heavens stood, the time was fortunate
To make request concerning Venus' works
(For there's a time for all things, say these clerks)
To any woman, to procure her love,
I cannot say; but the great God above,
Who knows there's no effect without a cause,
He may judge all, for here my voice withdraws.
But true it is that this fair blooming May
Was so affected and impressed that day
For pity of this lovesick Damian,
That from her heart she could not drive or ban
Remembrance of her wish to give him ease.
"Certainly," thought she, "whom this may displease
I do not care, for I'd assure him now
Him with my love I'd willingly endow,
Though he'd no more of riches than his shirt."
Lo, pity soon wells up in gentle heart.
   Here may you see what generosity
In women is when they advise closely.
Perhaps some tyrant (for there's many a one)
Who has a heart as hard as any stone,
Would well have let him die within that place
Much rather than have granted him her grace;
And such would have rejoiced in cruel pride,
Nor cared that she were thus a homicide.
   This gentle May, fulfilled of all pity,
With her own hand a letter then wrote she
In which she granted him her utmost grace;
There was naught lacking now, save time and place
Wherein she might suffice to ease his lust:
For all should be as he would have it, just.
And when she'd opportunity on a day,
To visit Damian went this lovely May,

And cleverly this letter she thrust close
Under his pillow, read it if he chose.
She took him by the hand and hard did press,
So secretly that no one else could guess,
And bade him gain his health, and forth she went
To January, when for her he sent.
   Up rose this Damian upon the morrow,
For gone was all his sickness and his sorrow.
He combed himself and preened his feathers smooth,
He did all that his lady liked, in sooth;
And then to January went as low
As ever did a hound trained to the bow.
He was so pleasant unto every man
(For craft is everything for those who can),
That everyone was fain to speak his good;
And fully in his lady's grace he stood.
Thus Damian I leave about his need
And forward in my tale I will proceed.
   Some writers hold that all felicity
Stands in delight, and therefor, certainly,
This noble January, with all his might,
Honourably, as does befit a knight,
Arranged affairs to live deliciously.
His housing, his array, as splendidly
Befitted his condition as a king's.
Among the rest of his luxurious things
He built a garden walled about with stone:
So fair a garden do I know of none.
For, without doubt, I verily suppose
That he who wrote *The Romance of the Rose*
Could not its beauty say in singing wise;
Nor could Priapus' power quite suffice,
Though he is god of gardens all, to tell
The beauty of that garden, and the well
Which was beneath the laurel always green.
For oftentimes God Pluto and his queen,
Fair Proserpine and all her faëry
Disported there and made sweet melody
About that well, and danced there, as men told.
   This noble knight, this January old,

Such pleasure had therein to walk and play,
That none he'd suffer bear the key, they say,
Save he himself; for of the little wicket
He carried always the small silver clicket
With which, as pleased him, he'd unlock the gate.
And when he chose to pay court to his mate
In summer season, thither would he go
With May, his wife, and no one but they two;
And divers things that were not done abed,
Within that garden there were done, 'tis said.
And in this manner many a merry day
Lived this old January and young May.
But worldly pleasure cannot always stay,
And January's joy must pass away.

   O sudden chance, O Fortune, thou unstable,
Like to the scorpion so deceptive, able
To flatter with thy mouth when thou wilt sting;
Thy tail is death, through thine envenoming.
O fragile joy! O poison sweetly taint!
O monster that so cleverly canst paint
Thy gifts in all the hues of steadfastness
That thou deceivest both the great and less!
Why hast thou January thus deceived,
That had'st him for thine own full friend received?
And now thou hast bereft him of his eyes,
For sorrow of which in love he daily dies.

    Alas! This noble January free,
In all his pleasure and prosperity,
Is fallen blind, and that all suddenly.
He wept and he lamented, pitifully;
And therewithal the fire of jealousy
Lest that his wife should fall to some folly,
So burned within his heart that he would fain
Both him and her some man had swiftly slain.
For neither after death nor in his life
Would he that she were other's love or wife,
But dress in black and live in widow's state,
Lone as the turtledove that's lost her mate.
But finally, after a month or twain,
His grief somewhat abated, to speak plain;

For when he knew it might not elsewise be,
He took in patience his adversity,
Save, doubtless, he could not renounce, as done,
His jealousy, from which he never won.
For this his passion was so outrageous
That neither in his hall nor other house
Nor any other place, not ever, no,
He suffered her to ride or walking go,
Unless he had his hand on her alway;
For which did often weep this fresh young May,
Who loved her Damian so tenderly
That she must either swiftly die or she
Must have him as she willed, her thirst to slake;
Biding her time, she thought her heart would break.

   And on the other side this Damian
Was now become the most disconsolate man
That ever was; for neither night nor day
Might he so much as speak a word to May
Of his desire, as I am telling here,
Save it were said to January's ear,
Who never took his blind hand off her, no.
Nevertheless, by writing to and fro
And secret signals, he knew what she meant;
And she too knew the aim of his intent.
O January, what might it now avail
Could your eyes see as far as ships can sail?
For it's as pleasant, blind, deceived to be
As be deceived while yet a man may see.
Lo, Argus, who was called the hundred-eyed,
No matter how he peered and watched and pried,
He was deceived; and God knows others too
Who think, and firmly, that it is not so.
Oblivion is peace; I say no more.

   This lovely May, of whom I spoke before,
In warm wax made impression of the key
Her husband carried, to the gate where he
In entering his garden often went.
And Damian, who knew all her intent,
The key did counterfeit, and privately;
There is no more to say, but speedily

Some mischief of this latchkey shall betide,
Which you shall hear, if you but time will bide.
   O noble Ovid, truth you say, God wot!
What art is there, though it be long and hot,
But Love will find it somehow suits his turn?
By Pyramus and Thisbe may men learn;
Though they were strictly kept apart in all,
They soon accorded, whispering through a wall,
Where none could have suspected any gate.
But now to purpose: ere had passed days eight,
And ere the first day of July, befell
That January was under such a spell,
Through egging of his wife, to go and play
Within his garden, and no one but they,
That on a morning to this May said he:
"Rise up, my wife, my love, my lady free;
The turtle's voice is heard, my dove so sweet;
The winter's past, the rain's gone, and the sleet;
Come forth now with your two eyes columbine!
How sweeter are your breasts than is sweet wine!
The garden is enclosed and walled about;
Come forth, my white spouse, for beyond all doubt
You have me ravished in my heart, O wife!
No fault have I found in you in my life.
Come forth, come forth, and let us take our sport;
I chose you for my wife and my comfort."
   Such were the lewd old words that then used he;
To Damian a secret sign made she
That he should go before them with his clicket;
This Damian then opened up the wicket,
And in he slipped, and that in manner such
That none could see nor hear; and he did crouch
And still he sat beneath a bush anon.
   This January, blind as is a stone,
With Maia's hand in his, and none else there,
Into his garden went, so fresh and fair,
And then clapped to the wicket suddenly.
   "Now, wife," said he, "here's none but you and I,
And you're the one of all that I best love.
For by that Lord Who sits in Heaven above,

Far rather would I die upon a knife
Than do offence to you, my true, dear wife!
For God's sake think how I did choose you out,
And for no love of money, beyond doubt,
But only for the love you roused in me.
And though I am grown old and cannot see,
Be true to me, and I will tell you why.
Three things, it's certain, shall you gain thereby;
First, Christ's dear love, and honour of your own,
And all my heritage of tower and town;
I give it you, draw deeds to please you, pet;
This shall be done tomorrow ere sunset.
So truly may God bring my soul to bliss,
I pray you first, in covenant, that we kiss.
And though I'm jealous, yet reproach me not.
You are so deeply printed in my thought
That, when I do consider your beauty
And therewith all the unlovely age of me,
I cannot, truly, nay, though I should die,
Abstain from being in your company,
For utter love; of this there is no doubt.
Now kiss me, wife, and let us walk about."
    This blooming May, when these words she had heard,
Graciously January she answered,
But first and foremost she began to weep.
"I have also," said she, "a soul to keep,
As well as you, and also honour mine,
And of my wifehood that sweet flower divine
Which I assured you of, both safe and sound,
When unto you that priest my body bound;
Wherefore I'll answer you in this manner,
If I may by your leave, my lord so dear.
I pray to God that never dawns the day
That I'll not die, foully as woman may,
If ever I do unto my kin such shame,
And likewise damage so my own fair name,
As to be false; and if I grow so slack,
Strip me and put me naked in a sack
And in the nearest river let me drown.
I am a lady, not a wench of town.

Why speak you thus? Men ever are untrue,
And woman have reproaches always new.
No reason or excuse have you, I think,
And so you harp on women who hoodwink."

   And with that word she saw where Damian
Sat under bush; to cough then she began,
And with her slender finger signs made she
That Damian should climb into a tree
That burdened was with fruit, and up he went;
For verily he knew her full intent,
And understood each sign that she could make,
Better than January, her old rake.
For in a letter she had told him all
Of how he should proceed when time should fall.
And thus I leave him in the pear tree still
While May and January roam at will.

   Bright was the day and blue the firmament,
Phoebus his golden streamers down has sent
To gladden every flower with his warmness.
He was that time in Gemini, I guess,
And but a little from his declination
Of Cancer, which is great Jove's exaltation.
And so befell, in that bright morning tide,
That in this garden, on the farther side,
Pluto, who is the king of Faëry,
With many a lady in his company,
Following his wife, the fair Queen Proserpine,
Each after other, straight as any line
(While she was gathering flowers on a mead,
In Claudian you may the story read
How in his grim car he had stolen her)—
This king of Faëry sat down yonder
Upon a turfen bank all fresh and green,
And right anon thus said he to his queen.

   "My wife," said he, "there may no one say nay;
Experience proves fully every day
The treason that these women do to man.
Ten hundred thousand stories tell I can
To show your fickleness and lies. Of which,
O Solomon wise, and richest of the rich,

Fulfilled of sapience and worldly glory,
Well worth remembrance are thy words and story
By everyone who's wit, and reason can.
Thus goodness he expounds with praise of man:
'Among a thousand men yet found I one,
But of all women living found I none.'

    "Thus spoke the king that knew your wickedness;
And Jesus son of Sirach, as I guess,
Spoke of you seldom with much reverence.
A wild fire and a rotten pestilence
Fall on your bodies all before tonight!
Do you not see this honourable knight,
Because, alas! he is both blind and old,
His own sworn man shall make him a cuckold;
Lo, there he sits, the lecher, in that tree.
Now will I grant, of my high majesty,
Unto this old and blind and worthy knight,
That he shall have again his two eyes' sight,
Just when his wife shall do him villainy;
Then shall he know of all her harlotry,
Both in reproach to her and others too."

    "You shall," said Proserpine, "if will you so;
Now by my mother's father's soul, I swear
That I will give her adequate answer,
And all such women after, for her sake;
That, though in any guilt caught, they'll not quake,
But with a bold face they'll themselves excuse,
And bear him down who would them thus accuse.
For lack of answer none of them shall die.
Nay, though a man see things with either eye,
Yet shall we women brazen shamelessly
And weep and swear and wrangle cleverly,
So that you men shall stupid be as geese.
What do I care for your authorities?

    "I know well that this Jew, this Solomon
Found fools among us women, many a one,
But though he never found a good woman,
Yet has there found full many another man
Women right true, right good, and virtuous.
Witness all those that dwell in Jesus' house;

With martyrdom they proved their constancy.
The *Gesta Romanorum* speak kindly
Of many wives both good and true also.
But be not angry, sir, though it be so
That he said he had found no good woman,
I pray you take the meaning of the man;
He meant that sovereign goodness cannot be
Except in God, Who is the Trinity.
　　"Ah, since of very God there is but one,
Why do you make so much of Solomon?
What though he built a temple for God's house?
What though he were both rich and glorious?
So built he, too, a temple to false gods,
How could he with the Law be more at odds?
By gad, clean as his name you whitewash, sir,
He was a lecher and idolater;
And in old age the True God he forsook.
And if that God had not, as says the Book,
Spared him for father David's sake, he should
Have lost his kingdom sooner than he would.
I value not, of all the villainy
That you of women write, a butterfly.
I am a woman, and needs must I speak,
Or else swell up until my heart shall break.
For since he said we gossip, rail, and scold,
As ever may I my fair tresses hold,
I will not spare, for any courtesy,
To speak him ill who'd wish us villainy."
　　"Dame," said this Pluto, "be no longer wroth;
I give it up; but since I swore my oath
That I would give to him his sight again,
My word shall stand, I warn you that's certain.
I am a king, it suits me not to lie."
　　"And I," said she, "am queen of Faëry.
Her answer shall she have, I undertake;
No further talk hereof let us two make.
Forsooth, I will not longer be contrary."
　　Now let us turn again to January,
Who in the garden with his lovely May
Sang, and that merrier than the popinjay,

"I love you best, and ever shall, I know."
And so about the alleys did he go
Till he had come at last to that pear tree
Wherein this Damian sat right merrily
On high, among the young leaves fresh and green.
   This blooming May, who was so bright of sheen,
Began to sigh, and said: "Alas, my side!
Now, sir," said she, "no matter what betide,
I must have some of these pears that I see,
Or I may die, so much I long," said she,
"To eat some of those little pears so green.
Help, for Her love Who is of Heaven Queen!
I tell you well, a woman in my plight
May have for fruit so great an appetite
That she may die if none of it she have."
   "Alas!" said he, "that I had here a knave
That could climb up, alas, alas!" said he,
"That I am blind."
                   "Yea, sir, no odds," said she,
"If you'd but grant me, and for God's dear sake,
That this pear tree within your arms you'd take
(For well I know that you do not trust me),
Then I could climb up well enough," said she,
"So I my foot might set upon your back."
   "Surely," said he, "thereof should be no lack,
Might I so help you with my own heart's blood."
   So he stooped down, and on his back she stood,
And gave herself a twist and up went she.
Ladies, I pray you be not wroth with me;
I cannot gloze, I'm an uncultured man.
For of a sudden this said Damian
Pulled up her smock and thrust both deep and long.
   And when King Pluto saw this awful wrong,
To January he gave again his sight,
And made him see as well as ever he might.
And when he thus had got his sight again,
Never was man of anything so fain.
But since his wife he thought of first and last,
Up to the tree his eyes he quickly cast,
And saw how Damian his wife had dressed

In such a way as cannot be expressed,
Save I should rudely speak and vulgarly:
And such a bellowing clamour then raised he
As does a mother when her child must die:
"Out! Help! Alas! Oh, help me!" he did cry,
"Outlandish, brazen woman, what do you do?"
    And she replied: "Why, sir, and what ails you?
Have patience, and do reason in your mind
That I have helped you for your two eyes blind.
On peril of my soul, I tell no lies,
But I was taught that to recover eyes
Was nothing better, so to make you see,
Than struggle with a man up in a tree.
God knows I did it with a good intent."
    "Struggle!" cried he, "but damme, in it went!
God give you both a shameful death to die!
He banged you, for I saw it with my eye,
Or may they hang me by the neck up, else!"
    "Then is," said she, "my medicine all false;
For certainly, if you could really see,
You would not say these cruel words to me;
You catch but glimpses and no perfect sight."
    "I see," said he, "as well as ever I might—
Thanks be to God!—and with my two eyes, too,
And truth, I thought he did that thing to you."
    "You are bewildered still, good sir," said she,
"Such thanks I have for causing you to see;
Alas!" she cried, "that ever I was so kind!"
    "Now, dame," said he, "put all this out of mind.
Come down, my dear, and if I have missaid,
God help me if I'm not put out indeed.
But by my father's soul, I thought to have seen
How Damian right over you did lean
And that your smock was pulled up to his breast."
That each of you must tell us, at the least,
A tale or two, or break his sworn behest."
    "I know it," said the franklin; "I am fain,
And pray you all, you do not me disdain,
Though to this man I speak a word or two."
    "Come, tell your tale, sir, without more ado."

"Gladly, sir host," said he, "I will obey
Your will, good host; now hearken what I say.
For I'll not be contrary in any wise,
At least so far as my wit shall suffice;
I pray to God that it may please you; rough
Though it may be, I'll know 'tis good enough."

The Franklin's Tale

The Franklin's Prologue

These ancient gentle Bretons, in their days,
Of divers high adventures made great lays
And rhymed them in their primal Breton tongue;
The which lays to their instruments they sung,
Or else recited them where joy might be;
And one of them have I in memory,
Which I shall gladly tell you, as I can.
　　But, sirs, because I am an ignorant man,
At my beginning must I first beseech
You will excuse me for my vulgar speech;
I never studied rhetoric, that's certain;
That which I say, it must be bare and plain.
I never slept on Mount Parnassus, no,
Nor studied Marcus Tullius Cicero.
Colours I know not, there's no doubt indeed,
Save colours such as grow within the mead,
Or such as men achieve with dye or paint.
Colours of rhetoric I find but quaint;
My spirit doesn't feel the beauty there.
But if you wish, my story you shall hear."

The Franklin's Tale

In old Armorica, now Brittany,
There was a knight that loved and strove, did he,
To serve a lady in the highest wise;
And many a labour, many a great emprise
He wrought for her, or ever she was won.
For she was of the fairest under sun,
And therewithal come of so high kindred
That scarcely could this noble knight, for dread,

Tell her his woe, his pain, and his distress.
But at the last she, for his worthiness,
And specially for his meek obedience,
Had so much pity that, in consequence,
She secretly was come to his accord
To take him for her husband and her lord,
Of such lordship as men have over wives;
And that they might be happier in their lives,
Of his free will he swore to her, as knight,
That never in his life, by day or night,
Would he assume a right of mastery
Against her will, nor show her jealousy,
But would obey and do her will in all
As any lover of his lady shall;
Save that the name and show of sovereignty,
Those would he have, lest he shame his degree
   She thanked him, and with a great humbleness
She said: "Since, sir, of your own nobleness
You proffer me to have so loose a rein
Would God there never come between us twain,
For any guilt of mine, a war or strife.
Sir, I will be your humble, faithful wife,
Take this as truth till heart break in my breast."
Thus were they both in quiet and in rest.
   For one thing, sirs, I safely dare to say,
That friends each one the other must obey
If they'd be friends and long keep company.
Love will not be constrained by mastery;
When mastery comes, the god of love anon
Beats his fair wings, and farewell! He is gone!
Love is a thing as any spirit free;
Women by nature love their liberty,
And not to be constrained like any thrall,
And so do men, if say the truth I shall.
Observe who is most patient in his love,
He is advantaged others all above.
Patience is virtue high, and that's certain;
For it does vanquish, as these clerks make plain,
Things that oppression never could attain.
One must not chide for trifles nor complain.

Learn to endure, or else, so may I go,
You'll have to learn it, whether you will or no.
For in this world, it's certain, no one is
Who never does or says sometimes amiss.
Sickness, or woe, or what the stars have sent,
Anger, or wine, or change of temperament
Causes one oft to do amiss or speak.
For every wrong one may not vengeance wreak;
Conditions must determine temperance
In all who understand good governance.
And therefore did this wise and worthy knight,
To live in quiet, patience to her plight,
And unto him full truly did she swear
That never should he find great fault in her.

Here may men see an humble wise accord;
Thus did she take her servant and her lord,
Servant in love and lord in their marriage;
So was he both in lordship and bondage;
In bondage? Nay, but in lordship above,
Since he had both his lady and his love;
His lady truly, and his wife also,
To which the law of love accords, we know.
And when he was in this prosperity,
Home with his wife he went to his country,
Not far from Penmarch, where his dwelling was.
And there he lived in bliss and all solace.

Who could relate, save those that wedded be,
The joy, the ease, and the prosperity
That are between a husband and a wife?
A year and more endured this blissful life,
Until the knight, of whom I've spoken thus,
Who at Kayrrud was called Arviragus,
Arranged to go and dwell a year or twain
In England, which was then known as Britain,
To seek in arms renown and great honour;
For his desire was fixed in such labour;
And there he lived two years (the book says thus).

Now will I hold from this Arviragus,
And I will speak of Dorigen his wife,
Who loved her husband as her heart's own life.

For all his absence wept she and she sighed,
As noble wives do at a lone fireside.
She mourned, watched, wailed, she fasted and complained;
Desire for him so bound her and constrained,
That all this wide world did she set at naught.
Her friends, who knew her grief and heavy thought,
Comforted her as they might do or say;
They preached to her, they told her night and day
That for no cause she killed herself, alas!
And every comfort possible in this pass
They gave to her, in all their busyness,
To make her thus put by her heaviness.

　　With passing time, as you know, every one,
Men may so long with tools engrave a stone
That thereon will some figure printed be.
And so long did they comfort her that she
Received at last, by hope and reason grown,
Imprinted consolations as her own,
Whereby her sorrow did somewhat assuage;
She could not always live in such a rage.

　　And, then, Arviragus, through all her care,
Had sent her letters home, of his welfare,
And that he would come speedily again;
Otherwise had this sorrow her heart slain.

　　Her friends saw that her grief began to slake,
And prayed her on their knees, for dear God's sake,
To come and wander in their company
And drive away her gloomy fantasy.
And finally she granted that request;
For well she saw that it was for the best.

　　Now stood her castle very near the sea,
And often with her good friends wandered she
For pleasure on the cliffs that reared so high,
Whence she saw many a ship and barge go by,
Sailing their courses where they wished to go;
But that was part and parcel of her woe.
For to herself full oft, "Alas!" said she,
"Is there no ship, of many that I see,
Will bring me home my lord? Then were my heart
Recovered of its bitter pains that smart."

At other times there would she sit and think,
And cast her two eyes downward from the brink.
But when she saw the grisly rocks all black,
For very fear her heart would start aback
And quake so that her feet would not sustain
Her weight. Then on the grass she'd sit again
And piteously upon the sea she'd stare,
And say, with dull sighs on the empty air:
"Eternal God, Who by Thy providence
Leadest the world with a true governance,
Idly, as men say, dost Thou nothing make;
But, Lord, these grisly, fiendish rocks, so black,
That seem but rather foul confusion thrown
Awry than any fair world of Thine own,
Aye of a perfect wise God and stable,
Why hast Thou wrought this insane work, pray tell?
For by this work, north, south, and west and east,
There is none nurtured, man, nor bird, nor beast;
It does no good, to my mind, but annoys.
See'st Thou not, Lord, how mankind it destroys?
A hundred thousand bodies of mankind
Have died on rocks, whose names are not in mind,
And man's a creature made by Thee most fair,
After Thine image, as Thou didst declare.
Then seemed it that Thou had'st great charity
Toward mankind; but how then may it be
That Thou hast wrought such means man to destroy,
Which means do never good, but ever annoy?
I know well, clerics gladly do attest,
By arguments, that all is for the best,
Though I can never the real causes know.
But O Thou God Who made'st the wind to blow,
Keep Thou my lord! This is my argument;
To clerks I leave disputing on what's meant.
But O would God that all these rocks so black
Were sunken down to Hell for my lord's sake!
These rocks, they slay my very heart with fear."
Thus would she say, with many a piteous tear.

 Her friends saw that to her it was no sport
To wander by the sea, but discomfort;

And so arranged to revel somewhere else.
They led her along rivers and to wells,
And such delightful places; and told fables,
And danced, and played at chess, and played at tables.
  So on a day, all in the morningtide,
Unto a garden which was there beside,
Wherein they'd given command that there should be
Food and whatever else was necessary,
They went for pleasure all the livelong day.
And this was on the morning sixth of May,
And May had painted with his soft warm showers
This garden full of foliage and of flowers;
And work of man's hand had so curiously
Arrayed this lovely garden, truthfully,
That never was another of such price,
Unless it were the very Paradise.
The scent of flowers and the fair fresh sight
Would have made any heart dance for delight
That e'er was born, unless too great sickness
Or too great sorrow held it in distress;
So full it was of beauty and pleasance.
After their dinner all began to dance,
And sing, also, save Dorigen alone,
Who made alway her same complaint and moan.
For him she saw not through the dancing go,
Who was her husband and her love also.
Nevertheless, she must a time abide,
And with good hope held, let her sorrow slide.
  Amid these mazes, with the other men,
There danced a squire before this Dorigen,
That was more blithe, and prettier of array,
In my opinion, than the month of May.
He sang and danced better than any man
That is, or was, since first the world began.
Therewith he was, description to contrive,
One of best conditioned men alive;
Young, strong, right virtuous, and rich, and wise,
And well beloved, and one to idealize.
And briefly, if I tell the truth withal,
Unknown to Dorigen—nay, least of all—

This pleasant squire, servant to Queen Venus,
The name of whom was this, Aurelius,
Had loved her best of anyone alive
Two years and more (since she did first arrive),
But never dared he tell her of his state;
Without a cup he drank his draught of fate.
He had despaired, for nothing dared he say,
Save that in songs he would somewhat betray
His woe, as of a general complaint;
He loved, but none loved him, though he went faint.
Of such a subject made he many lays,
Songs and complaints, rondels and virelays,
How that he dared not his deep sorrow tell,
But languished, as a fury does in Hell;
And die he must, he said, as did Echo
For her Narcissus, daring not tell her woe.
In other manner than you hear me say
Dared he not unto her his woe betray;
Save that, perchance, there would be times at dances,
Where young folk honoured all that makes romances,
It may well be he looked upon her face
In such wise as a man who sued for grace;
But nothing knew she of his love's intent.
Nevertheless it chanced, ere thence they went,
Because it happened he was her neighbour,
And was a man of worship and honour,
And she had known him in the time of yore,
They fell to talking; and so, more and more,
Unto his purpose drew Aurelius,
And when he saw his time addressed her thus:
    "Madam," said he, "by God Who this world made,
So that I knew it might your sad heart aid,
I would, that day when your Arviragus
Went overseas, that I, Aurelius,
Had gone whence never I should come again;
For well I know my service is in vain.
My guerdon is the breaking of my heart;
Madam, have pity on my pains that smart;
For with a word you may slay me or save,
Here at your feet would God I found my grave!

Time to say more, at present naught have I;
Have mercy, sweet, or you will make me die!"
    So then she looked upon Aurelius:
"Is this your will?" asked she, "And say you thus?
Never before have I known what you meant.
But since, Aurelius, I know your intent,
By that same God Who gave me soul and life,
Never shall I become an untrue wife
In word or deed, so far as I have wit:
I will remain his own to whom I'm knit;
Take this for final answer as from me."
But after that she said thus, sportively:
    "Aurelius," said she, "by God above,
Yet would I well consent to be your love,
Since I hear you complain so piteously,
On that day when, from coasts of Brittany,
You've taken all the black rocks, stone by stone,
So that they hinder ship nor boat—I own,
I say, when you have made the coast so clean
Of rocks that there is no stone to be seen,
Then will I love you best of any man;
Take here my promise—all that ever I can."
    "Is there no other grace in you?" asked he.
    "No, by that Lord," said she, "Who has made me!
For well I know that it shall ne'er betide.
Let suchlike follies out of your heart slide.
What pleasure can a man have in his life
Who would go love another man's own wife,
That has her body when he wishes it?"
    Deep sighs Aurelius did then emit;
Woe was Aurelius when this he heard,
And with a sorrowful heart he thus answered:
    "Madam," said he, "this were impossible!
Then must I die a sudden death and fell."
And with that word he turned away anon.
Then came her other friends, and many a one,
And in the alleys wandered up and down,
And nothing knew of this decision shown,
But suddenly began to dance anew
Until the bright sun lost his golden hue;

For the horizon had cut off his light;
This is as much as saying, it was night.
And home they went in joy and with solace,
Except the wretch Aurelius, alas!
He to his house went with a woeful heart;
He saw he could not from his near death part.
It seemed to him he felt his heart grow cold;
Up toward Heaven his two hands did he hold,
And on his bare knees did he kneel him down
And in his raving said his orison.
For very woe out of his wits he fled.
He knew not what he spoke, but thus he said;
With mournful heart his plaint had he begun
Unto the gods, and first unto the sun.
He said: "Apollo, governor and god
Of every plant, herb, tree, and flower in sod,
That givest, according to thy declination,
To each of them its time of foliation,
All as thy habitation's low or high,
Lord Phoebus, cast thy merciful bright eye
On wretched Aurelius, who is lost and lorn.
Lo, Lord! My lady has my swift death sworn,
Without my guilt, save thy benignity
Upon my dying heart have some pity!
For well I know, Lord Phoebus, if you lest,
You can thus aid me, save my lady, best.
Now vouchsafe that I may for you devise
A plan to help me, telling in what wise.
"Your blessed sister, Lucina, serene,
That of the sea is goddess chief and queen
(Though Neptune is the deity in the sea,
Yet empress set above him there is she).
You know well, Lord, that just as her desire
Is to be quickened and lighted by your fire,
For which she follows you right busily,
Just so the sea desires, and naturally,
To follow her, she being high goddess
Both of the sea and rivers, great and less.
Wherefore, Lord Phoebus, this request I make—
Without this miracle, my heart will break—

That at the time of your next opposition,
Which will be in the Lion, make petition
To her that she so great a flood will bring
That full five fathoms shall it over-spring
The highest rock in Armoric Brittany;
And let this flood endure two years for me;
Then truly to my lady may I say:
'Now keep your word, the rocks are gone away.'
    "Lord Phoebus, do this miracle for me;
Pray her she run no faster course, being free—
I say, Lord, pray your sister that she go
No faster course than you these next years two.
Then shall she be even at the full alway,
And spring flood shall endure both night and day.
And save she vouchsafe, Lord, in such manner
To grant to me my sovereign lady dear,
Pray her to sink, then, every rock far down
Into that region dark and cold, her own,
Under the earth, the place Pluto dwells in,
Or nevermore shall I my lady win.
Thy temple in Delphi will I, barefoot, seek;
Lord Phoebus, see the tears upon my cheek,
And on my pain be some compassion shown."
And with that word in swoon he tumbled down,
And for a long time lay there in a trance.
    His brother, who knew all his suppliance,
Found him, and took him, and to bed him brought.
Despairing in the torment of his thought,
Let I this woeful fellow creature lie,
To choose, for all of me, to live or die.
    Arviragus, with health, in honour's hour,
As he that was of chivalry the flower,
Came home again, with other gentlemen.
O happy are you now, my Dorigen,
Who have your pleasant husband in your arms,
The vigorous knight, the worthy man-at-arms,
That loves you as he loves his own heart's life.
Nothing he chose to question of his wife
If any man had said, while he was out,
Some words of love; of her he had no doubt.

He tended not that way, it would appear,
But danced and jousted, made for her good cheer;
And thus in joy and bliss I let them dwell
And of love-sick Aurelius will I tell.

In weakness and in torment furious
Two years and more lay wretched Aurelius
Ere foot on earth he went—aye, even one;
For comfort in this long time had he none,
Save from his brother, who was a good clerk;
He knew of all this woe and all this work.
For to no other human, 'tis certain,
Dared he his cause of illness to explain.
In breast he kept more secret his idea
Than did Pamphilius for Galatea.
His breast was whole, with no wound to be seen,
But in his heart there was the arrow keen.
And well you know that of a sursanure
In surgery is difficult the cure,
Unless they find the dart or take it out.
His brother wept, and long he sought about
Till at the last he called to remembrance
That while he was at Orléans in France—
For many young clerks are all ravenous
To read of arts that are most curious,
And into every nook and cranny turn
Particular strange sciences to learn—
He thus recalled that once upon a day,
At Orléans, while studying there, I say,
A book of natural magic there he saw
In a friend's room, a bachelor of law
(Though he was there to learn another craft),
Which book he'd privately on his desk left;
And which book said much of the operations
Touching the eight and twenty variations
That designate the moon, and such folly
As is, in our days, valued not a fly;
For Holy Church provides us with a creed
That suffers no illusion to mislead.
And when this book came to his remembrance,
At once, for joy, his heart began to dance,

And to himself he said in privacy:
"My brother shall be healed, and speedily;
For I am sure that there are sciences
Whereby men make divers appearances,
Such as these prestidigitators play.
For oft at feasts, have I well heard men say
That jugglers, in a hall both bright and large,
Have made come in there, water and a barge,
And in the hall the barge rowed up and down.
Sometimes there seemed to come a grim lion;
And sometimes flowers sprang as in a mead;
Or vines with grapes both red and white indeed;
Sometimes a castle built of lime and stone;
And when they wished it disappeared anon.
Thus seemed these things to be in each man's sight.
    "Now, then, conclude I thus, that if I might
At Orléans some old school-fellow find,
Who has these mansions of the moon in mind,
Or other natural magic from above,
He could well make my brother have his love.
For with a mere appearance clerks may make
It seem in man's sight that all rocks that break
The seas of Brittany were banished, so
That right above them ships might come and go,
And in such wise endure a week or two;
Then were my brother cured of all his woe.
For she must keep the word she gave at feast.
Or he'll have right to shame her, at the least."
    Why should I longer speak of this event?
He to the bedside of his brother went,
And urged him eagerly to get him gone
To Orléans; he started up anon
And forward on his way at once did fare
In hope to be relieved of all his care.
    When they were come almost to that city,
Perhaps two furlongs short of it, or three,
A young clerk walking by himself they met,
Who, in good Latin, heartily did greet,
And after that he said a wondrous thing.
"I know," said he, "the cause of your coming."

And ere a farther foot the brothers went,
He told them all the soul of their intent.
This Breton clerk asked after school fellows
Whom he had known through former suns and snows;
And he replied to this that dead they were,
Whereat he wept, for sorrow, many a tear.
Down from his horse Aurelius leaped anon,
And onward with this wizard he was gone
Home to his house, where he was put at ease.
To him there lacked no victuals that might please;
So well appointed house as was that one
Aurelius in life before saw none.
He showed him, ere he went to supper here,
Forests and parks full of the dim wild deer;
There saw he harts of ten with their horns high,
The greatest ever seen by human eye.
He saw of them a hundred slain by hounds,
And some with arrows bled, with bitter wounds.
He saw, when vanished all were these wild deer,
Some falconers by river flowing clear,
Who with their hawks had many herons slain.
And then he saw knights jousting on a plain;
And after this he did him such pleasance
That he showed him his lady in a dance
Wherein he also joined, or so he thought.
And when this master who this magic wrought
Saw it was time, he clapped his two hands, lo!
Farewell to all! the revels out did go.
And yet they'd never moved out of the house
While they saw all these sights so marvelous,
But in his study, where his books would be,
They had sat still, and no one but they three.
Then unto him this master called his squire,
And asked him thus: "Is supper ready, sir?
Almost an hour it is, I'll undertake,
Since I bade you our evening meal to make,
When these two gentlemen came in with me
Into my study, wherein my books be."
"Sir," said this squire then, "when it pleases you
It is all ready, though you will right now."

"Then let us sup," said he, "for that is best;
These amorous folk must sometime have some rest."
     After the supper they discussed, they three,
What sum should this said master's guerdon be
For moving all rocks Breton coasts contain
From the Gironde unto the mouth of Seine.
He played for time, and swore, so God him save,
Less than a thousand pounds he would not have,
Nor eagerly for that would take it on.
     Aurelius, with blissful heart, anon
Answered him thus: "Fig for a thousand pound!
This great wide world, the which, men say, is round,
I'd give it all, if I were lord of it.
The bargain is concluded and we're knit.
You shall be truly paid, sir, by my troth!
But look you, for no negligence or sloth,
Delay no longer than tomorrow morn."
"Nay," said this clerk, "upon my faith I'm sworn."
     To bed went this Aurelius and undressed,
And well-nigh all that night he had his rest;
What of his labour and his hope of bliss
The pain had left that woeful heart of his.
     Upon the morrow, when it was full day,
To Brittany took they the nearest way,
Aurelius, with this wizard at his side,
And thus they came to where they would abide;
And that was, as the books say, I remember,
The cold and frosty season of December.
     Phoebus was old and coloured like pale brass,
That in hot declination coloured was
And shone like burnished gold with streamers bright;
But now in Capricorn did he alight,
Wherein he palely shone, I dare explain.
The bitter frosts, with all the sleet and rain,
Had killed the green of every garden yard.
Janus sat by the fire, with double beard,
And drained from out his bugle horn the wine.
Before him stood the brawn of tuskèd swine,
And "Noël!" cried then every lusty man.
     Aurelius, in all that he could plan,

Did to this master cheerful reverence,
And prayed of him he'd use all diligence
To bring him from his pains that so did smart,
Or else with sword that he would slit his heart.
  This subtle clerk such ruth had for this man,
That night and day he sped about his plan,
To wait the proper time for his conclusion;
That is to say, the time to make illusion,
By such devices of his jugglery
(I understand not this astrology)
That she and everyone should think and say
That all the Breton rocks were gone away,
Or else that they were sunken underground.
So at the last the proper time he found
To do his tricks and all his wretchedness
Of such a superstitious wickedness.
For his Toletan Tables forth he brought,
All well corrected, and he lacked in naught,
The years collected nor the separate years,
Nor his known roots, nor any other gears,
As, say, his centres and his argument,
And his proportionals convenient
In estimating truly his equations.
The eighth sphere showed him in his calculations
How far removed was Alnath, passing by,
From head of that fixed Aries on high,
That in the ninth great sphere considered is;
Right cleverly he calculated this.
  When he the moon's first mansion thus had found,
The rest proportionally he could expound;
And knew the moon's arising-time right well,
And in what face and term, and all could tell;
This gave him then the mansion of the moon—
He worked it out accordingly right soon,
And did the other necessary rites
To cause illusions and such evil sights
As heathen peoples practised in those days.
Therefore no longer suffered he delays,
But all the rocks by magic and his lore
Appeared to vanish for a week or more.

Aurelius, who yet was torn by this,
Whether he'd gain his love or fare amiss,
Awaited night and day this miracle;
And when he knew there was no obstacle,
That vanished were these black rocks, every one,
Down at the master's feet he fell anon
And said: "I, woeful wretch, Aurelius,
Thank you, my lord, and Lady mine Venus,
That have so saved me from my dreadful care."
And to the temple straightway did he fare,
Whereat he knew he should his lady see.
And when he saw his opportunity,
With fluttering heart and with an humble cheer
He greeted thus his sovereign lady dear.
"My own dear lady," said this woeful man,
"Whom I most fear and love best, as I can,
And whom, of all this world, I'd not displease,
Were it not that for you I've such unease
That I must die here at your feet anon,
I would not tell how I am woebegone;
But I must either die or else complain;
You slay me, for no crime, with utter pain.
But on my death, although you have no ruth,
Take heed now, ere you break your promised troth.
Repent you, for the sake of God above,
Ere me you slay, because it's you I love.
For well you know your promise apposite;
Not that I challenge aught, of my own right,
In you, my sovereign lady, save your grace;
But in a garden, in a certain place,
You know right well what you did promise me;
And in my hand you plighted troth," said he,
"To love me best, God knows you promised so,
Howe'er I may unworthy be thereto.
Madam, I say it for your honour's vow
More than to save my heart's dear life right now;
I have done all that you commanded me;
And if you will, you may well go and see.
Do as you please, but hold your word in mind,
For quick or dead, as you do, me you'll find;

In you lies all, to make me live or die,
But well I know the rocks are vanished, aye!"
    He took his leave, and she astounded stood,
In all her face there was no drop of blood;
She never thought to have come in such a trap.
"Alas!" said she, "that ever this should hap!
For thought I never, by possibility,
That such prodigious marvel e'er might be!
It is against the way of all nature."
And home she went, a sorrowful creature.
For utter terror hardly could she go,
She wept, she wailed throughout a day or so,
And swooned so much 'twas pitiful to see;
But why this was to not a soul told she;
For out of town was gone Arviragus.
But to her own heart spoke she, and said thus,
With her face pale and with a heavy cheer,
All her complaint, as you'll hereafter hear:
    "Of thee," she cried, "O Fortune, I complain,
That, unaware, I'm bound within thy chain;
From which to go, I know of no succour
Save only death, or else my dishonour;
One of these two I am compelled to choose.
Nevertheless, I would far rather lose
My life than of my body come to shame,
Or know myself untrue, or lose my name;
By death I know it well, I may be freed,
Has there not many a noble wife, indeed,
And many a maiden slain herself—alas!—
Rather than with her body do trespass?
    "Yes, truly, lo, these stories bear witness;
When Thirty Tyrants, full of wickedness,
Had Phido slain in Athens, at a feast,
They gave command his daughters to arrest,
And had them brought before them, for despite,
All naked, to fulfill their foul delight,
And in their father's blood they made them dance
Upon the pavement—God give them mischance!
For which these woeful maidens, full of dread,
Rather than they should lose their maidenhead,

Unseen they all leaped down into a well
And drowned themselves therein, as old books tell.
  "They of Messina did require and seek
From Lacedaemon fifty maids to take,
On whom they would have done their lechery;
But there was none of all that company
Who was not slain, and who with good intent
Preferred not death rather than give consent
To be thus ravished of her maidenhead.
Why should I then hold dying in such dread?
  "Lo, too, the tyrant Aristoclides,
Who loved a maiden called Stimphalides,
Whenas her father had been slain by night,
Unto Diana's temple she took flight
And grasped the image in her two hands so
That from this image would she not let go.
No one could tear her hands from that embrace
Till she was slaughtered in that self-same place.
Now since these maidens showed such scorn outright
Of being defiled to make man's foul delight,
Well ought a wife rather herself to slay
Than be defiled, I think, and so I say.
  "What shall I say of Hasdrubal's fair wife,
Who in Carthage bereft herself of life?
For when she saw that Romans won the town,
She took her children all and leaped right down
Into the fire, choosing thus to die
Before a Roman did her villainy.
  "Did not Lucretia slay herself—alas!—
At Rome, when she so violated was
By Tarquin? For she thought it was a shame
Merely to live when she had lost her name.
  "The seven maidens of Miletus, too,
Did slay themselves, for very dread and woe,
Rather than men of Gaul should on them press.
More than a thousand stories, as I guess,
Could I repeat now of this matter here.
  "With Abradates slain, his wife so dear
Herself slew, and she let her red blood glide
In Abradates' wounds so deep and wide,

And said: 'My body, at the least, I say,
No man shall now defile,' and passed away.
"Why should I of more instances be fain?
Since that so many have their bodies slain
Rather than that they should dishonoured be?
I will conclude it better is for me
To slay myself than be dishonoured thus.
I will be true unto Arviragus,
Or else I'll slay myself in some manner,
As did Demotion's virgin daughter dear
Because she would not violated be.
    "O Cedasus, it rouses great pity
To read of how your daughters died, alas!
That slew themselves in such another case.
    "As great a pity was it, aye and more,
That a fair Theban maid, for Nicanor,
Did slay herself in such a kind of woe.
"Another Theban maiden did also;
For one of Macedonia her had pressed,
And she, by death, her maidenhead redressed.
    "What shall I say of Nicerates' wife,
Who, for like cause, bereft herself of life?
    "How true, too, was to Alcibiades
His love, who chose to drain death to the lees
And would not let his corpse unburied be!
Lo, what a wife was Alcestis," said she.
    "What says Homer of good Penelope?
The whole of Hellas knew her chastity.
    "Pardieu, of Laodamia they wrote thus,
That when at Troy was slain Protesilaus,
No longer would she live after his day.
    "The same of noble Portia may I say;
Without her Brutus could she no wise live,
To whom in youth her whole heart she did give.
    "The perfect wifehood of Artemisia
Was honoured throughout all old Caria.
    "O Teuta, queen! Your wifely chastity,
To all wives may a very mirror be.
The same thing may I say of Bilia,
Of Rhodogune and of Valeria."

Thus Dorigen went on a day or so,
Purposing ever that to death she'd go.
   But notwithstanding, upon the third night
Home came Arviragus, this worthy knight,
And asked her why it was she wept so sore.
And thereat she began to weep the more.
   "Alas!" cried she, "that ever I was born!
Thus have I said," quoth she, "thus have I sworn"—
And told him all, as you have heard before;
It needs not to re-tell it to you more.
   This husband, with glad cheer, in friendly wise,
Answered and said as I shall you apprise:
"Is there naught else, my Dorigen, than this?"
   "Nay, nay," said she, "God help me, as it is
This is too much, though it were God's own will."
   "Yea, wife," said he, "let sleep what's lying still;
It may be well with us, perchance, today.
But you your word shall hold to, by my fay!
As God may truly mercy have on me,
Wounded to death right now I'd rather be,
For sake of this great love of you I have,
Than you should not your true word keep and save.
Truth is the highest thing that man may keep."
But with that word began he then to weep,
And said: "I you forbid, on pain of death,
That ever, while to you last life and breath,
To anyone you tell this adventure.
As I best may, I will my woe endure,
Nor show a countenance of heaviness,
That folk no harm may think of you, or guess."
   And then he called a squire and a maid:
"Go forth anon with Dorigen," he said,
"And bring her to a certain place anon."
They took their leave and on their way were gone,
But nothing knew of why she thither went.
Nor would he to a soul tell his intent.
   Perhaps a lot of you will certainly
Hold him a wicked man that wilfully
Put his wife's honour thus in jeopardy;
Hearken the tale, ere you upon her cry.

She may have better luck than you suppose;
And when you've heard all, let your judgment close.
　　This squire I've told you of, Aurelius,
Of Dorigen he being so amorous,
Chanced, as it seems, his lady fair to meet
In middle town, right in the busiest street,
As she was going forth, as you have heard,
Toward the garden where she'd pledged her word.
And he was going gardenward also;
For he was always watching when she'd go
Out of her house to any kind of place.
But thus they met, by chance perhaps or grace;
And he saluted her with good intent,
And asked her, now, whither it was she went.
　　And she replied, as if she were half mad:
"Unto the garden, as my husband bade,
My promise there to keep, alas, alas!"
　　Aurelius then pondered on this case,
And in his heart he had compassion great
On her and her lamenting and her state,
And on Arviragus, the noble knight,
Who'd bidden her keep promise, as she might,
Being so loath his wife should break with truth;
And in his heart he gained, from this, great ruth,
Considering the best on every side,
That from possession rather he'd abide
Than do so great a churlish grievousness
Against free hearts and all high nobleness;
For which, and in few words, he told her thus:
　　"Madam, say to your lord Arviragus
That since I see his noble gentleness
To you, and since I see well your distress,
That he'd have rather shame (and that were ruth)
Than you to me should break your word of truth,
I would myself far rather suffer woe
Than break apart the love between you two.
So I release, madam, into your hand,
And do return, discharged, each surety and
Each bond that you have given and have sworn,
Even from the very time that you were born.

My word I pledge, I'll ne'er seek to retrieve
A single promise, and I take my leave
As of the truest and of the best wife
That ever yet I've known in all my life.
Let every wife of promises take care,
Remember Dorigen, and so beware!
Thus can a squire perform a gentle deed
As well as can a knight, of that take heed."

   Upon her bare knees did she thank him there,
And home unto her husband did she fare,
And told him all, as you have heard it said;
And be assured, he was so pleased and glad
That 'twere impossible of it to write.
What should I further of this case indite?

   Arviragus and Dorigen his wife
In sovereign happiness led forth their life.
Never did any anger come between;
He cherished her as if she were a queen;
And she to him was true for evermore.
Of these two folk you get from me no more.

   Aurelius, whose wealth was now forlorn,
He cursed the time that ever he was born;
"Alas!" cried he, "Alas! that I did state
I'd pay fine gold a thousand pounds by weight
To this philosopher! What shall I do?
I see no better than I'm ruined too.
All of my heritage I needs must sell
And be a beggar; here I cannot dwell
And shame all of my kindred in this place,
Unless I gain of him some better grace.
And so I'll go to him and try, today,
On certain dates, from year to year, to pay,
And thank him for his princely courtesy;
For I will keep my word, and I'll not lie."

   With sore heart he went then to his coffer,
And took gold unto this philosopher,
The value of five hundred pounds, I guess,
And so besought him, of his nobleness,
To grant him dates for payment of the rest,
And said: "Dear master, I may well protest

I've never failed to keep my word, as yet;
For certainly I'll pay my entire debt
To you, however after I may fare,
Even to begging, save for kirtle, bare.
But if you'd grant, on good security,
Two years or three of respite unto me,
Then all were well; otherwise must I sell
My heritage; there is no more to tell."
    Then this philosopher soberly answered
And spoke in this wise, when these words he'd heard:
"Have I not fairly earned my promised fee?"
"Yes, truly, you have done so, sir," said he.
"Have you not had the lady at your will?"
"No, no," said he, and sighed, and then was still.
"What was the reason? Tell me if you can."
    Aurelius his tale anon began,
And told him all, as you have heard before;
It needs not I repeat it to you more.
    He said: "Arviragus, of nobleness,
Had rather die in sorrow and distress
Than that his wife were to her promise false."
He told of Dorigen's grief, too, and how else
She had been loath to live a wicked wife
And rather would that day have lost her life,
And that her troth she swore through ignorance:
"She'd ne'er before heard of such simulance;
Which made me have for her such great pity.
And just as freely as he sent her me,
As freely sent I her to him again.
This is the sum, there's no more to explain."
    Then answered this philosopher: "Dear brother,
Each one of you has nobly dealt with other.
You are a squire, true, and he is a knight,
But God forbid, what of His blessed might,
A clerk should never do a gentle deed
As well as any of you. Of this take heed!
    "Sir, I release to you your thousand pound,
As if, right now, you'd crept out of the ground
And never, before now, had known of me.
For, sir, I'll take of you not one penny

For all my art and all my long travail.
You have paid well for all my meat and ale;
It is enough, so farewell, have good day!"
And took his horse and went forth on his way.
　　Masters, this question would I ask you now:
Which was most generous, do you think, and how?
Pray tell me this before you farther wend.
I can no more, my tale is at an end.

Here the Maker of this Book Takes His Leave

Now do I pray all those who hear this little treatise, or read it, that, if there be within it anything that pleases them, they thank Our Lord Jesus Christ, from Whom proceeds all understanding and all goodness. And if there be anything that displeases them, I pray them, also, that they impute it to the fault of my ignorance and not to my intention, which would fain have better said if I had had the knowledge. For our Book says, "All that is written is written for our instruction;" and that was my intention. Wherefore I meekly beseech you that, for the sake of God's mercy, you pray for me that Christ have mercy upon me and forgive me my trespasses—and especially for my translations and the writing of worldly vanities, the which I withdraw in my retractations: as, *The Book of Troilus*; also *The Book of Fame*; *The Book of the Nineteen Ladies*; *The Book of the Duchess*; *The Book of Saint Valentine's Day, Of the Parliament of Birds*; *The Tales of Canterbury*, those that tend toward sin; *The Book of the Lion*; and many another book, were they in my remembrance; and many a song and many a lecherous lay—as to which may Christ, of His great mercy, forgive me the sin. But for the translation of Boethius's *De Consolatione*, and other books of legends of saints, and homilies, and of morality and devotion—for those I thank Our Lord Jesus Christ and His Blessed Mother and all the saints of Heaven; beseeching them that they, henceforth unto my life's end, send me grace whereof to bewail my sins, and to study for the salvation of my soul:—and grant me the grace of true penitence, confession, and expiation in this present life; through the benign grace of Him Who is King of kings and Priest over all priests, Who redeemed us with the precious blood of His heart; so that I may be one of those, at the day of doom, that shall be saved: *Qui cum patre*, etc.

AMERICAN LITERATURE

Little Women — Louisa May Alcott
The Last of the Mohicans — James Fenimore Cooper
The Red Badge of Courage and *Maggie* — Stephen Crane
Selected Poems — Emily Dickinson
Narrative of the Life and Other Writings — Frederick Douglass
The Scarlet Letter — Nathaniel Hawthorne
The Call of the Wild and *White Fang* – Jack London
Moby-Dick — Herman Melville
Major Tales and Poems — Edgar Allan Poe
The Jungle — Upton Sinclair
Uncle Tom's Cabin — Harriet Beecher Stowe
Walden and *Civil Disobedience* — Henry David Thoreau
Adventures of Huckleberry Finn — Mark Twain
The Complete Adventures of Tom Sawyer — Mark Twain
Ethan Frome and *Summer* — Edith Wharton
Leaves of Grass — Walt Whitman

WORLD LITERATURE

Tales from the 1001 Nights — Sir Richard Burton
Don Quixote — Miguel de Cervantes
The Divine Comedy — Dante Alighieri
Crime and Punishment — Fyodor Dostoevsky
The Count of Monte Cristo — Alexandre Dumas
The Three Musketeers — Alexandre Dumas
Selected Tales of the Brothers Grimm — Jacob and Wilhelm Grimm
The Iliad — Homer
The Odyssey — Homer
The Hunchback of Notre-Dame — Victor Hugo
Les Misérables — Victor Hugo
The Metamorphosis and *The Trial* — Franz Kafka
The Phantom of the Opera — Gaston Leroux
The Prince — Niccolò Machiavelli
The Art of War — Sun Tzu
The Death of Ivan Ilych and Other Stories — Leo Tolstoy
Around the World in Eighty Days — Jules Verne
Candide and *The Maid of Orléans* — Voltaire
The Bhagavad Gita — Vyasa

BRITISH LITERATURE

Beowulf — Anonymous
Emma — Jane Austen
Persuasion — Jane Austen
Pride and Prejudice — Jane Austen
Sense and Sensibility — Jane Austen
Peter Pan — J. M. Barrie
Jane Eyre — Charlotte Brontë
Wuthering Heights — Emily Brontë
Alice in Wonderland — Lewis Carroll
The Canterbury Tales — Geoffrey Chaucer
Heart of Darkness and Other Tales — Joseph Conrad
Robinson Crusoe — Daniel Defoe
A Christmas Carol and Other Holiday Tales — Charles Dickens
Great Expectations — Charles Dickens
Oliver Twist — Charles Dickens
A Tale of Two Cities — Charles Dickens
The Waste Land and Other Writings — T. S. Eliot
A Passage to India — E. M. Forster
The Jungle Books — Rudyard Kipling
Paradise Lost and *Paradise Regained* — John Milton
The Sonnets and Other Love Poems — William Shakespeare
Three Romantic Tragedies — William Shakespeare
Frankenstein — Mary Shelley
Dr. Jekyll and Mr. Hyde and Other Strange Tales — Robert Louis Stevenson
Kidnapped — Robert Louis Stevenson
Treasure Island — Robert Louis Stevenson
Dracula — Bram Stoker
Gulliver's Travels — Jonathan Swift
The Time Machine and *The War of the Worlds* — H. G. Wells
The Picture of Dorian Gray — Oscar Wilde

ANTHOLOGIES

Four Centuries of Great Love Poems

BORDERS.
CLASSICS

The text of this book is set in 11 point Goudy Old Style, designed by American printer and typographer Frederic W. Goudy (1865–1947).

The archival-quality, natural paper is composed of recyclable products made from wood grown in sustainable forests; the manufacturing processes conform to the environmental regulations of the country of origin.

The finished volume demonstrates the convergence of Old-World craftsmanship and modern technology that exemplifies books manufactured by Edwards Brothers, Inc. Established in 1893, the family-owned business is a well-respected leader in book manufacturing, recognized the world over for quality and attention to detail.

In addition, Ann Arbor Media Group's editorial and design services provide full-service book publication to business partners.